My Other Life: A Combat Soldier in Vietnam

9/3/21

To Marty,
my fellow Central
Y and East High swimmer
and friend. Those days are
long gone, but I remember them well.
All the best,
Rick

My Other Life: A Combat Soldier in Vietnam

by

Richard Alexander

The Darwin Press, Inc.

Princeton, New Jersey

Publisher's Cataloging-In-Publication Data
(Prepared by The Donohue Group, Inc.)

Alexander, Richard (Richard James) 1944-

My other life : a combat soldier in Vietnam / by Richard Alexander.

pages : color illustrations ; cm

ISBN: 978-0-87850-216-5

1. Alexander, Richard (Richard James) 1944- 2. Vietnam War, 1961-1975--Personal narratives, American. 3. Vietnam War, 1961-1975--Veterans--United States. 4. Vietnam War, 1961-1975--Psychological aspects. I. Title.

DS559.5 .A449 2015
959.704/3092

Published by:
The Darwin Press, Inc.
Princeton, NJ 08540-2202 USA
www.darwinpress.com
Printed in the United States of America

This book is lovingly dedicated to Mom, Dad, Lee and Sue

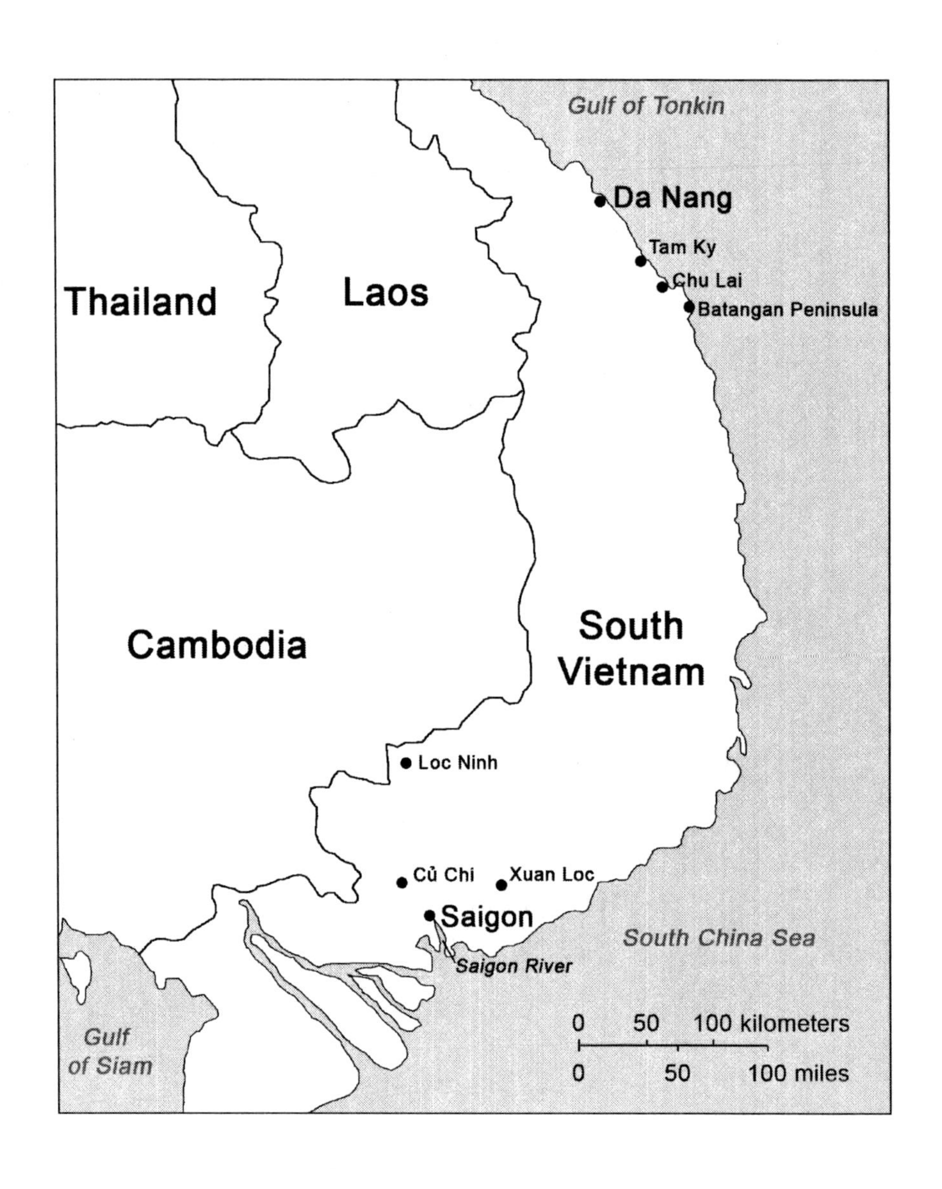
Gulf of Tonkin
Da Nang
Tam Ky
Chu Lai
Batangan Peninsula
Thailand
Laos
Cambodia
South Vietnam
Loc Ninh
Củ Chi
Xuan Loc
Saigon
South China Sea
Saigon River
Gulf of Siam
0 50 100 kilometers
0 50 100 miles

TABLE OF CONTENTS

All of the events described in this book actually happened and involved people that I knew. But because memory is often clouded and ambiguous—especially after almost fifty years—specific details as I was reconstructing those events sometimes eluded me. With the exception of close friends, family, and several soldiers with whom I served, people's names have been changed to protect their privacy.

Preface

This memoir has been swirling around inside my head for forty-six years now. Even though I've told much of it to friends and family (it's not like I can't talk about it or am unwilling to go there), it seems like once I get started I'm never quite sure how far to go; how much to divulge; what layer to take it to—for my audience's comfort and/or my own. I mean some stuff is pretty doggone funny . . . to my way of thinking anyway. And other stuff—well—I'm talking about being in a *war*, and as rumor has it, for those who haven't witnessed it first hand, there's some nasty, gut wrenching shit that goes on in war. Some people want to hear about it; others reveal through their facial expressions. (I can see it in their eyes: *Please* don't go there, *please. I feel bad that you had to experience all that, but . . .* Okay, okay, I won't.)

Many years back, a friend of mine—he was just an acquaintance then—asked me if I'd seen the movie, *Full Metal Jacket?* "Did I *see* it?" I told him. "I was *there.* I lived that shit." Oh boy! The look in his eyes was like, Wow! Do tell. I'm interested.

He called me at work and asked me if I'd be willing to share my experiences in Vietnam with his history class at a local prep school. "I know I'm putting you on the spot, Rick," he said, "and understand completely if you don't want to. I mean, the last thing in the world I want to do is open up old wounds and make you relive . . . ."

What I thought, sitting at my desk, was . . . "No. No way. Sorry Andy. I don't think I can handle it. No, definitely not." What I *said*, suddenly breathing heavily, already imagining myself sitting nakedly and bearing my soul to a bunch of curious teenagers, was, "Sure. Of course. I'd be glad to." Then, looking around, my heart pounding after we'd picked a day and time, I said to myself, "Jesus Christ. Why the fuck did I just go and do *that*?"

Andy explained to me that the class's assignment was to find a Vietnam veteran and interview him. But the class had balked. Even if they found a Vietnam veteran to interview, which didn't sound all that easy, they were afraid that the veteran, especially as he began answering their questions, might snap, flip out, and possibly harm them. I mean it's not like they hadn't heard of this kind of thing happening, or there wasn't a precedent of Nam vets flipping out, going on rampages. Anyway, Andy changed the assignment. A real live Nam vet was going to visit their class and speak to them. Their assignment was to come up with some questions.

According to Andy, the class expected their guest to show up on a motorcycle and with a bandana wrapped around his head, a long, scraggly beard, pony tail, tattoos, fatigue shirt, the whole bit, and stoked up on something when he would begin to start mumbling incoherently, "the war, man, it was fucked up, man" (which of course it was), "nobody gives a shit, man." They were quite blown away when this rather clean cut, gray haired gentleman wearing khakis, penny loafers, and a button-down shirt arrived, looking nervous, not quite sure what he was doing there. My heart was pounding. It was like, oh man, the first time—anytime—I've visited the Vietnam War Memorial and suddenly it all comes rushing back. I'm back over there again.

Andy introduced me. I sat down, took a deep breath, glanced at my notes and . . . next thing I knew the bell was ringing. I looked around, unsure of where I was. What just happened? I wasn't sure. Oh yes, I'm . . . .

Walking with Andy out to my car, I apologized; told him I was sorry.

"Sorry?" he said. "Are you kidding me? That's the most incredible class I've ever seen. Those students were glued; they will never be in another class like that. Do you realize what a great teacher you are?"

I don't even know what I said. I just let it rip. Pour out of me. One moment Andy said I was crying; the next moment he and the class and I were laughing; at times I was ranting and raving.

I taught that class once a year for five years.

All those bright eyes staring at me. Listening to my every word. I wonder if any of them ended up in Iraq or Afghanistan. Know what bugs me? Those enticing, propagandistic television ads by the military showing young men and women jumping out of helicopters and what not; firing exotic —whoa! now *that* could mess up your whole day—weapons. Instead of showing neat, adventuresome, how-cool-is-*that* shit, they should show a soldier scooping up the ashes of a friend who was burned to death from the floor of a personnel carrier and emptying them into a body bag; or gravely wounded soldiers finishing out their days in some forgotten ward of a V.A. hospital. But you know what? It wouldn't make any difference. None. None whatsoever. In the same way that after one time I never had to worry about being ordered to go down inside a tunnel again because there was always an ample supply of gung-ho fellow platoon members who were just dyin' to take on that challenge (you got it, bro! You have definitely, damn sure fucking *got* it!), in the same way a surprising number of soldiers raised their hands in—"me", "me", "me"—fashion when asked who wanted to crawl around under the earth (but be careful, there might be booby traps set up down there) there's an endless supply of incredibly brave, but heedless, ready an' rarin' t'go young people just chomping at the bit to go jumping into the fray. Bring it on motherfucker. Semper fi an' all that. Remember how in the movie, *The Deer Hunter*, Christopher Walken (Nickie) turns to—whomever—as they're sitting at the bar (this is, of course, before they all head over and discover the true nature of what's awaiting them) and says, cockily, like he's invincible, "I hope they send me where the bullets're flyin' an' the fightin's the worst." There will never be a problem filling the ranks. Ever. Even if . . . Yeah, even if despite all the glorious, high minded causes bandied about by politicians and generals and whomever else, the war being fought ends up being fought for nothing, for naught!

* * *

In writing this memoir, trying to recall my experiences and the people I knew during *that year*, it's as if I'm recalling—in some sort of reverse *déjà vu* fashion—what happened in some other life. I've been here before, I'll think, as I walk along a path in some wooded area, or hear rain drops splashing in a nearby puddle, or while breathing in hot, muggy air. In my mind suddenly I'm walking through a jungle on patrol, or cleaning a weapon (disassembling and reassembling a fifty-caliber machine gun for instance—*Jesus*). *Could I really* do *that*? How about blind-folded; the fifty-caliber and M-60 machine guns, the M-16 rifle and the M-79 grenade launcher?

"Emily, when you were in Vietnam" (my daughter Emily was in Vietnam with the Semester-At-Sea program her junior year at Penn State) . . . "when you were in Vietnam, sweetie, it was brutally hot, right? I mean, tell me. Come on. It's the hottest place you've ever been, right?"

"Dad, I was . . . I was in India, too. Remember? And Cambodia. Oh my God. Angkor Wat. I thought I was going to die. And Guatemala."

"Yeah, but . . ." and I'll think of her over there, my oldest daughter, crawling around in one of the Chu Chi tunnels—or traveling by bus (a *bus*? You mean a *tour bus*?), along the same road my outfit came down from the Cambodian border at the beginning of the Tet Offensive—and I'll tell her how when I first got over there, I panicked. "I could hardly breathe it was so hot and muggy. How am I going to make it through a whole year like this? I wondered. I felt as if I was drowning."

And she will look at me and say, "Yes, Dad, it was hot. Brutal." Then, "Dad. *Dad.* It was hot, Dad. Brutal." And I'll nod my head, remembering. Oh, I was hot over there alright.

Acknowledgements

I would like to express my heartfelt gratitude to my good friend Ed Breisacher, who provided me with an endless supply of inspiration and encouragement in writing this book, and worked tirelessly to help me complete it. I would also like to thank Jim Plastine for his competent technical assistance.

1.
I Wanted To Go

Not a day has gone by during the past forty-six years that I haven't thought about that place over there—*the Nam,* as those of us who fought over there called it. Not Nam. Not Vietnam. *The Nam.* I'll hear that sound, the sound of a helicopter flying overhead, and whammo! There I am yelling at some whacked out door gunner who's perched menacingly at the opening on the side of the gunship hovering above me, firing his M-60 machine gun *way* too close to where I'm sitting inside the armored personnel carrier driver's compartment. "You come any closer asshole," I shout at this adrenalized—and whatever the hell else he's on—cowboy getting his jollies as red-orange tracer rounds streaming down from his sixty make it look as if he's trying to pee on me, "and I'll climb up out of this here hatch and empty a sixteen clip into your sorry ass." He can't hear me, this dude, of course, with the deafening noise that, not just he, but our platoon firing fifties and sixties into the tree line below him is making, but as we lock eyeballs, me looking up over my shoulder and squinting at him through blinding sunlight, him pausing for a moment, giving the brrrrrap of his machine gun a brief rest and then aiming in another direction. I know he knows what I'm thinking and is heeding my warning. And here comes another gunship. And *another.* Why? What's the point? The Phantoms have already swooped down—twice—and released that God awful, horrifying, jelly-like shit (napalm) the lieutenant called in—oh that stuff's nasty, thick black clouds of smoke rising from big orange fireballs as the canisters floated above our heads and exploded less than twenty feet away (uh, would prefer to not have any of that stuff get on me thank you very much). All this occurring, of course, while the two or three V.C. (Viet Cong) who fired the rockets at us are sitting safely inside a tunnel, waiting for our *give em everything we got* counter attack to be over. Soon as we *Americans* calm down (stop showing off), the medevac choppers come in to pick up the wounded (no dead this time), the V.C. will venture out again and . . . .

Ah, that thudding sound, rotor blades smacking the air. I hear it and suddenly I'm lying on a hospital bed in intensive care listening to the loud drumming of medevac choppers as they bring in the wounded. One of those brought in wakes up in the bed next to me and realizing that he's lost both his legs, starts screaming, "I want to die, I want to die," at the top of his lungs. Major Tompkins comes over and reads the riot act to the kid, and tells him: "How dare you broadcast that you want to die in front of all these brave, wounded men who are worse off than you and probably won't make it." Woe Nellie. Hold on. Are you *shitting* me? Later, when the boy is asleep, finally, and the major comes over to check on him, I reach over and grab the major's arm. "Major, tell me," I say, "Please tell me that what I just saw and heard, didn't just happen. That I . . . Please tell me I was dreaming." I look at the major with pleading eyes. "I . . . was hallucinating, right?" . . . No. I wasn't.

But that noise. Of a helicopter off in the distance getting closer. Does it make me think of dust-offs? Choppers coming in and bringing out the dead and wounded? You bet. But also, the incredible silence that seemed to fall over wherever we were after the choppers were gone, had left; the unbearably sad and lonely feeling I had—like I'd been abandoned, left to fend for myself—after my friend, Blackman (bless his only-been-in-the-country-a-month heart), was helicoptered out with a million-dollar wound after our first fire fight. For real? You're outa here? Leaving me? Looking around at that Godforsaken place and thinking, oh wow, oh wow, there's no way in hell I'm ever going to get myself out of here alive or in one piece.

Choppers. I'll hear one and—oh boy, here we go again—find myself standing in the back of an armored personnel carrier next to a machine gun as Henry Ross (Hank), speaking on the radio below, tells the pilot of a Chinook helicopter coming under intense fire as the pilot is trying to lower the supplies (petro, c-rats, beer, ammo) dangling in a net underneath, "if you don't get your sorry ass down here with *my* beer, I'm going to come out there and shoot you down myself." "Who *is* that?" the enraged, indignant pilot wants to know. He gets to a certain point—almost there, the gasoline drums at the bottom of the net almost touching the ground—and then is forced to rise, pulling the net back up. Which just pisses the hell out of Hank, who feels that the pilot is fucking with him. The pilot makes it down, the supplies are unloaded, Hank gets his beer, and Captain McNulty promises the pilot that the drunken soldier, who has been threatening him, will be severely punished.

Well, not exactly. Hank, you see, is a special kind of dude. Unlike anyone else *ever* in this man's Army. Untouchable it would seem. Infamous—or famous, depending on whose viewpoint . . . throughout the regiment. A living legend. And he was my friend. We were crew members together. *Wait a sec. Hold on.* **You** *knew Hank Ross? The Ross element*? Yes. Yes, I did. Indeed I did.

Those were our days. That was my year! Other things, besides the sound of helicopters, can bring me back over there too, of course. There are all sorts of triggers that reawaken those long-ago memories, but more often than not, with no apparent trigger at all, suddenly there I am. Sergeant Morrison is yelling over the intercom at me, "What the fuck are you *doing*? Trying to get us all killed?" I was pissed off at him for making me his driver—*I'm going to make you the best damn driver in all Vietnam, soldier, he says.* (Oh yeah? Not if *I* can help it.) I'm speeding, blindly, recklessly (can't see a fucking thing through the thick clouds of dust being shot up from the treads of our armored personnel carriers—tracks we called them—down a steep, narrow dirt road that winds next to the side of a hundred-foot drop-off). That road, which amazingly I and my fellow crew members didn't go flying off of (they were poised, Sergeant Morrison, Simon, and Hank to jump off the top of the track onto the road if they had to) led to a white, sandy beach where we were ferried, one track at a time, across a small inlet to the Batangan Peninsula, where we discovered it was almost impossible to drive—even an inch—or take a step without setting off a mine or booby trap, which members of our troop did regularly.

Or I'll be out on the Batangan, cowering shamefully in the driver's compartment as right up above me in the Track Commander's hatch my friend Murphy is alternating firing the fifty-caliber and his M-16 only inches above my head. Oh, he's pissed. And rightly so. By not regularly tightening the treads of our track with a grease gun, which was one of my crucial maintenance duties as a driver, one of the treads came flying off during the night, on a "keep-the-road-cleared-and-open mission" while I was back getting some beauty sleep. What a rude awakening I had when torn from whatever I was dreaming—whatever stage of the "going home" process I was on—Murphy turned over the cot, with me on it. "Hope you got yourself plenty of rest," he shouted at me (as I waited for a knee or fist to hit me in the mouth, and cautiously lifted myself off the ground and dusted myself off), "because, guess what, asshole, you're on duty for the next eight hours."

Or I'll be kneeling next to St. James who, after flying out of the back of the track, "Double Deuce," after it set off a mine as we were starting up a ridge; it was as if he'd been shot out of a cannon with one leg going one way, the rest of him another. Here he was, lying in some tall grass about thirty feet from the stricken track, which had been flipped over onto its *back,* and taking his last sputtering breaths before Donnie, our medic, pulled a poncho liner up over his face.

Or I'll find that old rage rising to the surface again, watching Sergeants Waters and Hanover gun down an unarmed Viet Cong boy whom I'd taken prisoner—jus' t'show me how it's done, doncha know.

* * *

I *wanted* to go to Vietnam. Yup. Was looking forward to it. In fact—oh please, don't look at me like that—the night before I left, I had a dream in which I received new orders telling me that I wasn't going. There'd been a mistake and I was to report back to Fort Knox and finish out my tour of duty there. I remember waking up in a—please tell me it ain't so, that I'm dreaming—cold sweat, breathing heavily and then looking around in the dark and realizing that, whew! Thank goodness, I was only having a bad dream. Okay, okay, hold on! Finding out that you didn't have to go to Vietnam, after all, was a bad dream? You got it, kimosaube. I'm speaking in retrospect here. Before . . . before all that happened.

I brought the war upon myself, of course. Flunking out of school—well—allowing myself to be placed on academic suspension for the upcoming 1965-66 school year with what was happening in Southeast Asia, I was pretty certain that Uncle Sam would soon come knocking, saying, I WANT *YOU*! So, feeling that—who knows?—the Army might do me some good, help me grow up as they say, help me set some more meaningful priorities for myself (my father was certainly thinking that way), so I wrote to the draft board and asked them to please speed things up.

I was staying with a friend in Newport, California, when my father called and informed me that I'd gotten a letter from the draft board. "You want me to open it?" he asked.

"Yeah, sure. Go ahead." I was to report to the Selective Service office in Rochester, New York, on April 18. It was April 2nd, the day after April Fools. I had two weeks. Which meant I had to get my ass in gear. My heart was pounding. The *Army*? Three weeks from now I'll be in the *Army*? Okay, okay, I know. This is what I requested, but, wow, jeez man, what if I was only joking?

Knowing I'd had a little leeway before the draft board got their act together after I asked them to place me at the front of the list, I spent three weeks in Boulder, Colorado, flipping burgers and having one last hurrah before having to—oh boy! What I didn't know—stand at attention in formation while some dumbass drill sergeant made snide remarks about my sexual orientation and spouted out horrible, demeaning things about my mother.

From Denver I traveled by Greyhound bus to Los Angeles,

and then from L.A. I traveled by bus out to Newport where I stayed with a friend—a fraternity brother who had flunked out of the University of Colorado the same time I did, but was enrolled at Orange Coast Community College, which meant he still had a student deferment. Hold on. Could I have done something like that? Sure. Of course. But I didn't. Fuck it. Tell me, where did my give-a-shit attitude at such a crucial time in my life come from? *Better get in step, boy and I didn't say Leroy.*

(A brief note here. After my bus pulled into the L.A. terminal at two or so in the morning, I picked up my luggage, walked outside, and asked a black patrolman standing on the corner where I might catch a bus to Newport. "Say *what?*" the officer asked, looking at me, wondering if what he was seeing—*me*, a young white man standing there before him—was for real. "Look, if I was you," he said, still shaking his head in disbelief, "I'd hightail my white ass back inside that terminal there an' stay put till mornin'. Dig? You start walkin' down these streets at this hour, any hour. . ." He looked into my eyes. "You have no idea where you are, do you, son? No, you don't. Maybe someone inside can explain it to you. Meanwhile, unless you've got a death wish, are planning on committing suicide . . . and even if you *are*, I'm ordering you back inside that building." Wow. What if that officer hadn't been there and stopped me. Would I have crossed the street and . . . Indeed I would have. "Say, can you fellas tell me where I might catch the bus going out to Newport?")

Hard to say how far I would have gotten, or what my life expectancy on those streets that night would have been. But I'll tell you one thing: I have since dreamed of what might have happened. Walking along, oblivious—Jesus, was I *that* naïve?—and being confronted by a bunch of gangland thugs who were still all charged up and full of hatred following the race riots that the police and the National Guard had quelled only three weeks before and were still simmering, ready to blow again. Mentally walking along in the dark in a place like that is, of course, the stuff that nightmares are made of. And then—well—let's see, twelve months later?—I was assigned to a track on which two of the crew members were young blacks who were from cities in which race riots were currently taking place. When I told Simon what happened to me in Watts, he broke out laughing and declared I was even dumber than he'd thought. He was already shaking his head and thinking what a dumb shit I was, after I'd explained to him how come I would be in Vietnam fighting in the first place.

Anyway, after my father read the draft board's instructions to me, I did something that may have been worthy of entry into the Guinness Book of World Records. Which was, I traveled by Greyhound bus from Los Angeles to New York City. Say *what?* Yup. Straight through, bro, for 72 hours. Stiff. Raggedy. Didn't sleep all that well. Saw the country that I was about to serve though, that—well—as it turned out I ended up fighting for. All kinds of thoughts swimming in my head as I sat looking out the window on that bus. Those buses. As I woke up in—um, let's see—were we still in New Mexico? Finally, dragging my ass off the bus in the Port Authority in New York City. Praise the Lord! Walking over to gate number 9, greeting the driver as I boarded a bus to Princeton, New Jersey, and completing the final leg of my pre-service marathon journey.

Even though I was living with my parents in Princeton, New Jersey, my draft board was located in Rochester, New York, where I'd grown up and registered. The day before I was to report to the draft board, I took a bus (oh boy, here we go again) from the Port Authority (wasn't I just *here*?) to the bus terminal in Rochester where I was picked up by my uncle. He drove me over to his home where I spent the night, and then the next morning—at the crack of dawn—he drove me over to the old, grey building in which selective service had its offices. And off I went, just as my father and two of his brothers had twenty-two years before. My dad had three brothers, two of whom were in the Army during WWII. Dad was an Army quartermaster lieutenant, who graduated from Officer Candidate School (OCS) in 1944, the year I was born, and he strongly recommended that I do the same. Hey, you're going in? Might as well make the most of it, he used to joke self-deprecatingly around his brothers, who enjoyed teasing him about how his only wound during the war was the broken ear drum he received while playing sharks and minnows in the clear, warm waters of the Pacific while stationed in Hawaii. In 1946 he was assigned to the aircraft carrier, *USS Saidor*, from which he and other officers standing on deck wearing special goggles to protect their eyes from the blinding light from the explosion, as they witnessed the Bikini Atom Bomb tests during Operation Crossroads. I still have the coconut dad sent me from Bikini Atoll when I was two years old. On the side of the brown, now rock-hard coconut—I imagine him reaching over and picking it off a tree or bending down and grabbing it where it had fallen and was half buried in sand—he'd carved the letters, BIKINI and then below that the year, 1946. I'm pretty sure the coconut is not radioactive, because he'd obviously picked it up and carved on it before watching the mushroom-cloud spectacle from aboard ship twenty miles away. Ironically, one of the ships destroyed during the tests was the destroyer on which my father-in-law had been the ship's supply officer, a ship on which seventeen shipmates of his were killed during a kamikaze attack. Up until several years before his death in 2004—almost sixty years after the Bikini tests—my father continued to receive questionnaires from the Army periodically, wanting to know if he or any of his children had suffered any of the listed symptoms for radiation sickness. "I, of course, am excluded, you know," I'd point out teasingly to my brother and sister when dad proudly made us aware that he'd once again received one of these questionnaires. And they'd go, "yeah, yeah. Thanks." The fact that *I* was born two years *before* the tests and they were born—well, let's see—one and four years *after*—well—fortunately whatever level of radiation my dad had been exposed to never seemed to be a health-wise issue for him or Lee or Sue.

My uncle Dick was an Army M.P., who was stationed in London during the Blitz, and my uncle Bob was the only survivor of an infantry battalion during the Battle of the Bulge when he was removed from the battlefield after passing out with a burst appendix. While he was recovering in a London hospital, Uncle Dick visited him. According to my father, Uncle Bob never spoke about the war and what happened to him while in Europe until I came back from Vietnam and started relating my experiences. My guess is, hearing his nephew explain, often tearfully, what he'd just gone through was a little hard to take. Not that he wasn't deeply sympathetic. He and I were very close and, after all, we had that very special bond that came from each of us having *fought* for our country and been in combat. Although—woe! The Bulge. Gotta say, based on what I've read (and what my uncle shared with me), my experience in Vietnam, with respect to carnage and slaughter (and, yes, hardship in many ways, fighting day in and day out in sub-zero weather), seemed to pale in comparison.

At any rate, I had dinner with my aunt and uncle, after which Uncle Dick and I stayed up late reminiscing and looking at photographs, and then in the morning Uncle Dick was only too glad—proud, honored—to hand the family-service-to-our-country torch over to me. My dad and all three of his brothers were staunch Republicans and ascribed to the hawkish domino theory that if South Vietnam fell to the communists, so would the rest of Southeast Asia.

Sooooooo, from the selective service office where I "signed in" after Uncle Dick left me off—"Good luck, Rick. Come on. Don't be so glum. It won't be *that* bad"—and after a female clerk behind one of the desks looked up at me, like, oh you poor bastard, and then ran a line through my name on the list in front of her—*Yup. That's me, sweetheart. I'm here. I showed up*—and after some concerned, caring soul handed me a Bible and said a prayer for me as I was leaving the building, I and a dozen or so other draftees boarded a bus and were driven to Buffalo, New York. In Buffalo, we were greeted by an Army sergeant, who led us into a building where, after being given physicals—standing in line with dropped pants and underwear, while a dude who looked like Doctor Strangelove grabbed our balls and told us to cough—we were herded into a room that had a large American flag hanging from a pole in front of it and sworn in. *Oh shit! Let the fun begin. I, Richard James Alexander, just got inducted into the fucking Army.*

That night, the night after I'd raised my right hand and swore to—whatever it was I'd promised, with God and whoever else as my witness—I spent sleeping on a cot in a flea bag hotel. I remember waking up in the morning and thinking as I looked out through the filthy windows at whatever Buffalo street it was . . . thinking, oh boy, you've done it now, haven't you? Truly you have. Where is all this going to lead? No place good, I feared.

The Army picked up the tab for breakfast at a greasy spoon next to the hotel (*Gee, thanks. That's really big of you*), and as I was sitting at a table sipping coffee and nibbling on some sort of stale pastry, Timmy Cahill, whom I'd known since grammar school but hadn't seen since—well—since he and I were standing next to each other in the little league field one Saturday morning and he turned to me and said, "Jesus Christ! Who *is* this fucking clown?" (referring to my dad, who was trying to hit fly balls out to us before practice and kept missing the ball or sending out little dribbles). Timmy got up from where he was sitting, put a quarter in the Juke box, punched a few numbers and looking over at me, said, "this is for you, Rick." Moments later, Barry Sadler—remember him?—started telling us about "fearless men who jump and die" and other heroic deeds as he sang the "Ballad of the Green Berets." "Thanks," I said, and we all just sat there envisioning God knows what and wondering what was in store for us. (With respect to my dad's trying to hit fly balls to Timmy and me six or so years before, I reminded my dad years later of the not quite up to par batting sessions he'd held many years before, and he laughed that wonderful belly laugh of his. Dad had a wonderful sense of humor, could laugh at himself and though he was an excellent all-around athlete, hitting fly balls to his son—who was out in the field fucking *dying*. Geez, Dad, come on—and whoever else was out there with me—well, that was not his strength.)

At any rate, over at the Buffalo train station where we waited in the lobby for a train to Grand Central Station in New York City—from which we would walk over to the Port Authority and catch a bus to Fort Dix—I made eye contact with a young man who was standing by himself over in the corner, and he came over and introduced himself.

"Howdy," he said, reaching over and shaking my hand. "You guys headed for Dix?"

"Fraid so," I said.

"Yeah, me too." Mind if I join you?"

"Not at all." He was by himself because he'd enlisted and been told by his recruiter to join us riff-raff draftees who were headed for the same basic training location as him. In fact, he'd been told to "round us up" and lead the way. He'd signed up for three years, which meant he was guaranteed the airborne training he'd asked for. Guaranteed also was that he'd be assigned to either the 173rd or 101st Airborne when he got to Vietnam, assuring that he'd see plenty of action and be in the thick of things.

At the Vietnam War Memorial many years later, I struggled with whether I should see if his name was in one of the thick, wall location books. I liked believing, as far as I was concerned, he'd made it, come home, was married and . . . sure, I was puzzled, worried, when he didn't write back to me a second time after he arrived in Vietnam. In his first letter to me after I arrived in Vietnam, he wrote from Fort Benning that it wasn't fair, me being over there and him not. He'd signed up to go, had enlisted to go to Vietnam and fight, and I hadn't. Then I got a letter from him stating that he was there, finally, that he was up north with the 101st. "Damn, it's hot over here," he wrote. "You were right. It's like being trapped in a sauna." That was the last I heard from him. Which made no sense. We'd been writing to each other since basic training. But I hoped and didn't want to know the truth, if the truth was what I feared it might be. Which it *was*. Forty years later I was searching the Vietnam War Memorial web site and found his name. But I thought it might not be him. I mean, Douglas Henning PFC? That didn't make sense; didn't seem possible. No way was he still a private. He would've been at least a corporal by then. But then I scrolled down and saw a picture. The one taken of him at Fort Dix after we finished our basic training. Oh no, oh no. My heart was pounding. He *was* killed over there. I thought of us standing next to each other in the Buffalo train station; me looking into his startlingly blue eyes. He was eighteen. My mom loved him. He came and stayed with my parents and me several times during weekend passes. We'd kept in touch during the eight months I was stationed at Fort Knox. Fuck! He really *was* killed. He really was. Not living in Buffalo, I really couldn't look him up.

* * *

My first year in the Army, from April 19, 1966, until the same day and month a year later when I received orders for Vietnam, was filled with personal contradictions. On the one hand, I was intrigued by what I imagined it was like being a combat soldier in Vietnam. I had this strange urge to discover for myself what it would be like to be over there: on patrol; in a fire fight; standing in a jungle clearing with my shirt off like soldiers I'd seen in photographs; sitting on top of a bunker; on top of an armored personnel carrier as it's noisily knocking down trees and cutting a path through a jungle—smitten by Hemmingway's old adage that war is man's greatest adventure. On the other hand, there I was, all through those first four months of training, having to "low crawl" to chow because I couldn't wipe off the smirk that was always on my face. Who *were* those clowns telling me what to do, constantly yelling at me? Because of my obvious lack of enthusiasm when charging dummies with a fixed bayonet; the lackadaisical manner in which I yelled, "kill! Kill! Kill!"—as I stuck the dummy. *You end up in the Nam, yer dead meat, soljer.* Yeah, yeah, yeah!

Seems as if I had a bad attitude, doesn't it? Certainly not the right attitude for going over and fighting in a war. And, after all, wasn't the training cadre, the in-our-face drill sergeants only doing their job? There to help prepare wise-ass, college dropout punks like myself—no matter how much they hated us—so that when the time came—*it **will** come. Guaran-fucken-teed*—we had the best chance possible to make sure that those little slant-eyed motherfuckers we were fighting over yonder died or were wounded for *their* country, and not the other way around. Thus the incessant, often clever, brainwashing remarks that I often found humorous, but could never in a million years buy into. And for which right from the get-go I developed a raw hatred for. A lean, mean, killing machine?—that's what you assholes are trying to turn me into? Forget it. "Neva hatche," as the South Vietnamese used to say.

During my first few days at Fort Dix, as I was trying to avoid being nabbed by one of the seemingly hundreds of non-coms snooping around, trying to find some still wet-behind-the-ears sucker like me to do their work for them prior to beginning my eight-week basic training, I and another fresh-off-the-street, didn't know his ass from his elbow, dude, stepped off to the side of the road when a sergeant driving by in a pick-up, pulled over, and leaning out the window asked us if we wanted to help him deliver laundry. "It's a good gig," he said, smiling. Seemed like an awfully friendly chap. "Better'n KP or picking up cigarette butts, which is what yer gonna be doin' if ya don't make yerself scarce some place soon. You fellas jus' get here? Well, I'll make life easy for ya the next few days 'fore ya start yer trainin'. Hop in. I'm Sergeant . . ." (he told us his name, we told him ours as we shook hands, and then he drove off). He wasn't lying. Driving around the base helping him deliver and pick up laundry was a good gig. Of course, unbeknownst to us there was a method to his friendly, welcoming persona. Which, okay, we should've picked up on. But even if we had—it was worth it being with him and not having to be stuck in the back of a hot, sweaty, smelly kitchen laboring over endless grease laden pots and pans. After we finished, the sergeant asked us if we wanted to do the same thing tomorrow.

"Sure. Fuck yes," I said.

"Okay, great. I'll pick you up—how bout in front of those barracks over there? 8:00 okay? By the way, I'm a little short on cash and . . . " I forget the reason he needed it, but it sounded plausible, he'd been good to us, had watched over us, said he'd pay me back tomorrow when he picked us up. So, in response to his seemingly reasonable request, I reached into my back pocket, pulled out my wallet, handed him a crisp ten dollar bill and, I know, I know, there's one of us born every minute, right? Or is it every hour? Probably the former.

So, I would imagine you've already formulated in your mind, the puzzled, disappointed expressions that came over our faces when waiting at the appointed time and place, the helpful, jovial laundry service sergeant didn't show up. "You *sure* this is where he said?"

"Yes, I'm sure."

"And this . . . Shit! It's 8:45. Were we . . . ?"

"We were here at the right time, yes. We've been duped. You ain't never seein' that ten dollars again."

So be it. Lesson learned. I feel a little embarrassed even now thinking about that incident—when I told my dad, he just laughed. Welcome to the Army—but the main thing I remember about that day, was the story the sergeant told us during one of our many breaks and how he was the first soldier—there would be many more later—I'd looked at with the certain awe that came from being around someone who'd actually been in combat over there; who'd actually been in combat in Vietnam—*the Nam.* The way he'd said, *the Nam*—it was the first time I'd heard Vietnam referred to that way and had a certain, "I was *there*, bro"—in the shit authenticity to it—though now I don't believe for a minute the story he told. (I may have believed it at the time, because; it was fun believing it: The *Argosy, True Adventure* magazine cover images he evoked telling how he and a friend had been captured during the monsoons and escaped by bashing their captors' heads in with entrenching tools has never left me.

* * *

So, did I want to go over there and experience the harrowing adventures that the laundry-service sergeant claimed he'd had? No I did not!

Well, maybe. I'm not sure. I was intrigued by what was going on in that tiny country that I'd never even heard of until six months before. Also, somewhere in my subconscious—no—not my subconscious since I knew what I was doing . . . somewhere in my not too deep (couldn't have been too deep because I knew it was there) psyche I was compelled to do everything I could to—not just wake up one morning and find myself in Vietnam—but find that I was an infantry lieutenant over there. Where was this *coming* from? Had I watched too many war movies?

Anyway, while I was taking the psychological profile test to determine my strengths and weaknesses and what type of service I would be best suited for as an officer, I surprised myself by answering the questions in such a way that I would end up with a profile that matched perfectly with what the Army was looking for in an infantry officer. Was I a hunter? You bet. Did I feel comfortable around guns? Yes. Did I own a gun? Of course. Was I interested in fixing cars? Yes. Was I handy at fixing things around the house? Definitely. In other words, I was "mechanically" inclined. Yes. On and on and on, I painted a picture of myself that was pretty much the exact opposite of who I was and what I was interested in. Of my abilities and lack of abilities. I readily figured out the strategy of the Army psychologists who had developed the test and had fun—messing up I guess you'd call it—what they were trying to do. But why? *Why?* To this day I do not have an answer. I was bored, I guess, and it was a game. But—an *infantry* officer? An L-tee in—*the Nam?* Where the life expectancy . . . .

When I went for my interview in front of the OCS (Officer Candidate School) selecting board, they kept asking me about the infantry. Definitely zeroed in on that. Which made Dad nuts when I told him. "I thought you were interested in quartermaster?"

"I am," I said. "That's my first choice. But you have to pick one of the combat arms as your second choice and I picked the infantry."

Jeez, my father must have thought. What's *with* this kid?

Good question, Pop. What *was* with me?

Why did I have such a need to be something I wasn't?

Well, you can fool some of the people some of the time etcetera, etcetera—however that saying goes. But just before I left Fort Dix, the ten or so officers who had interviewed me (*grilled* my ass, focusing on my apparent proclivity toward the infantry) and recommended me for the next phase on my way to becoming an officer, questioned their judgment and hard earned evaluation skills when they found out how miserably I'd performed on the firing range, and was one of only a handful of trainees who almost had to repeat the eight-week training we'd just gone through because of it. After suffering the embarrassment and humiliation of being inept at the most important skill an infantry soldier is required to be proficient in, not to mention how miserable and depressed I was when informed that I was going to have to repeat the entire eight weeks I'd just been through, those of us who had come up short on the range the previous day—there were only five of us—were rounded up and escorted to a room where the company commander informed us that he'd been thinking a lot about our failure to get the minimum marksman score, how maybe we'd just had a bad day, and since we'd come so far and he valued us as soldiers (yeah, yeah, yeah, all staged, he did this every cycle, I'm sure), he was giving us another chance, so he could claim for his own proficiency rating that he had a one hundred percent on-time graduation rate. *Way t'go Cap'm*! So, once again, off we went to the range to see if this time—let's see, breathe in, hold breath, squeeze—we could cut muster and move on with the rest of the class. Oh, the harsh, unbelieving looks leveled at us from our fellow trainees as we climbed into the back of the truck that drove us away with our hearts pounding. *Please, please, God, help me to see what I'm supposed to be firing at and don't let me fail again.*

As a potential OCS candidate I was required to have advanced individual training (AIT) in one of the three combat arms (infantry, armor, or artillery). Thus, I received orders following basic training for armored reconnaissance training at Fort Knox, Kentucky, where, daily, for eight long weeks, I was practically the sole target of the training cadres' wrath for not, in their estimation, giving them the utmost, undivided attention they felt they deserved during their endless, mind numbingly boring, by-the-numbers training sessions. Yes, despite the fact that I needed to know and become proficient in the skills they were teaching us (because I—like the other trainees in class—might in the very near future actually have to utilize those skills) since there was a war going on and I could very well end up fighting in it. But also—hello, wake up whoever you are—I was planning on becoming an officer, something that the training officers were very much aware of and resented. Yet, despite these two very compelling reasons why I should have been concentrating and paying attention, I was often caught daydreaming—thinking of Janey Simpson who was still in Boulder—instead of paying attention to—well—how to disarm a mine, or strip down and put back together a fifty-caliber machine gun, which, along with an M-16 and M-60 machine gun, I was able to do in less than a year from then, blindfolded. I didn't want to be there. It was as if I'd been accepted at college and had enrolled in a course of study I thought I was interested in, but then after I got there realized I'd made a terrible mistake. Tough shit. Not a whole lot of Army provisions for that kind of dilemma. Anyway, for five weeks I suffered the embarrassment and humiliation of being torn from my time with Janey—from the letters I was mentally composing to her—to have to come up in front of the class and demonstrate what the training NCO had just taught us.

"What in the *fuck* are you doing here, soldier?"

"Yeah. Been asking myself that same question a lot lately, sarg."

Until, finally, much to the satisfaction and relief of the training cadre, I said, to hell with it and had them remove my name from the OCS list. Poor Dad. Just when he thought I was finally grabbing hold of the reins and doing something that would have a long lasting, positive impact on my life, I quit. Dear Mom and Dad—I could see the disappointment in my father's eyes as he read the letter that Mom had most likely already opened and read. "Maybe," Mom would have tried to console him, "maybe it's just not for him, honey."

"Yeah, but . . . ."

I have no idea what I wrote. Something about this Army crap not being for me. I didn't want to have to spend an extra year in the Army just so I could be an officer and so I didn't say anything about how, given my attitude, I wouldn't have made it three weeks in OCS. Make that a week. Not that I'm proud of that. I'm not. It's just . . . it wasn't for me is all. Anyway, the legacy of my having withdrawn from OCS—oh how heavily that had weighed on me, how relieved I was to no longer have all that hanging over my head—was that my MOS (Military Occupation Status) was now 11Delta20, Armored Reconnaissance, which meant that if I ended up in Vietnam—which I *did*— I'd be assigned to a combat outfit—which I *was*. So be it.

Meanwhile, for the eight months preceding my orders for

Vietnam, I had the best damn assignment a disillusioned soldier like me could possibly have. Unlike my miserable AIT (Advanced Individual Training) experience, which for the most part I've tried to block out, I don't like seeing myself in such a blundering, un-warrior-like fashion. I remember just about everything that took place while I was stationed about a mile up the road from where I was quartered during AIT.

I remember standing in the turret of the A1E1 tank whose treads were splattering mud all over the jeep that was close behind us, as my friend L.D. Bryant, sitting in the driver's compartment below me, sped recklessly, chewing up the pavement along one of the base's highways. "Slow down, L.D.," I shouted over the intercom. "Jesus, man. What are you doing? There's a fuckin' colonel behind us. His driver's honking. They want us to pull over."

Ah! Those days. L.D. and I—and Russ and Leonard and Jeremy and all the other college, OCS drop outs (fuckups), who the Army wasn't sure what to do with while we waited for our overseas assignments—were having a ball while test-driving the newest, considered to be the most combat-ready, tanks and personnel carriers rolling off the GM production lines in Detroit; being *told* (it was our *job*, we were being challenged) to see if we could run the giant, thirty- and sixty-ton vehicles that had been turned over to us (go ahead, it's yours, don't be shy) into the ground.

How long could these state-of-the-art machines operate optimally with clowns like us at the helm? That was the million-dollar question that we spent eight months helping the engineers assigned to the Armor Board's Test and Evaluation Command to answer.

The man-made "bottoms," a marshy, low-land area that the engineers flooded periodically in order to simulate conditions in

Vietnam during the monsoons, served as a proving ground for the armored vehicles, where we ran punishing trials each day, and based on the data that was collected from the vehicle's gauges and other baseline indicators, and then analyzed, following our non-stop romps, the engineers made recommendations on how performance could be improved. It was from that muddy, swampy area that the tank L.D. was driving and I was commandeering had just emerged—we'd been driving around in muck for eight hours—and were headed back to the Armor Board's motor pool. It was one hell of a gig. Trying to abuse tanks. Personnel carriers. I dug it. No KP, no guard duty. Whooie! I mean, at some point I did want to go overseas, but this was the perfect assignment. Every other weekend off. Say, anyone up for going to Louisville this weekend? Or, as it turned out, I'm off to Lexington, in case anyone wants to join me. Through a friend, whose name I don't remember, I became an honorary member of a University of Kentucky fraternity. Which is how I met Diane. With whom I spent several wonderful weekends together.

But back to L.D. I remember him telling me as we stood next to the statue of some Confederate soldier in Nashville early one morning—we'd driven there on a whim, like we did everything else during those days when we were free to do so—when we weren't plowing through mud in the bottoms, listening to those engines scream, as if hollering for help, as their treads spun helplessly—yet again—in some quagmire, "You know, Allie," he said, those unrestrained blue eyes of his gazing devilishly into mine, "if this was a hundred years ago, I'd have te shoot yer sorry Yankee ass. You know that, don't ya?"

"Yeah, well, lessen I 'append te shoot yer rebel, lost the mother fucking war, first."

L.D. He had told me as we were haulin' ass down whatever

highway we were on—he and some of his University of Tennessee drop-out friends had cars—that he didn't like my friends and that I was the only Yankee he'd ever met that he even halfway liked, that he could even consider being friends with.

L.D. I remember how I ended up in jail following a drinking contest we'd had. Our friend Skaggs—Sergeant Skaggs—was an NCO who had seen combat in Vietnam with the 25th Infantry Division and was a few years older than us—and one of the few NCOs at the Armor Board who didn't drink himself into oblivion every night. He got wind of L.D.'s challenge to me and graciously offered to be the designated driver to and from one of the hundreds of gin mills lining both sides of Highway 31, which ran from Fort Knox to Louisville. Based on the unusually high number of fatalities due to drunken driving on it each year, Highway 31 was considered the most dangerous highway in America.

Two weeks prior to our contest—each of us drinking a shot glass full of beer every minute (me on the sixty, L.D. on the thirty) until Skaggs, who was sitting with us at the table, pouring, declared the winner to be. . . *L.D.* hands down. It was like calling a fight. One thousand and one, one thousand and two . . . you okay, Allie? OK, as I said, the four of us walked out of a gin-mill strip joint late one evening just as the driver of a VW Bug with four other soldiers crammed into it, pulled out onto the highway and was immediately struck by a tractor trailer barreling toward them. Good God! As horrific as anything I would end up seeing in Vietnam. The headless bodies of two of the soldiers lying, bleeding where they'd been thrown through the windshield onto the wet pavement; their heads . . . .

Very sobering. A year or so later while I was in the Nam, L.D. sent me a letter informing me that two of our Armor Board friends had been killed on that highway, and I thought of all the wild and crazy nights we'd spent getting drunk together in those sleazy strip joints. But the night Skaggs watched L.D. gradually drink me under the table as we downed shots of beer he kept setting up—easy at first, but then, wow!—two MPs and a civilian cop entered the building and working in tandem (let's see, who are we going to catch tonight) began checking to see if any of the drunken, rowdy young men cheering the dancer who had just whipped off her g-string on stage was a soldier off post without a pass.

"You fellas from Fort Knox?" one of the MPs came over and asked.

"No, "said Skaggs, offering to be our spokesman. L.D. chimed in also. Always with all the angles, L.D. Ain't no sorry ass flatfoot and two dufus, baby-faced MPs gonna get the best a me.

"Then yer civilians?"

"Yes."

"Visiting I suppose?"

"You got it, pal."

"Okay," the civilian cop said, "May I see some identification? Plus yer draft status card."

"You bet." So everyone—except me, of course—pulled out their wallets and handed over what the cop wanted. On top of being drunk, I wasn't able to produce an I.D. showing that I was a civilian, and upon further scrutiny from the MPs—much to the dissatisfaction of L.D. (***What*** *in the fuck're you doin', Allie?*), announced to the three self-satisfied assholes glaring at me. "Okay, I'm a soldier, yes."

"At Knox?"

"Where the fuck else?"

"And you . . . ?"

"My pass? I seem . . . " I continued to fumble with my wallet. "I seem to have misplaced it."

"Uh, I think you better come with me, soldier."

So off I went, along with some other drunken soldier who didn't have a pass. As we were being driven to Louisville—after having been pushed out into the cold air like criminals and then shoved into the back of an Army patrol car—the soldier sitting next to me complained that he'd just gotten back from *the Nam* (there it was again, that phrase, evoking all sorts of—you were *there*, in the shit?—images). "Now look. Ain't this somethin'? I do a little celebratin', have myself a little fun and—what the *fuck,* man—I'm bein' taken t'jail by a couple a rinky dink rent-a-cop-mother fuckers who think they're hot shit." As he talked, he pulled out his wallet and showed me how damaged it and the cards within it were from getting soaked during the monsoons. "Six months fightin' in the rain, sittin' out all night on ambush." As he rambled on I thought of him sitting in mud next to a path in the jungle somewhere and imagined the sound of rain pelting his helmet and pattering against the big leaves above him; I could feel the rain that was dripping off his helmet running down the back of his neck. What was it like being out there? How scared was he? Or do you get used to it?

As the MP driving left the highway and pulled onto a city road, the soldier next to me put his hand over his mouth, leaned forward and asked the driver to stop and open the door; he had to puke. I looked over at the soldier and then moving as far away from him as I could, shouted to the MP not driving, "Jeez, man, he's *serious*, open a fuckin' door," but the MP just glanced dismissively over his shoulder at me and said skeptically, shaking his head, "hey, I wasn't born yesterday, you know." And right then, right at that moment, the soldier leaned as far forward between the front seats as he could and let loose.

"Aw man," the driver realizing what had just happened yelled. "Fuck! Fuck!" Stopping the car, he checked his hands and sleeve to see if they had any vomit on them. The foul, rank mess the soldier in the back seat had just made was not only all over the arm rest but covered his lap as well. "What the fuck's the matter with you?" he shouted, looking over his shoulder to see if there might be another eruption. The soldier, using his shirt sleeve to wipe his mouth, seemed to be pulling back, retreating, but then suddenly he lurched forward, thrust his head as far into the front of the car as he could, and aiming at the driver, began retching again.

Yup. Maybe you fellas weren't born yesterday, but I gotta tell ya, judging from my vantage point here—and I seem to have weathered this clean, don't seem to have a drop on me—you and the inside of your precious vehicle here are currently stinkin' t'igh 'eavens and I'll be most grateful to get the fuck out of here.

In the Louisville jail that the Army had contracted with, to "hold" caught-off-post-without-a-pass dopes like me overnight, I was thrown into a cell with other drunks and miscreants where, with my head spinning (the good ol' whirlies), I spent the night on a steel framed bed with a moldy mattress wondering what in the hell had just happened. Sometime during the night a drunken street bum—one of the regulars I presumed—lashed out at me for getting up and inadvertently peeing in *his* sink. "What the fuck're you doin'?" he shouted indignantly. "That's where I wash. I have to *live* here, you know?"

"Sorry. It was a mistake. I thought . . . ."

Yeah!

Like I said, those days! *Dad, I. . . I just didn't want to wait around for six months before, well . . . I'm not up for OCS is all. This is better, even though . . . .* Oh well, L.D. damned near laughed hisself to death when I got back to the barrack and told him. A sergeant from the Armor Board came and picked me up. "Little too much to drink there, eh Allie?" opined Sergeant Carter. He was a friend of Skaggs. At the movies he would always have tears in his eyes when the national anthem was played. Approximately a year from when he picked me up and drove me back to base after my Article 15 offence. (I had to do twenty hours of hedge trimming and cutting grass.)

A year or so following that fiasco, I ran into Skaggs as he was returning to Vietnam—I saw him at regimental field headquarters near Loc Ninh on the Cambodian border just before the Tet Offensive, where he informed me that Carter, who had come over with him, had been shot in the head and killed on his first day in the bush.

What stays with me most about my night in Louisville, however, is the lost feeling I had sitting on the edge of the bed with my head spinning and listening to the clanking noise the jailer's keys made—loud, at first, but then the fading sound of steel doors being slammed shut as the jailer moved further and further away from where I was.

* * *

Back to the Armor Board. Even though I was very fortunate to have landed the "piece a cake" service I had there during my "waiting" period, the escalating war was never far from my thoughts. I read about it in *Stars and Stripes* and magazines I was able to get hold of, and watched what was going on over there on the T.V. that was in the day room, and remained obsessed with talking to soldiers who had seen combat over there.

"Your finger was sliced off during a fire fight?" I said to Skaggs once as we were sitting in the diner we often went to off base, imagining as I gazed deep into his eyes, the circumstances in which he'd received his million-dollar wound. He was the gunner of an assault team and kneeling next to a tree with an M-60 when he felt a sharp pain in the middle of his hand and looked down and . . . holy shit! Blood was springing up from . . . from where he no longer had a middle finger. He found the finger. It was just . . . lying there. On the ground. In that powdery red dust that got into everything. He handed it to the medic—"Here. I'm not sure anything can be done with this, but hold onto it for me, would ya?" But it ended up being unsalvageable. "They tried to sew it back on, but—well—you can see the result. Considering. I mean, given what's going on over there . . . Look at it this way, Allie. That piece of shrapnel—what *else* could it have been? —from the artillery that had been called in and was exploding *way too close to where I was thank you very much*, could have caused a lot more damage to my body than just . . . " He continued to explain that he was shipped back to the States, against his wishes. "I wanted to stay. That's where I belong. I'm a soldier. " I imagined him over there, walking along in the jungle, sweating in unfathomable heat, holding an M-60, swinging it back and forth, listening. He was *there* and had made it. Come home.

The overseas assignments for the two groups stationed at the Test and Evaluation Command, prior to the group I was in, were

Germany and Thailand, either of which I would have been okay with. Patrolling the western side of the Berlin Wall in a jeep for a year, or spending a year in the most exotic, far away land I could imagine, I could have dug either one. Nonetheless, when I received orders for Vietnam, it was not the nightmarish dread that most of those who received orders with me felt. No, don't ask me to explain, but I felt a strange, almost joyful exhilaration, a thrill that I wouldn't have felt if it had been for either of the other two. Vietnam. I was going to Vietnam. *Me.*

It was the middle of February. I kept looking at my orders to make sure I wasn't misreading them. In retrospect, strange behavior since I was *savoring* them. I was to report to Oakland Army Base on April 19. From there, I knew, I'd be flown to Tan San Knut Air Force Base in Saigon, where I'd board a bus and be taken to the 90th Replacement Company in Long Bien. Not too great. I was going over. To Vietnam. *The Nam.* Those soldiers I'd seen in newsreels and photographs; standing with their shirts off in jungle clearings, or walking along on patrol; sitting on top of personnel carriers; jumping with their rifles from helicopters and running head down through fields and rice paddies—that would be *me* soon.

"Hello . . . Mom? Hi Mom. Dad?" Dad picked up the phone in the bedroom. He'd just gotten home from work. Mom was in the kitchen. "I'm . . . going over. To Vietnam. I just got orders. I'm to report to . . . ."

Mom was crying. I could hear her sobbing.

"Mom, it's okay. I . . . I kind of want to go. I'll be fine."

"When do you leave?"

* * *

It was snowing out. There was already a foot of snow on the ground. I was standing in the dark in a phone booth. Across the street a tank was being driven into the motor pool. It was only partly visible. Snow was really coming down.

"I have a month before I leave. Orders came down—well—in my case I'll be in Vietnam for a year and then, that'll be it. I'll come home—God willing—and be discharged. Mom, it'll be okay, I promise."

Yeah, I promised. And Dad promised. Like somehow we knew.

At any rate, I was going over and I was glad. Unlike—well—Freelander, who immediately said, "fuck it! I'm not going," and then proceeded to not go. When he didn't show up with the rest of us at Oakland Army Base, I was shocked. He'd been serious. He really *had* gone to Mexico the way he said he was going to. It wasn't just drunk talk. I wonder whatever happened to him.

"Oh you poor bastard," L.D. said to me after I received my orders. "I was afraid that would happen." He was hoping we'd all be sent to Thailand. Spend our last year in the Army hanging out in Bangkok. He was excluded from going to Vietnam because his brother was a Marine there.

Just before I left Fort Knox—to go home for my month's leave before flying to San Francisco and then reporting to Oakland Army Base for shipment over—L.D. and his wife, Carol, and I were playing hearts in the tiny kitchen of the trailer they'd rented off base. Their TV was on, and it seemed every five minutes there was a newsreel showing combat. Remember those days? Live from South Vietnam . . . L.D. turned to me and said, "that's *you*, Allie. In what? Thirty-five days? That's you, my man. Take a good look." And I watched and thought, oh shit, that *will* be me, soon, and then, of course, it *was*. L.D. was right.

* * *

Also, just before I left—while I was "clearing base" (getting shots, etc.)—I was informed that Russell Di-Pasquale (one of my good Yankee friends whom L.D. didn't like) was almost killed when the jeep he was driving out to the field turned over and that he was over at the base hospital with a broken leg. Russ, who had received the same orders as me, was disappointed that he couldn't go. We'd been looking forward to going over together. Since we both had the same MOS, maybe we'd be assigned to the same outfit together. Russ's leg was broken badly. When I visited the hospital, I found him lying helplessly on a bed with his leg up in the air in some sort of sling contraption. When I saw him a year later—we wrote letters back and forth during my year over there—he was extremely pissed off at the orthopedic surgeon who'd operated on him and wanted to sue the Army. "Look," he said when we met in the Helicopter Club at the top of what was then the Pan Am Building after I got back, "my right leg. See how it's shorter. Those incompetent motherfuckers messed me up. I'm a gimp. Did you notice the way I was walking?"

Lying on the bed next to Russ when I visited him was a black dude who with two months to go in Vietnam had gotten his left foot blown off. Russ tells this guy, "Hey, my friend here, he's on his way over, off to the *Big Green*, and—well—you have any advice for him?"

He looks me in the eye, this guy, studies me—probably thinking, oh you poor bastard—and says, "yeah, man, sure, *defi-*

nitely, I have some advice for you. Remember your ABC's." I'm looking at this guy, trying to imagine the calamitous circumstances in which he lost his foot, and his eyes widen suddenly as if he knows some terrible, nasty secret (I find out later, of course, that he *does*), and he says to me, "Always Be Cool."

Umm . . . Always Be Cool. Good advice I find out, in a land where there is always underlying tension and fear and bitterness and resentment—and the tempers of angry, frustrated, armed-to-the-hilt soldiers are constantly flaring up during bitter arguments over such vital matters as . . . who gets what C-rats (who gets the beans'n'franks'n'fruit cocktail in other words) . . . who gets the last beer; the last . . . Bud, or Pabst, or Miller, or Hamm's that's lying at the bottom of the cooler all by its wee lonesome; or who . . . gets to listen to their own particular favorite type music, without the interference of someone else's. Large powder keg, that one. With any number of fellas—those who like listening to Loretta Lynn, Merle Haggard, and Johnny Cash (the Grand Old Opry crowd) on one side; and those who have more of an inclination toward the music of soul performers, on the other—ready to light a match to it, in a hot second, if they feel the sanctity of their music heroes has in any way been compromised or diminished. Best to just remain cool in certain tinderbox situations, and when certain mentally unstable folks start rantin'n'ravin', givin' indications that their not unusual edginess might be escalating to a new phase . . . .

Russell shook my hand and wished me luck and said he wished he was going over with me. "Bring me back an ear," he said, and the next thing I knew I was looking out the window of the plane that flew me from Louisville to Newark, New Jersey.

2.
Welcome to Blackhorse

Dad drove me out to Kennedy Airport in his Mercury Grand Prix. Long haul. To be just sitting there. Waiting to arrive at the airport so I could head off to war. Say again! It was raining. Perfect weather for the occasion. Each of us sitting in the car silently. Not much to say. Mom's best friend, Hartson, drove from Rochester to stay with her for a week following my departure. Hartson. Hartson Adams. An angel. Like my Mom. Best friends since childhood those two. Her husband, Art, and my father best of friends also. And their four children, Nance, Bill, Debby, and Wendy like brothers and sisters to Lee, Sue, and me. Hartson was like a second mother to me and like a grandmother to Emily and Julie after Mom died. Oh how Mom suffered. Could there possibly be any torture worse than what she went through those two years dying of cancer? Well, that year worrying each moment of every day for a year while I was in Vietnam, perhaps. Hartson came and stayed with us during that last week before Mom died. Hartson. Not wanting to interfere with my going off to fight in a war and leave-taking with Mom in the morning, she and I said goodbye the night before. I also said goodbye to Sue the night before. Tearful hugs. And in the morning when that dreaded time finally came, Mom, sobbing, held onto me and wouldn't let me go. I finally had to pull myself away. "Bye Mom. I love you."

At Kennedy Airport Dad offered to pay for a shoeshine if I so desired. You know, for my black shoes. That went with my khaki uniform that Mom had washed and ironed for me the night before. I'd heard her upstairs working while I was lying in bed unable to sleep.

"No, that's okay," I said. "But thanks."

"You sure?"

"I'm sure. Dad, you can go," I said. "I'm just going to, you know, wander around for a while."

"Sure?"

"Yeah, it's time. Bye Dad."

I held out my hand and he took it and then we hugged. We looked into one another's eyes. Father, son . . . Son, father. "I'll see you . . . ."

"See you in a year," he said.

"Yup. A year. Take care." I watched him walk down the stairs, cross the lobby and push his way through the revolving glass doors onto the street.

* * *

On the flight to San Francisco, I looked out the window at the white mist off in the distance. Niagara Falls. I thought of growing up near there, in Rochester. Trips to Niagara Falls. Standing on deck getting soaked as the Maid of the Mist pulled up close to the crashing Horseshoe Falls. "You kids stay with your father," Mom used to say as we climbed down to the bottom of the American Falls. As I flew over Boulder, I looked down and thought of Janey (how colossally I'd messed up that relationship) and how I could have still been down there walking among those red-tile-roofed buildings. Yet the truth was—okay, except for being with Janey. Did she even *know* that I was in the Army? Not to mention . . . ? No—I was glad I wasn't. I felt special. Privileged. I was a soldier going off to fight in a war. I didn't want to be sitting in a class room down there. Did I? Well, sort of. No, I was happy where I was. Thirty thousand feet above. Flying to. . . *hey, Dave. Check it out. See that plane flying up above you? The one just starting to cross the mountains? That's me, bro. I'm up here. Lookin' down on your ass. Wish me luck.*

In San Francisco International Airport as I was waiting for my duffle to come down the shoot I ran into Tim Cronin who was doing the same thing.

"Headin' over?" I asked.

"Yup. You?"

"Fraid so."

"So you're . . . ."

"On my way to Oakland."

"Me too. May I join you?"

"Sure. Of course."

So, there we were, Timothy Cronin and I, standing outside the terminal with our duffels. After sitting next to each other on a bus that took us over the Oakland Bay Bridge and left us off at the Oakland Army Base; spending two days and three nights being housed in a gigantic warehouse (the same one used to house soldiers being shipped to the South Pacific during WWII); being issued jungle fatigues and boots and pistol belts and standing in formation each morning waiting for our names to be called (*okay, listen up. The following soldiers have been assigned to—remember this number. Flight number . . . and are to report to . . .*); Timmy and I sharing a bunk in the center of hundreds of others (we needed coordinates to find our way back to where we slept, which was a tad confusing when trying to find our way after having been drinking over at the Enlisted Men's Club); hearing our names called and discovering that because we'd arrived at the same time we'd been assigned seats next to each other; a twenty-two hour flight, during which we stopped in Hawaii and Manila, with lights out, where we watched Phantom jets pull up alongside to escort us to Ton San Knut Air Force Base, in Saigon; sitting on the plane for close to an hour, sweating (Jeez was it hot, unbearable. Was this a test? To see if we could handle it? *No, I can't! No, I can't! No, I can't!*); sitting on that plane—that Braniff Boeing 707—with the engines and therefore the air conditioning off, and listening to and watching fighter jets taking off, and hearing bombs exploding off in the distance; after climbing down the steps that were *finally* wheeled over to us and stepping onto the runway—*this is it! We're here. On South Vietnamese soil*, taking everything in while being led through the terminal, which was crowded with Americans and South Vietnamese (*Look, man. Pajamas, conical straw hats*); being crammed into small, smelly, dilapidated buses that were waiting for us to be driven twenty or so miles in the dark to the 90th Replacement Company in Long Bien (peering curiously out the windows and catching our first glimpses of South Vietnamese standing outside their thatched huts in villages); standing exhaustedly next to a tall table inside a tent and filling out forms and answering, "if I die in a combat zone, box me up and ship me home," questions and then finding an empty cot in one of the tents to go crash on; and after being rudely awakened at dawn by shouting non-commissioned officers (NCOs), and wondering where in the hell I was (you're in Vietnam, dude. You're *here*. This is it). I stood next to Timmy in formation in the broiling sun and waited to hear what outfit I was going to be assigned to. Not a support company in Saigon where I'd have a beautiful live-in probably. Nope. That—with my Military Occupation Status (MOS)—didn't seem to be an option.

The way it worked, the way you were informed of what was—not your fate exactly. No, it would be overly dramatic to put it that way. Okay, the way you found out which outfit you were going to be joining (who you were going to be in the field playing Russian roulette with each and every day for the next year), was this: A sergeant—from the outfit you were being assigned to—stepped up to a podium that was in front of where we were standing and shouting into a megaphone called off the names of those who were to come up front and form a line behind him. "Okay," a sergeant from the 25th Infantry Division shouted, "when I call your name I want you to sound off like you've got a pair. Got that? And as you're hightailing your ass up here, I want you to show me how excited you are to have been assigned to the most ass-kicking combat outfit in Vietnam."

Yeah, yeah, yeah. Let's get this fucking over with. Torture standing here. Not sure I'm going to make it in this heat. Sun beating down. And it's still early. A year of *this*? *I love you, Janey. The reason I . . . .*

Oh my goodness. And who's *this*? Sergeant from the 173rd Airborne. Who uh . . . whose ranks got seriously depleted on some hill the day before. Timmy and I read about it in the *Stars and Stripes*. And—holy shit!—as the sergeant calls off the names of replacements, of these young soldiers who will be immediately sent to the Central Highlands—to (like my friend Doug Henning) do what they signed up to do—one by one (complying with the sergeant's request that when they hear their names called they act like the gung-ho, brainwashed motherfuckers they are), they shouted, "here sergeant," and then running to the front, moving their hands up and down as if they were pumping the rifles that they hadn't even been issued yet (soon enough), cried, "I want to die! I want to die!"

"I hope you *do*," I said to Timmy under my breath. Did I really? I'm not sure. No, not really. I don't know. Maybe I did. It's just . . . I hated them: What they'd become; been turned into. Airborne. Big fucking deal. So you jumped out of an airplane. So you could then come over here and . . . okay, I know, I know, get em while they're young. Before they think too much. Like me.

Oh God. What had I gotten myself into? *Janey, you don't even know I'm here, do you, sweetheart? That anti-war rally we went to . . . didn't even know where this place was. I don't even remember what was said. All I remember is, oh my God, your beautiful legs, your . . . that tight skirt you were wearing. . . .*

Timmy had his name called the next day, by a sergeant from the 9th Infantry Division. He just looked over at me and shook his head. The *9th?* We both knew what *that* meant. "See you in a year," I said just before he climbed onto the truck that drove away taking him to the mosquito- and snake-infested, leech-crawling, steaming swamps and marshlands of the dreaded Mekong Delta.

"Take care, Rick. Hope you end up with something better than *this*."

God speed, my friend. How could I fucking *not?*

My name was called the next day, by a sergeant from the 11th Armored Cavalry Regiment. No surprise. You come over with an MOS of 11Delta20, you end up in a track outfit.

So, let's see. I looked at the large, glass encased map that was over by the pick-up area, where trucks from the various outfits came to fetch the new recruits.

As Murph and I and several other recruits were waiting for the convoy to come pick us up and take us to base camp, a scruffy looking dude, whose jungle fatigues were not brand spanking new looking like the ones we had on, was also waiting. He'd been on "R & R" and was heading back to whatever troop he was in.

"You headed for Xuan Loc?" he asked, checking us out.

"Yup," I said. "You?"

"A hundred twelve and a wake up," he said. "Been doin' this shit eight months. Gonna be harder now that I just got back from Bangkok. You guys wanna good place t'go when—well—sorry t'rub it in," he shrugged, "little early to be talking about "R & R," but when the time comes, I highly recommend Bangkok. Whooie! Nonstop, if ya know what I'm sayin'. Anyway, some guys, they won't even go on "R & R" on account of . . . like *me*, right now. Too hard to come back. Best to go right up to the end, jus' before yer wake-up, then go home. Anyway, the Cav. Any questions?"

Needless to say, we had a bunch. What would we be doing exactly?

"Well, you'll be assigned to an armored personnel carrier most likely. Tracks we call them. You been around tracks before?"

We told him we had.

"Well, so you'll be assigned to a track, which means you'll either be . . . no, take that back. To start out you'll be a gunner, a left or right gunner. Any a you fired a sixty before?"

Yes again.

"From Knox, I guess. 11Delta20?"

It went on like that. He'd been a driver the whole time. He was with the Cav when it first came over. They'd trained together at Fort Meade, Maryland, and then had come over by ship. He'd helped build the base camp we were going to. "It's huge," he said. "When we first got there, there was nothing but jungle.

We formed perimeters, like we do now in the field—covered wagon style—while the jungle was being cleared. Each squadron took a third of the perimeter. By the way, where we're going is called Blackhorse. The reason being—see this insignia? We're the Blackhorse regiment. Which consists of three squadrons, each having three troops of armored personnel carriers—tracks we call them—and a company of tanks. Each of the nine troops consists of three platoons, and each platoon has eight tracks and their crews. A crew is made up of the driver (the toughest most dangerous job in Vietnam. You won't hear too many soldiers arguing against that), the T.C. (Track Commander) and a left and right gunner. You guys—like I said, that's what you're going to be—sit on either side of the back flap next to an M-60 machine gun. The T.C. sits in the turret behind a fifty. At any rate, we laid concertina wire, built sandbag bunkers, set up tents . . . it's like a city there now."

I have two different movies running simultaneously inside my head. In one I'm sitting in the back of a truck with Murphy and several other recruits as the convoy we're in alternately hauls ass—so we aren't sitting ducks—and moves slowly through jungle villages and old rubber tree plantations on our way to base camp. Even though the heat is unbearable and I can hardly breathe—and the fine, powdery dust being thrown into the air from the treads of the tracks escorting us is settling on us, getting in my eyes and mouth—I'm feeling happy, exhilarated by the surroundings; young and old women and children and old men wearing pajamas and conical straw hats stepping from thatched huts and waving to us; the enormous leaves of the close-by trees; the roar of the powerful engines; soldiers sitting on top of their tracks, T.C.s inside the turrets . . . Heady stuff. Like a dream. Magical. For the moment anyway. But what if . . . . ?

No "what ifs" right then, during that initial convoy ride.

You mean if we came under attack?

Yeah, if, all of a sudden . . . .

Nothing was going to happen. It was as if I was on a Disney World ride. We were safe. You think the Army would—on that initial journey anyway—put us in harm's way? Come on. We hadn't even been assigned rifles yet.

On through the city of Xuan Loc and then driving into base camp through the gate.

Jesus. Huge place. The soldier returning from "R & R" and sitting next to us was right; a big sprawling dust bowl. He gets off, and we are driven to first regimental and then squadron headquarters for processing, and then to a section of the perimeter just beyond the airstrip where the Echo Troop tents and motor pool are located. That's one movie reel playing inside my head.

The other is the newsreel I watched brokenheartedly on T.V. years later, of South Vietnamese clutching their belongings as, on the same road I'd just been on and would be on so many times during convoy escort duty, tried desperately to flee to Saigon before the communists came; of the ARVN making their last stand (very possibly—*most likely*) from within the Blackhorse basecamp, the communists blasting their way through the wire surrounding the besieged fort in their final attack; and then of the gleeful, gloating communists commandeering American tanks and personnel carriers as they rolled unimpeded down that same road toward Saigon.

* * *

The first Blackhorse trooper Murphy and I met was Sergeant Hannah, the scarlet-faced, bulbous-nosed, gin-swilling staff sergeant who, before his undistinguished, lackluster tour in Vietnam (where he was primarily in charge of burning shit), had served in WWII and Korea. Okay, okay, he was in charge of the rear, which essentially meant he was in charge of no one—a few newbies like Murph and me, while everyone else was out in the field. He did take time out from his drinking to greet us, "Welcome 'te Echo Troop, fellas." Take us to the supply tent and issue us an M-16, ammo and ammo magazines, helmet liner and steel pot, flak vest, poncho liner, and then give us a rundown. "Find 'yerself a tent," he said, "Troops're all out in the field. They're takin' a beatin' out there. Shouldn't be in a hurry t'join 'em. Take a shower if ya want. Under them fifty-gallon drums o'er yonder. But don't be usin' up all the water. Troops'll be back in a couple a days an' I reckon I don't need t'tell ya they will have themselves a strong case 'a the ass—we're talkin' the ass like a Russian bull should there be no water left. Fair warnin'. Be spare. Chow's in the mess tent yonder."

Following that uplifting meeting with Sergeant Hannah, I poked my head in the front flap of one of the tents and lying buck naked in a pool of sweat on one of the twenty or so cots was a tall, somewhat heavy set, red headed, freckled Irishman, who glanced over at me, startled (I, uh, interrupting something?) and motioned with his hand for me to come in. "Come on, come on, have a seat," he yelled. The dude was obviously from New England with the accent he had. "Anywhere. Place's empty as you can see. Troops're all out at Junction City. You heard about it? Probably been watching it on TV. Know more 'bout what's goin' on than I do. Big sweepin' operation. A motherfucker out there. In the Iron Triangle. Up against the Cambodian border. I just learned yesterday that one of my best friends was killed. Burned to death. Incinerated. Don't mean to scare you, but ridin' on them things—which I've been doin' for eight months now—and which *you* will be doing soon (no rush, no rush, stay here as long as you can) is like riding on top of a gasoline bomb. The track he was on. One I'm assigned to—we were fellow crew members—blew. Went up in flame after hitting a mine. Have a seat. You just get here? Bout time we started gettin' recruits." He reached up, placed two fingers on the front of his neck and checked his pulse; then he leaned over and examined his limp, shriveled up penis. "Do me a favor," he said, glancing over at me.

"Yeah, sure." *Fucking weirdo.*

"Would you mind . . ." He once again raised himself to a sitting position, and then as if he couldn't hold himself up anymore, plopped his head back down on his pillow. "Hot in here, ain't it?" he said, using a filthy towel to wipe sweat from his brow.

"Yeah, I'd agree with that," I said.

"So where you from?" Finlay asked.

"New Jersey."

"Ah, New Jersey. I'm from Rhode Island. Not too far."

"No."

"You just get here?"

"Yes."

"I see you got your sixteen. Already t' go, eh? An' some clips. Yer set, what's yer name?" Rick. "Yer all set t'go out an' *get some,* aren't ya Rick? Create a little havoc. Waste someone. Put a hurtin' on their ass. Don't mind me. I'm broiling in here. Fuckin' sweat box. Go grab yourself a beer. In that cooler over there. But first . . . if you wouldn't mind . . . . " He checked his pulse again. "I'd deeply appreciate it if you'd check out my, you know, dick. Hey, don't worry, I ain't no queer. That's not what's . . . no need frettin ' bout *that.*"

I glanced at his penis. Yup. He had one. Right where it should be. "Looks fine," I reported.

"How do you know? How can you see from so far away?"

"Listen, I think I hear Sergeant Hannah calling me."

"I *ain't* queer I told you, I just . . . . Come back!" he cried.

Was this a set-up? Were soldiers looking in on us and laughing? Was this some kind of initiation ritual? *Look at that fuckin' newbie. Ol' Finlay's got that motherfucker not knowin' whether he's comin' or goin'.*

What was going on, what I had witnessed inside that sweltering tent, was that the dude I had happened upon, who was lying naked on his cot dripping with sweat, was having a nervous breakdown. Two weeks prior to my encounter with him a doctor had told him that he had a—"whooie! Hope you had yourself a good time there young man"—giant, super-duper-sized dose of the clap and . . . .

Let me go back to the beginning.

Finlay was a devout Catholic, engaged to be married and a virgin, so when he went down to the bank of a river with a whore who Harvey and several others from the 2nd Platoon had arranged for him to be with, he felt guilty, that he'd betrayed not only his fiancée, but his parents and father whomever; nonetheless he'd *done it*; removed that terrible burden and had thoroughly enjoyed himself. Not half bad. And even though his fiancée and parents and the priest he'd grown up with would have been disappointed in him if they'd known—*oh Roger, how* could *you?*—he was fairly certain that they wouldn't have wanted him to die without ever having done it, which, given the circumstances, being in a war and all, was very possible; probable in fact.

So, for the next forty-eight hours—while standing in the

chow line, waiting for Sanchez or Regan to slap some strange looking glob onto his tray, while sitting inside the turret staring blankly at the walls of darkness during guard duty; or while sitting on the back flap of the carrier next to his M-60 machine gun, as the 2nd Platoon column plowed noisily through jungle or sped across rice paddies—Finlay relived, in his mind, the wondrous, sacred moments he'd shared with the beautiful young whore. Dreaming of her pretty face and long, dark hair flowing down past her shoulders—the feel of actually being inside her—he somehow managed to leave his feelings of guilt and betrayal back on the road overlooking the Long Dai River, and despite continued reminders of the girl's wretchedness in the form of incessant teasing—*Yo Finlay, wonder what yer honey's up to today?* Or, *you think she's back down on the bank of the river, or takin' the day off?. . . .* Despite continual reminders of the sleaze into which he'd allowed himself to be dragged—*I wonder just how many clients she has each day? What would be your guess? Fifty? A hundred?*—Finlay came to think of her as a saint, an angel of mercy, sent to him from the heavens.

Until it *happened,* that is. Until the infectious disease that, unbeknownst to him, the whore had passed on to him, possibly during his most ecstatic moments, manifested itself into the thick, white substance that he discovered oozing from the swollen redness at the end of his penis while showering.

Rumors ran rampant as Finlay, lying naked, sweating on a cot in a semi-conscious state, became the object of much speculation. Observing Finlay during the first couple of weeks of his "bed rest," as his lay-up was officially referred to (his lying on his cot staring blankly up at the top of the tent all day, thinking, what if the penicillin doesn't work and the infection continues to eat away at . . . "), members of the 2nd Platoon were mostly curious about Finlay's peculiar behavior and enjoyed quipping to each other about it. Finlay knew that he'd become infamous throughout—not only Echo troop but the whole 2nd Squadron—the *regiment*!

He could feel the wide gulf that had soon developed between him and his fellow platoon members. Even members of his own crew as he lay despondent on his cot seemed leery of him. Were they fearful of him because of his seemingly inconsolable state, because he was crazy? He was so absorbed with himself and his—what he perceived to be—unsolvable predicament, that he was hardly even aware that there was anyone else around him. Mentally he was already on that special island for the afflicted (that his teasers had warned him about) and living separately from the rest of mankind. It was at this juncture that I came across him.

Harvey gave me the scoop on Sergeant Hannah also. When Echo troop had first arrived he was a track commander (T.C.) on track Two-Eight. But when Lieutenant Marshall called him on the radio and said, "Uh, two-eight, this is, uh, two-six, do you read me, over," Sergeant Hannah wouldn't respond. Was he being obstinate?—he was an old, crusty motherfucker—or did he just not fully understand the concept? The lieutenant gave him every chance in the world to get his act together, demonstrate that he could master this not all that complicated skill, but for whatever reason—how 'bout his pickled brain from years and years of alcohol abuse?—he was left behind when the troops pulled out. Radio communication between the L-tee and T.C.s in the field was essential, so, sorry bub, I know you've got two wars behind you and beaucoup stories, but here in the Nam, for the wellbeing and safety of your fellow soldiers, you're being relieved of your command.

"Listen," said Harvey—we were sitting drinking beer on the sandbag wall in front of his tent—"I'm going to make a suggestion. When Sergeant Hannah asks for volunteers to burn shit during formation tomorrow and subsequent mornings, jump on it. Ah, you think I'm pullin' yer leg, fuckin' with ya. I'm not. It's the best detail goin'. Reason? You don't have to do anything. Jus' lean back against one a them shit-house walls, make yerself comfortable in whatever shade you find, an' read a book, whatever strikes yer fancy. Why? Because the good sergeant does the whole fuckin' thing for ya. Here's how it works. First he asks you if you've ever burned shit before. You say no. Even if you have. Then he tells you not to worry, he'll show you how. 'First ya pull the buckets a shit out, like this,' he'll tell ya as he's pullin' em out. You jus' stand there an' watch that shit-burnin' fool go t'work, t'ply his trade. There's three buckets that he'll haul out for ya, all the while sweatin' te beat the band. He might commence t'rest a moment before gettin' down to the actual burnin'. 'Then ya,'. . . an' he'll explain as he's pourin' Diesel in the buckets an' lightin' a match to it. Followed by remindin' you like he's whoopin' up some special brew that ya gotta stir, keep stirrin', but you don't need to do a fuckin' thing. Yer a fool if ya do. He'll go back inside his hutch for a half hour, swill down some more gin, then come back an' check. You don't move. Jus' stay put. Like I say, relax. Smells crappy, but hell, every place around here smells crappy. Next day he asks for volunteers, same thing. 'Ever burn shit before?' 'Nope,' you say an' off you go. Better'n pickin' up cigarette butts, fillin' sandbags. But wait a sec. Won't he remember me? Not in a million years, bro. He has no idea who's been watching him perform that ritual I jus' described day after day."

* * *

"Who in the fuck're *you*?" I was going through the serving line with Harvey—"say Rick, why don't we head on over to the mess tent for some chow"—when one of the K.P. servers, a big, burly, unshaved dude with thick, shaggy hair piled high on his head glared contemptuously at me from behind the trays of garbage he was helping ladle and made the above—rather rude, I thought—inquiry.

"Come on, Hank, be nice now," Harvey snapped at him, "this here's . . . what's yer las' name? This here's my man Rick Alexander, 11D20. We cen use . . . . "

Hank. That was *him* staring at me, checking me out like I'd just crawled out from under a rock. The Ross element. The defiant one I'd been hearing about.

"I 'ont give a fuck *who* you are," Hank informed me, his greenish eyes watching me from within his handsome, freckled face, "you jus' stay away from me, hear?"

So this was *him*, the defiant soldier whose capers and shenanigans over the past eight months would have earned anyone else a stint in—if not Leavenworth, at least Long Bien Jail (LBJ as the in-country stockade was referred to). But here he was, even after his most recent truck stealing, illegal use of an Army vehicle, brawling with (assaulting) M.P.s episode, standing before me in the serving line, giving me a ration of shit I, quite frankly, didn't think I deserved.

Oh, I'll stay away from you, asshole. No need for you to concern yourself about that. *How fuckin' far away from you do you want me to stand? This far enough?*

Harvey scolded him, said, "What the fuck's the matter with

you, Hank? Why you gotta be this way? My man, Rick. Look at 'em. He's got big, white teeth. Seems smart. We *need* new guys, Hank."

"Are you dufus?" said Hank, keeping his eyes on me, not letting me go.

"Yeah, I suppose," I said. "Sure."

"What I figured. Cen you function?"

"How's that?"

"Function. *Kill.*"

"Well, I guess. We'll find out won't we?"

"Less you get wasted beforehand."

Thing is, in reality all that trash talk was the antithesis of Hank, of who "he was," what he really stood for. Which within the next month I would find out. Meanwhile, I was a newbie. FNG (Fucking New Guy). One thing though, which those seasoned, been there eight months, got it figured out, functioning motherfuckers, would soon learn. I. Could. Take. *Any.* Thing. They. Had. Dig?

But Hank. Henry Ross. The Ross element. One day—soon actually—he and I would become close friends. As close as anyone could ever really be with Hank. And he would end up being one of the most remarkable people I have ever met. Where is Hank now I wonder? Still alive? Still cutting meat in some store in L.A.? He was a butcher. No, he'd be retired by now if alive. But most likely he's drunk himself to death. Had him a good start over in Nam. I can see him sitting at a bar in L.A., telling stories, which nobody believes are true (how could you?) even though they are, oh believe me they are, I was there, I witnessed them, and saying, as he moved his shoulders up and down, the way he used to do, "Now I ain't a hardly bullshittin'," or, if he was particularly agitated, annoyed about something—the bartender not filling his beer mug quickly enough, or being a little tardy in setting him up with another shot—"Now I ain't a *hardly* bullshittin'."

For the time being however, Hank was giving me a hard time and I was thinking that this legendary folk hero was nothing more than a mean, nasty, chip on his shoulders, bastard.

I didn't have to stay away from him as he requested however—though I would have gladly done so—because the following day he left for a week of "R & R" in Bangkok. He should have been heading off to LBJ in handcuffs and shackles. A week in *Bangkok*? What gives?

The story that Harvey and several other members of the 2nd platoon told me—well—first imagine Hank bouncing up and down in the cab of the two-and-a-half-ton truck he had hotwired and stolen from India Troop's motor pool one evening and driving down the rutted, presumably mine-filled dirt road connecting base camp and Xuan Loc. "I need t'get laid," he informed Harvey as the two of them left the club bar and began staggering the hundred or so meters over toward the section of the perimeter in which Hank was planning on carrying out his plan. As he drove the ten miles over the, like I say, presumably mine-filled road, the question, in retrospect, became: Had the Viet Cong or NVA (North Vietnamese Army) soldiers, who normally came out of the jungle and planted mines at night, sometime between dusk and dawn, for some reason forgone that activity that evening? Taken the night off? *You fellas have been working hard, killin' lots of Americans, so go an' do what you want to tonight.* Or, more likely, had the Viet Cong or NVA, upon seeing what they were seeing—witnessing a rather large vehicle of some sort flying by them without the headlights on as they set out late on their nightly mission—spoken to one another and decided that—Yo!—anyone crazy enough to be driving on the road they were working on at two o'clock in the morning (and being soldiers themselves they would have known what the most likely drunken soldiers flying heedlessly by them in the darkness were up to, were ultimately after), deserved a free pass, a brief halting of operations, so that the obviously crazed individual or individuals could get through and reach their destination. Whatever the reason, Hank made it and successfully ran the *gauntlet*, as Captain McNulty (who Hank was brought before following his arrest) called it. Miraculously, he'd made it into Xuan Loc—into Dodge—in one piece, much to the astonishment of the Army of the Republic of South Vietnam soldiers (ARVNs), who sitting inside the bunkers along the sides of the road next to the entrance to the city, heard the sound of what they were pretty certain was a truck, getting louder and louder, as, you know who raced desperately toward them. They heard this loud racket, clanking and sputtering noises as the engine misfired several times, and not only wondered what in the hell was going on—although a few did actually speculate that the "defiant one" might be in the process of pulling off yet another of his capers, but how whoever it was had managed to not set off one of the hundreds of mines that were planted in the road; how the clown or clowns charging full speed ahead as if they were being chased across a plain by hostiles and trying to make it into the safety of a fort, had come so far without being struck by a rocket.

Hank, Hank, Hank, you crazy bastard. He parked the truck in front of the *Good Times Bar*, found what he was looking for, why he'd just carried out this fool hearty, death-defying, self-ordered mission and then in the morning the six M.P.s, who after waiting for the Army Corps of Engineers to clear the road had driven to Xuan Loc in a convoy, received among them, two fat lips, several black eyes, and at least one broken nose when they stormed into the room Hank was staying in and arrested him. For . . . let's see, take your pick. Stealing a truck? Operating government property illegally? Operating a government vehicle while intoxicated? Being AWOL? Resisting arrest? Assaulting police officers? No way in hell he was going to get away with those types of crimes, right? *Wrong*. Why you talkin' bout the Ross element, bro?

Oh sure, he was busted, as per usual, from Spec 4 to Private First Class (hardly a free fall) and had to spend a few days in the hot sun performing the obligatory Article 15 routine of digging holes and filling them up again.

"Was it worth it, Hank?"

"Fuckin' A."

But one has to ask, how did he get away with shit like that? Anyone else . . . According to Harvey soldiers from all three Eleventh Cav squadrons—and from members of other outfits as well (the 1st and 25th Infantry Divisions, the 101st and 173rd Airborne)—enjoyed hearing of Hank's exploits—*Wait a second! Hold on. He did* what?—so that for those soldiers to hear, as they sat in foxholes, or were riding along on the tops of personnel carriers; for them to hear, as they sat on guard duty, or peeled potatoes, or were sitting inside the back of a truck as it sped along in a convoy, that the "defiant one" was being hauled off to prison for his (basically harmless, as they saw it) shenanigans, that he was possibly going to have to do hard time at a place like Leavenworth for the bold antics they delighted in hearing about . . . this was not a good thing, the Army brass decided (some feared rebellion; mutiny) so Hank was reluctantly let off the hook.

Factored into the officers' decision to tread lightly, possibly, was Hank's folk-hero status with the South Vietnamese, as word spread in nearby cities and towns of Hank's reputation for sticking up for them, for preventing—even at gun point several times when Hank deemed it necessary—American bullies (of which there were more than just a few, unfortunately) from crossing the line and . . . .

Oh what a world I was about to enter. That I'd already entered.

I was assigned to the second platoon track, Two-three. "Welcome aboard," the T.C. Simmons told me when I went to the motor pool to meet him and the other crew members. "I hear you're familiar with all the weapons and have been around these iron coffins. Just kidding. Two-eight became a funeral pyre out where we just were, so all that's weighing heavily on me at the moment. It passes. Ya get all hyper vigilant for a short while, then get back to normal again. Anyway—don't mean to be preachy—ya have any questions, just ask." He introduced me to Santana, the driver—"best damn driver in Nam. Avoids mines and when he takes us over paddy dikes, smooth as silk, you won't even know it, right Billy?"

"You say so boss."

"An' this here's the handsome fellow you'll be sittin' next to for hours on end on the back flap. Can make his sixty sing. Ten second bursts, right Wiggs? Excuse his name, Wigglesworth, and go ahead an' call him anything you want. Anyway, you'll be the left gunner, Rick. An' by the way, as you may have heard and probably noticed, we ride on top a these boxes so if we hit a mine we'll be thrown free. 'Less yer the driver, an' then yer just plain fucked. Hardest and most dangerous job in Vietnam sittin' down in that hatch and workin' them brake sticks all day long. An' a bit toasty down there too, eh Tana? At any rate, rule a thumb: I realize it's yer home now, but don't ever, *ever*, under any circumstances be down inside one of these things when it's moving. *Ever*. Even *here*. At base camp."

The irony is that, in less than a month, Simmons became paralyzed from the neck down after Two-three hit a mine and flung him into the air like a ragdoll. This happened after I'd left Two-three and was assigned to Two-six.

Simmons—jeez, I think about him often, as well as the many other 2nd platoon members who became paralyzed. A whole bunch. The most prevalent injury in track outfits due to the unfathomable force that occurs when a track sets off a mine. But yeah, I think about those guys. Every time I receive requests for and give money to organizations for paralyzed veterans. Where are they, man? They still alive? Hard to think of how life has been for them. I mean, I see their young faces just before . . . That's the thing, one moment they were sitting on top of a track dreaming away like the rest of us, and the next . . . no quarter given. Here's the situation. Deal with it. 'Least you're alive.

Simmons let me drive, watched me breakdown and reassemble my M-16, the 60 and 50, and gave me some pointers on firing the M-79 grenade launcher. Nifty weapon. I preferred to pop out grenades from that shot-gun-like weapon, to pulling pins and throwing grenades.

So I was all set. Ready to rock'n'roll as they say. Join my fellow warriors in combat. But where to? I mean, would we be heading back to the Cambodian border anytime soon? Or operating in the Xuan Loc area? On April 25, 1967, less than a week after I'd arrived at base camp, Captain McNulty had us gather in formation and let us know what was what. On April 28—in just three days—the entire 2nd Squadron was leaving base camp and heading up north. I remember scoffing at him, thinking, Jesus, who *is* this fuckin' turkey? Side walls, white walls whatever with that stupid eighth of an inch matting on top (what'd he do, get a haircut every day?), pressed jungle fatigues (okay, we were at base camp, but come on!), to say he had a military bearing wouldn't do him justice. He *was* a West Pointer I heard later, but wow! Are you *shitting* me? Lighten up dude.

We would be going by ship (LST) up the Saigon River, into the South China Sea, and then up along the coast to Chu Lai, which was one hundred miles south of Da Nang. Soon the monsoons would already be heading south—there were two seasons in South Vietnam, a dry season for six months and then a rainy season for six months—making it too difficult for our tracks to operate where we were, so we were being attached to the Americal Division to help support whoever needed it in the area around Chu Lai.

Off we went, and in my mind I watch our convoy hauling ass the way I imagine Hank did, along the road to Xuan Loc. Then, throwing up huge columns of dust, we sped between rubber trees and slowed down in jungle villages, as we made our way down Highway 1 into Saigon. I watch us moving slowly like we were in a parade along Saigon's To Do Street on our way to the docks (Americans waving at us and cheering from balconies, South Vietnamese women and children and old men running up to us and begging, looking for handouts). I remember sitting next to my machine gun, sweating miserably and covered with dust, joyously feeling like I was a conquering hero (oh how happy I was, this is where I wanted to be).

It's a good thing we don't know what awaits us, isn't it?

What's in store for us? And then in the upcoming years, they haunt my mind. I see what is going to happen to many of the soldiers riding in that convoy with me. I see myself years later, trembling, as I run the tips of my fingers over the names of some of those soldiers at the Vietnam War Memorial. I see myself eight years after that exhilarating, adrenalized, this-is-where-I-want-to-be jaunt in front of that give 'em hell, cheering crowd, demoralized, depressed, as on my small, black-and-white television screen, I watched in horror and disbelief as North Vietnamese soldiers, waving flags and shouting victory slogans, rode down that same street on top of American tanks and personnel carriers and in jeeps and the backs of trucks (the Cav's, some of them).

I couldn't watch.

But I *had* to. How could I not?

On. Off. On. Off. *On.*

Doomsday!

For the people I, along with hundreds of thousands of Americans, had grown to love and fought with and for and—that was *it*! That was *it*?

Up the Saigon River—in a Landing Ship, a Tank (LST), jammed with twenty-four personnel carriers and dozens of trucks and jeeps. No escape. Sun beating down relentlessly on the deck, steaming heat below—into the South China Sea (where eight years hence South Vietnamese refugees would battle the elements in crowded rafts as they waited, often in vain, to be picked up by foreign freighters and taken to a refugee camp), up the coast.

There's a war going on—that *I am* going to. Flashes from exploding bombs. Mountains in the distance. Fighting in them. Moored for a day and a half before going to shore (much speculation about what was going to happen when we did), driving across a white beach where headquarters had already been set up, and then finally hauling along a dirt road that cut through jungle and across rice paddies to our destination, a small hill in the middle of dried-up rice paddies on which the Marines were overrun the month before.

3.
There it is!

"Lonnie, where're you headed?" I saw him waiting near the helipad at the top of the hill, poised to run over and board a helicopter that had just landed and was blowing dust in his face.

"I'm going back to base," he shouted over to me. I was walking by and had seen him. He was already holding onto the top of his helmet to keep it from blowing off—or maybe he was shielding his eyes from the blinding, midday sun and swirling dust.

"Back to *base*?" I shouted, wondering if maybe I hadn't heard him correctly. At first I don't think he realized who it was; then it dawned on him. Hell, along with Murph, he and I had already spent ten days trying to figure out who we should listen to and who we should stay away from (wasn't that hard); while back at base camp; standing on the bow of the LST watching the dolphins; while being told as we looked out at the dried up rice paddies surrounding the hill we'd come to (Hill 58) that soon, if not already those paddies and the hills and valleys beyond would be filled with mines; while trying to comprehend—as we glanced over at the charred wreckage of an amphibious Marine assault vehicle—what had occurred on that hill less than a month before. "Way I understand it," Sergeant Phillips told us, trying to scare the bejesus out of us, "see that jungle across the way? One night the gooks came swarmin' out of there, across them paddies to where we're now standin'. Unsettlin', ain't it? An' where are them gooks right now? You got it. In them yonder hills. Jus' waitin' for us t'come out there an' try an' find 'em. No, take that back. We won't find 'em, but they'll be waitin' out there for us—are out there waitin' for us right now the sneaky bastards."

Anyway, there we were Lonnie and I, standing at the top of Hill 58 next to a helicopter about to take off and when I said, "back to *base*?" repeating his answer (to where he was going), he replied, "Yeah. To be in the band."

"Hold on! *Who*?"

"The band. They need. . . "

"*Band*?"

"A trombonist."

"Lemme get this straight, Lonnie. You're. . ."

"Gotta go, Allie. Take care. God's speed an' all that."

I watched him duck his head and run; the way—well—Murph and I would do during the upcoming months when we helped load medevac choppers with dead and wounded.

After I watched Lonnie sitting in the chopper, waving, dust swirling around, pelting me in the face as he was being lifted into the air, carried away. I watched him being flown across the paddies that *he* no longer had to concern himself with. (*Gosh, I won't be minesweeping down there, after all, will I*?). Over jungle and then above the hills to Chu Lai Air Force Base. And from there? I imagined him walking out the back of a C-130 and being greeted by a colonel and his entourage: "So glad we've found you, soldier. We've been without a trombonist for—oh jeez—three weeks now? And're just pleased as punch that you've agreed to leave your friends and Hill 58 to come and do this important assignment."

A week or so later I felt abandoned again. We were in a valley we frequently crossed during missions and started drawing fire. From AK-47s I was informed later. I couldn't make the distinction at the time, but knew we were being shot at. And that the bullets coming our way were flying out of more than one weapon. And then I heard a popping sound, followed by a whoosh, then more popping sounds and more whooshes and I said to myself, "that's it! Fuck. Ten days in country and I'm a goner. I love you mom and dad." Rockets. The gooks were firing rockets at us! Aiming for one of our gas tanks, one of our driver's compartments. *RPGs (rocket propelled grenades), you hear that popping sound, man, an' all you cen do is hope te high heavens one of 'em isn't comin' at you. Here's the deal, Allie: You hear a rocket explode. . . by the way, RPGs're armor piercing, meanin' ain't nothin' happenin' till they've bored a hole through two inches a steel, like they 'as bein' sucked in where you is if yer a driver, which a little advice to ya, my friend, you don' wanna be. Anyway, you* hear *the explosion an' yer o'er the hump. Fer that particular rocket. I ain't talkin' bout the next one and the one after that an' so on an' so forth. But you hear the boom from that first pop—gotta keep them pops straight—an' you know that you still haven't bought the farm yet. It's someone* else *who's been splattered all o'er the inside a the driver's compartment, who's gone up in flames when the rocket exploded inside the gas tank next to 'em.*

Holy shit! Since I hadn't heard an explosion, I'd thought I'm a goner. But wait a sec. Far as I could tell I was still—well—like all the other gunners when the shooting started I was standing down inside the back of the carrier, where I'd tripped and fallen (*Oh boy, here we go, this is* it) whle firing my sixty. Still there. Intact, far as I could tell. Arms, legs, hands, dick. Yet no explosion. The rockets must have sailed over our heads. Missed their targets. *Us.* One chance for the gooks with their hit-and-run tactics as we were passing by. Not that they wouldn't have others. They would. But for then . . . all I knew was I hadn't been blown to bits or burned and was *functioning*. Oh yeah, I was functioning. On all cylinders. Ten-second bursts. Just like you said, Simmons. Aiming for the tree line. Fifties pounding away. *Get some, T.C.s, get some.* Does this mean I'm a combat vet now? Reckon it does. *I guaran-fucking-tee, Allie, that you will have earned your CIB* (Combat Infantryman's Badge) *first time you go out in them hills*. Well, you were right, Davis. You called it. Not that it was that hard a call to make. And big fucking deal, right? I mean some housecat, who has a live-in and gets sniped at while walking over to the base PX to buy some more Jack Daniels cause he and his pals have run out, gets a CIB too, right?

The L-tee came over the radio telling us to hold our fire. "Save your ammo," he cried. Suddenly the shooting stopped. Someone was calling for a medic. This was a movie I was in, right?

Wiggs looked over at me. "You alright?"

I looked around. "Far as I can tell, yeah. Were those rockets?"

"You heard em? Good ear. You'll be hearin' that sound a lot as we. . . ."

Donnie, the medic ran by. We looked behind. "Someone's been hit," said Wiggs. "On Two-nine looks like." Wiggs threw up his arms. "Me, me!" he cried, "aim at me you assholes. I'll take a bullet any day. If it'll get my ass outa here. 'Fore a rocket or one a the gazillions a mines bein' planted all around where we been an' are goin' sends me home in a plastic bag."

The tree line where shots had come from—where I'd heard popping sounds—was all shot up. The 11th Cav had more fire power than any other outfit in Nam. Yet we were sitting ducks. It's not like the gooks wanted to engage us. They didn't. They hit and ran. They hadn't been very successful that time (several bullet wounds as I'd find out in a moment), but the rockets had missed their mark. Whoever was manning the launchers—a couple of dirt farmers most likely—were long gone. In a tunnel somewhere, probably.

Ah! A tunnel. One of *those.* How strange it is for me to think of my six-foot-three, one hundred eighty pound, claustrophobic-self climbing down into one of those dark (pitch black), narrow, underground cave-like structures that were often lined with booby traps . . . oh my, I *did* that? Reckon so, but only once. Why? Two reasons. One, as soon as I dragged my filthy, sweaty body out of that miserable hole in which I might very well have set off a booby trap of some sort and blown off my legs and been smothered by dirt caving in all around me, I vowed to never, *ever* do anything like that again. *Ever*! Meaning *what?* Meaning: I was *not.* Going down. Into one of those tunnels ever again. That I would have taken a court martial first. But I never had to. It never came up. Due to the endless supply of ready an' rarin' t'go volunteers for that rollicking fun-filled activity. *Y'all jus' live it up, ya hear. 'Ave yerself a ball. Slither aroun' down ther t'yer 'earts content*.

At any rate, it seems strange as I remember that nightmarish excursion and recall all the tunnels we came across (during my former life—that's how it seems) to think of Emily, my oldest daughter, climbing down into one of those tunnels forty years later. Her junior year in college she traveled around the world by ship in the University of Virginia's Semester-At-Sea program and one of the countries she visited was Vietnam. I have a photograph of her looking up at whoever took the picture as she is climbing up out of one of the Chu Chi tunnels. Her hair is pulled back and looks wet and her face is all shiny with sweat. My baby. Visiting—oh my—*there*? That place? Where . . . .

Okay, so the gooks who ambushed us that afternoon were now hiding in a tunnel and we could drop anything we had on them—bombs, artillery, napalm—and they'd be safe. Planning their next attack. Would we be going by there again? Was the sun that came up each morning hotter than blazes? Did Makefield say each and every morning as it was coming up, "Well, fellas, looks like it's gonna be another hot one?"

Yes. Would they hear us coming, the loud roar of our engines, for miles and be able to plan their next attack? Would they know our precise location by the columns of dust billowing up toward the sky?

Yes, and yes again.

Blackman walked by with Donnie, the platoon medic. His arm was in a sling. Nothing too serious it seemed. He glanced over at me. "My elbow," he shouted. "They got me."

"Shattered," Donnie called over to us.

Wiggs looked at me. "Say goodbye to your friend," he said. "He ain't comin' back."

Blackman shrugged like he was sorry, and then was hustled over by the command track. And as I watched the medevac chopper come in and get him; watched him hurrying over with Donnie and two other wounded soldiers (the gooks had obviously had Two-niner's crew in their sights); as I watched him being lifted and carried away, I was once again torn by conflicting emotions; raw envy for my friend who moments before was in the same boat that I was in and was now apparently headed to a hospital in Chu Lai and then stateside (nurses, clean sheets, TLC and the extraordinary feeling—that I could only imagine—of knowing it was over, that you'd made it), and a—how can you *do* this to me? You're going to leave me out here all by myself?—feeling abandoned. Already I knew that what had just happened to Blackman was an aberration; pure luck; he'd just won the lottery and it was ridiculous to even hope that something like that could happen to me. What were the chances? None. Zero. Zilch. Like ninety-nine percent of the rest of us I'd spend my tour out in places like that valley waiting for whatever was going to happen. . . to happen. I'd either be killed or seriously wounded. No million-dollar wound in the cards for me; of that I was pretty certain.

* * *

The first patrol I went out on—that Lonnie bless his trombone-playing heart was missing because he'd been whisked away to go off and play in the 11th Cav band—was an eye opener; what happened that insufferably hot, muggy afternoon in the small, bombed-out jungle village we ended up in on the other side of the paddies, I have carried around with me to this day; it set the tone for my whole tour. "Dear Lee," I remember mentally saying to my brother as we came upon the ruins of several bunkers that had obviously just been abandoned (I'd been—as I was wont to do and continued to do—mentally composing letters to Lee and Sue and my parents). Wearing steel pots and sweating under our flak vests we'd slogged across the sun-scorched paddies, carrying our weapons.

"Dear Lee, it looks like the V.C. just left this place. Scary to think of them looking over at Hill 58 where we are, watching our every move and scheming: "Look, here comes another column of those steel, box-shaped vehicles . . . they're leaving the gate and—

ah ha—they have their minesweepers in front of them trying to detect those mines we've been busy planting. And wait a sec. I think there's a foot patrol leaving too—heading this way?" Reason we know they left in a hurry, Lee, is . . . Oh my, look at this. A bowl with. . . those fish? Sardines? And—well—what's that mushy looking stuff, rice? With—aw shit there's bugs crawlin' around in it. No wonder they're so skinny. Okay, that's it. I'm no longer going to complain about the slop we're given to eat. Pass the ham and limas. Spooky, Lee. Knowin'. . . they were right here. The enemy. Where'd they go? They watching us? I feel like there are a thousand eyes on me right now. And. . . looks like Sergeant Waters has found. . . 'What's ya got there, sarg? 'Their version of a claymore,' he says. Meaning it's got rocks—well, stones and glass and whatnot in it. Not the eight hundred tiny steel balls packed neatly in C-4 that we have and which I will be helping to set up when I go out on night ambush patrol one of these evenings. Sit out on the ground all night listening, waiting. Can't wait. Hope I'm not too paranoid. Hold on a second, Lee. Dick brain over there is calling me. He and Sergeant Waters are the leaders of this patrol."

Sergeant Hanover and Sergeant Waters. Just prior to the patrol's setting out, Sergeant Hanover called over to me as I was walking back from the mess tent. I squinted to see who it was. The sunlight was blinding. It was that tall, skinny, curly grey-haired individual I'd seen on the ship but had no idea who he was. Well, a sergeant, someone who had free reign to fuck with me any time he wanted. And he was fixin' on doing just that at that moment. Damn. I'd almost made it. I'd come three quarters of the way down the sloping hill and was almost to Two-three's position on the perimeter when he stopped me—and like it'd been jus' buggin' the shit outa him an' he jus' *had* t'know—said, "You like niggers?"

"I got nothin' against black people," I said.

He shook his head back and forth, disgustedly, and then peering at me with his steely gray eyes, said, "I ain't sayin' nothin' 'bout no black people now. I said, 'you like niggers?"

I thought maybe he was putting me on. Another one of the endless hazing tricks played on newbies. That some of the blacks standing by their assigned tracks were shaking their heads, listening, thinking, there he goes again, messin' with the "fresh meat" (as we newbies were also referred to)—like they dug it and approved; thought it was funny; a joke. Hell, there wasn't no racism 'round here. Far from it. Ol' Sergeant Hanover, he just enjoy fuckin' with that newbie's head. Like all of a sudden I'd hear laughter and look over and see blacks high-fiving each other, saying, "man, they shore got you," and then come over and high-five Sergeant Hanover.

But no, no one was laughing and when Hanover looked at me and said, "well, since y'all don' seem t'mind bein' aroun'—*black* people as you calls em—ah might jus' 'ave t'see to it you get yer ass assigned to a nigger track." I just walked away. And then, there I was out on a patrol with that sorry bastard. What'd he want now?

"Okay, so newbie," he said, "here's the deal. While Sergeant Waters an' I destroy some a these 'ere bunkers an' see what else they left behind. They shore left in a hurry. I want you to . . . see that clearing there. Jus' outside them trees. Where the light is. I want you t'park yer green ass out there an' cover us. Watch whatever the fuck flank it is. Got that? Okay, git!"

In my mind, I see myself step cautiously from the shade at the edge of the jungle into the sudden brightness of a sunlit field. Shielding my eyes with my hand, I squinted into the blinding light. Sweat is pouring off me. Through bleary eyes, I glance around at the walls of jungle surrounding me; the propeller-sized leaves dangling from the limbs of tall trees; the tall (hopefully not snake-infested) grass; a mound of dirt that I just *knew* was full of vicious, man-eating red ants. I'd already been feasted upon several times by those miserable creatures and was on high alert to make sure I never was attacked by them again . . . a cluster of thick bushes and strangely configured small trees; and then suddenly, after studying for a few moments a large, gray, lichen-covered rock (of the type I used to come across while hiking in the Adirondacks), I look over and see—a *boy?* Nervously I wipe my eyes with the sleeve of my shirt and look again. A boy! Yes. There was a *boy* standing there in front of me; a filthy, bare-footed boy wearing tattered black pajamas. I blinked to make sure I was seeing right. I was. My heart pounded. The boy was unarmed. I started to swing my rifle around but was too frightened and stunned to move. The boy and I stood frozen. Neither of us moved. The boy was looking at me. I gazed into the boy's doe-like eyes. The boy's face and arms were smeared with dirt. My arms were shaking. My legs felt as though they were about to collapse. Lowering my M-16, I pointed it toward the boy, who was watching me, watching my every move, and just as I was about to step forward, Sergeants Hanover and Waters stepped out of the jungle and walked over and stood next to where I was standing.

"Well, well," said Sergeant Hanover, glancing over at the boy and grinning, "look at what we have *here*. Ain't this somethin'?" The boy remained frozen, his terror-filled eyes moving back and forth between the two sergeants and me.

Sergeant Hanover turned toward the gruff looking man standing next to him. "Wha'd'ya think, Sergeant Waters?" he asked. The two of them eyed the boy, leering at him as if he was an insect that had just crawled out from under a rock and startled them. "Looks like Private Alexander here's got himself a real live prisoner. Wouldn't ya say?"

"Sure's hell looks that way t'me," said Sergeant Waters. Using the sleeve of his dirt encrusted shirt he wiped sweat from his eyes so he could see better. "Yup." He tilted his head sideways. "Sho nuf does. Bit scrawny, I'd say, but. . ." He spat a gob of white foam that landed in the grass next to the boy's feet. "We ain't throwin' em back, is we sarg?"

"Naw." Sergeant Hanover glanced over at the barely noticeable entrance to the tunnel the boy had mistakenly climbed out of, then back at the boy, "young Luke the Gook 'ere ain't goin' nowheres, cept maybe t'join some'a his dead friends'n'brothers'n'sisters'n'Ma'n'Pa'n whoever the fuck else."

Sergeant Waters watched the boy shaking. "Dang," he said. The boy's hands and knees were twitching; his lips quivered. "Jus' look at im a-tremblin'." And then, leaning forward, feigning amazement, he hollered, "You *scared* boy?" In a quick, unexpected motion, Sergeant Waters raised the butt of his rifle to strike the boy and the boy jumped back, flinching. "I believe you *is* scared, ain't ya?" Sergeant Waters laughed. "Yup," he lowered his rifle slowly, "I do believe you is. An'ya *should* be." His icy blue eyes roamed around behind the boy suspiciously, and then darted back. "Lucky I don't 'ave the time er I'd string yo ass up like a nigga in one a them trees yonder."

Sergeant Hanover let out a yowl. "I'd motion fer that," he said. "Surely I would. No tellin' *what* this motherfucker an' 'is pals've been up to."

Sergeant Hanover stood for a long time watching the boy's eyes dart back and forth in fear, and then calmly, as if he'd suddenly become bored, he turned, aimed his cold, gray eyes at me, and with a huge smirk on his face, said, "Shoot em! Shoot the motherfucker!"

I gazed at the frightened boy, and then turned toward the sergeant. "Look, sarg., he's. . . ."

"*Shoot* em!"

"But he's. . . ."

"Shoot em!"

". . . he's unarmed and. . . ."

"That's an *order*, Private. You *hear* me?"

"But. . . ."

I pleaded with Sergeant Hanover to take the boy prisoner, stating how the boy was unarmed and maybe with an interpreter he could provide some valuable information, but neither of the sergeants was listening, they both just looked at each other, shaking their heads, until finally, with a kicked look in his eyes, that all too familiar, merciless, *gonna* **git** *me some* look, Sergeant Hanover gunned the boy down.

Sergeant Hanover drew in a long, deep, satisfying breath—like he'd just come out of a bunker after being with a whore—and then after studying the bloody heap lying in the grass in front of him, turned, and as if he'd just circled the bases after hitting a game-winning home run—and Sergeant Waters was waiting at home plate to greet him—he excitedly threw up his arm and joined Sergeant Waters in a jubilant high-five.

"Motherfucker just vanished," I heard Sergeant Hanover say in the mess tent that evening as he giddily described the KIA Captain McNulty had credited him with, "I mean, one moment the boy was just *standing* there, shaking in his. . ." He gave a toothless grin. "His bare feet. And the next moment. . . " He held up his arms and pretended he was firing a rifle. He moved his head back and forth, remembering. Glancing at Sergeant Waters, who was sitting at the table across from him, he shouted, proudly, "Wasn't much left'a the motherfucker, was there Sergeant Waters?"

Sergeant Waters' head moved back and forth the way Sergeant Hanover's had. "Nope," he said. "I'd seriously agree with that. Last I saw, ol' Luke the Gook was lookin' like raw meat. Hamburger. T'was a sight t'behold!"

I remember how, in my mind, I rose slowly from the table, walked over to where the two sergeants were sitting, and as they—and all of Echo Troop—watched in disbelief, calmly raised my rifle, pointed it at their smug faces, pulled the trigger, and with blood and brains and whatever else was inside their mean, wicked heads splattered across the mess tent, walked back to my table, sat down, and resumed eating. Hard as a rock roast beef and soggy, overcooked peas—what the *fuck* else?

Three weeks after the incident, Sergeant Hanover became paralyzed when Two-Four set off a mine and, upon hearing the Sergeant's fate, I cheered to myself, wishing I could go visit the sorry ass bastard as he lay helplessly on a hospital bed somewhere and inform him, face to face, eyeball to eyeball, that I was glad he was suffering and would no longer be able to get around—*War's a* ***bitch****, ain't it sarg.?*—and that—

"Whew! Damn! *Harsh*!" my friend, Tucker, said to me, as I confided my sentiments about the sergeant to him. "I mean—*whew*! Hold on! Dude's *low*, I agree. He an' some others round here don't exactly make ya proud t'be soldierin' over here, an

American, but with respect to that boy—come on, Allie. He was a V.C. A Viet Cong, who. . . who may very well've been the one who planted the mines or fired the rockets that killed—take yer pick. Who *knows* how many Americans he'd killed? A whole shit load I bet. He an' whoever *else* was down inside that hole with him." You're looking at me like, what's the big deal? As your friend Tucker reminded you the boy was a V.C., who . . . *him* or you, right? With respect to the incessant killing that took place, this was a *war*, my goodness, *tell* me something, you say. I mean, this wasn't any My Lai, where. . . .

Correct. It wasn't.

But trust me when I say, I saw something in those two sergeants' eyes that frightened me far more than what I feared was in store for me during the next twelve months (which was considerable) and induced in me the lingering rage that to this day has not subsided. The right-up-front cruelty and vicious, no-holds-barred sadism the sergeants and others of their ilk enjoyed dispensing over there was thankfully counter balanced by Hank and Sergeant Morrison and most of the others with whom I served, who by their actions gave me reassurance. I remember how that whole world sprang back at me like an exploding mine when eight years later a fellow state worker and fellow Vietnam veteran turned to me as we were sitting at a bar following work one evening and said, "I don't know if you were into "the kill thing" over there, but . . . ."

"No," I said abruptly. "No, I wasn't." And held up my hands to cut him off.

He gave me a smug, condescending look. Like, oh you're one of *them*? (One of those pansy motherfuckers who had his tender sensibilities smashed to bits in that manly world over there.) I knew what he was doing. It had happened to me before, though not for a long time. He wanted to do some bonding, like, he tells me something horrific (though not in his eyes) that he'd done (which he *did*, despite my giving him every indication that I didn't want him to; that I wasn't going to play his sick, demented game), and then if I was up to it, which I wasn't, I try to top it. Though who, even if they took the bait and played along, could top *his*? "Yeah, we use te round up women an' children in the villages an' put a flame thrower on em, see. Have us a roast. Then we'd go over an' piss on their sorry gook ashes." Nice, man. Of course, the drunken asshole sitting on the stool to my left overheard this—non-confession. (No, no. Just brag, boast). He reached over in front of me (*get your filthy, smelly, lowlife body away from me you worthless, piece a shit I hope you die degenerate*) and gave him a high five. "I'm with ya, bro. Screamin' Eagles. Seventy, seventy-one."

I hated them, oh how I hated them (as you may have gathered). Tell me, what was I *doing* in a sleazy joint like that anyway?

I pictured Hightower and his fellow Green Berets (though by no means, no means at all, were they all like him) getting their jollies killing and terrorizing villagers. I'd known guys like him over there. Psychopaths.

Which begs the question? Who's better suited to winning wars, crazy fucks like him, who NEVER HESITATE, never even give a second thought (who *get off* on all that shit; dig it), or the majority of soldiers who are weighted down with, among other things, a conscience?

The day after the boy was killed the second platoon went out on a small recon mission to see what was out there and report back on what kind of impact the artillery rounds were having—whooshing over our heads and exploding all night long. That was our lullaby, the sweet dreams Echo troop was having. And I know now, of course, to draw fire so whoever was out there could be pinpointed and then destroyed. If only it had been that easy. But the truth was—as I have already pointed out, how unstealthy our tracks were (here they come, here they come! Get ready)—more often than not as we went out to "*get some*" as everyone was fond of saying (sixteen M-60s and eight fifty-calibers aiming at the nearest trees or wherever we thought they were) they got us. Spray painted in white letters on the sides of one of the first platoon's tracks I remember were the words, "GO GET EM DONE GOT EM," a good slogan under the circumstances and one which the brass really liked; one they would have picked as their winner if they'd had a contest. *Come on over here, General Westmoreland, an' look at this one. Whooie! Now doesn't that say it all?*

"*Shore does, colonel. Shore does.*"

At any rate, during that small, take a peek mission—out one day, back the next—Murphy and I were taught how to mine sweep. As predicted, the area surrounding us—not just the paddies, but what lay beyond—was becoming inundated with mines. And to lessen the odds that one of our tracks might set one of them off, minesweeping was an integral part of our daily routine, especially in the paddies, and the "only way through" the passageway we took through the wall of jungle on the other side. The rule of thumb was that we tried to get into the enemy's heads: Any place the V.C. thought we might end up taking our tracks through; the "rabbit hole" entrance to the area we operated in beyond the paddies, any place we might be drawn to because of shade—that lonesome tree o'er yonder (say fellas, there might even be a breeze under them leaves); any road or path we might use in order to avoid having to knock down trees and go through jungle when we were tired and in a "don't give-a-shit-anymore" mode, a mine would be there. So, especially as we heard explosions shaking the earth nearby at night and in the morning, we watched in amazement and horror as villagers from across the way darted across the paddies and frantically collected chunks of beef that the water buffalos wandering around haplessly just outside the gate had provided, it behooved us to locate the mines and blow them up before—well—before it was *us* setting them off. (Many thanks to the buffalos, however, who in inadvertently sacrificing themselves, made our minesweeping job a little bit easier—one less of those nasty motherfuckers to find and destroy—and going beyond the wire surrounding Hill 58 a little more safe. So to you big, dumb, clumsy, hardworking, loveable beasts of burden, a debt of gratitude.)

Minesweeping (by us humans, we soldiers) was done in tandem. You had the actual sweeper (that was me) as we worked our way across the paddies, moving the detector back and forth across where the treads of the carriers behind us would go, listening for the tell-tale beeping sound that meant there was metal below. Heart pounding. Holy shit. There may be a *mine* down there. Right below where we're standing. "Murph," he was walking along next to me, holding a bayonet. "Here. Here, my man. See what's there. Metal of some sort." He crouched down and stuck the bayonet into the dirt. "Keep digging," I said. There's *something* down there. This beeper's goin' crazy."

"Yup." Murph looked up. Upon further examination the object he dug out and held up was a C-ration can. Beef and potatoes. "Keep going," I said. Not meaning to be bossy. When Simmons was explaining what to do before we went out, he told us how the gooks like to play tricks. Plant stuff on top of the mines as a sort of decoy. But as Simmons pointed out, "what's the chance that a C-ration can or some other metal object you might find is just randomly buried in the dirt out there. None. Anything metal you find that isn't a mine, keep diggin'. There's a strong chance—a hundred percent I'd say, that they're fuckin' with ya."

Sure enough a little more digging and, wow! There *was* a mine.

As Murphy carefully brushed away dirt with his fingers, I motioned for Nelson, who was leaning against the turret of Two-one, the lead track, with his legs dangling over the side, to come join us.

"Good job," he said, kneeling down and squinting at the small hole and the top of the mine that had been uncovered in it. "Go stand behind the track," he said—which we did—and then after slapping a chunk of the silly putty-type C-4 explosive he was holding onto the mine's metal top, and jabbing a blasting cap that was at the end of a small roll out wire into it, he stood up, cautiously worked his way back to where Murph and I were standing, shouted, "fire in the hole!" pressed his thumb against the trigger mechanism he was holding and blew the mine up.

When the dust that rose from the explosion settled, there was a large crater where the mine had been. We detected and dug and motioned for Nelson to come over and do his thing two more times, Murph and I, switching roles so we'd each get the hang of both of them, and then when we arrived at the rabbit hole, the narrow, tunnel-like path that cut through thick brush and trees and connected the rice paddies with the hills and valleys beyond, I had the honor of holding the bayonet and watching Murph move the detector back and forth. Pushing away vines and limbs and stepping over fallen logs and debris, I tried not to think that hiding behind the trees next to us might be a V.C. waiting for us to take one or two more steps (*come on, come on, closer, closer, that's it*) so they could command detonate a mine and pulverize us, blow us into tiny bits the way a sweep team from the third platoon had been. (Most of the mines we encountered were "contact detonated," meaning they couldn't be set off unless a heavy vehicle of some sort ran over them. A mine that was "command detonated" meant that a wire with a trigger mechanism was connected to it and some gook hiding close by could set it off any time they wanted.)

After we'd made it through all that thick growth without any beeps from the detector, the engines of the tracks behind us whining as the vehicles flattened bushes and knocked down trees, we came to a clearing. Murph and I swept a path diagonally across the clearing, avoiding the tread marks made by other tracks before we busted randomly through a stand of trees and entered a field of six-foot-high elephant grass.

Sergeant Morrison told Murph and me to climb back up onto our assigned tracks.

"Good job," said Simmons, perched behind the fifty. Wigglesworth jumped down inside the back and fetched three beers from the cooler: one for me, one for Simmons, and one for himself. Then as we sat next to our guns, sucking down ice-cold Pabst Blue Ribbons, the drivers, who were unable to imbibe (bein' as how they were too busy concentrating, keeping the treads of their vehicles in the tracks being made in front of them), followed the Two-one through the trees and into a sea of elephant grass.

Say, not bad, you say, I mean—it's what? A hundred and twenty degrees out there? Sun beating down, you're sweaty, thirsty as all get out and your fellow gunner reaches over and hands you an ice cold beer? Yeah. Being assigned to tracks had its advantages. Made all the more evident when we had guests.

Guests you say?

Yes, guests. Check it out. Don't ask me when or where—I don't remember exactly—but several times along the way (during the upcoming months), we had visitors; specifically, grunts (cause that's what they were, they pounded ground, didn't they?) from the 101st and 173rd Airborne joining us on our tracks. Here's how it worked: several of those young (okay, everyone was young), gung-ho, "bring it on motherfucker" types (like those recruits who yelled, "I wanna die, I wanna die," as they were running up to the front of the formation at the 90th Replacement Company), were assigned to ride on top of our tracks with us and when the shit hit the fan, which they were hopin' it would, they'd deploy (jump down off the tracks an' go get em), chase them over to our carriers which we'd line up, our fifties and sixties pointed in the direction we expected them to come. That's how it was supposed to work, though it seldom did. With regard to our cocky—hey, I'm airborne—guests (so what, you jumped out of an airplane meaning you volunteered to be cannon fodder), they were not at all pleased about having to ride next to us—what they condescendingly referred to as "legs." For two reasons: the first being—well—as I just mentioned they didn't want to have to rub elbows with us lowly dirt poundin' motherfuckers. Except, wait a sec. Haven't you noticed, *you're* the ones who pound dirt, while we. . . Oh well that's how they saw it. How they were trained (brainwashed) to think of themselves. As to the second reason, they readily admitted that they wanted no part of riding on top of armored personnel carriers. Too dangerous. They would have rather walked.

So they rode with us—not like we were digging this arrangement either (they stank even more than we did)—being all cocky and superior, refusing to make eye contact. If we'd been in a bar they would have been aching to get into a fight, kick our asses, show us "legs" a motherfucking thing or two. Meanwhile, Wiggs and I had us a time taking turns jumping down into the back (when the vehicle was not moving, of course) and grabbing ice cold beers for just Wiggs, Simmons, and me.

"Allie, cen I get ya another cool one or are ya set for now?"

"Ya know, Wiggs, with this heat an' all, I think I'll take a pass for the moment. Have too many, I'll feel like taking a nap. Which I may do next to my gun here after our guests're deployed. Thanks for asking though."

Finally, one of the Screaming Eagles, a young black guy who was leaning against the turret, couldn't take it anymore and shouted above the roar of the engine, "okay, okay, you guys win. Fuck, man! What we gotta do t'get one a you t'offer us one a them cold Buds yer servin' up t'each other there?"

"Well," said Wiggs, looking over at the big liquid eyes staring pleadingly at him from within a young black face glistening with sweat beneath his helmet, "a little respect. Tone down 'yer attitude a bit. You don't think we heard all those snide remarks 'bout havin' t'ride with a bunch a lousy grunts—which we clearly *ain't.* We ain't got no wings on our chests, but. . . ."

"Okay, okay, my pals an' I be considerin' it a distinct honor t'be ridin' wid y'all folks t'day an' would be most appreciative if y'all could see it in yer ass kickin', armored cav hearts t'offer up a few a them cold Buds te some mighty thirsty soldiers 'fore we 'ave te depart with y'all an' go take care a business."

"Wha'd'ya think, Allie? Should we. . . . ?"

"Sure. Beers all around."

* * *

Elephant grass. We cut a huge swath through it. If the V.C. had been hiding in it we wouldn't have seen them. They could have wreaked havoc on us. Trouble was, they'd have had no place to run and hide after doing so. We would have been able to mow them down. Nonetheless, it was spooky going through there. Not knowing who was lurking.

Sitting on top of the track. On the left side of the back flap. Machine gun loaded and ready to start firing. Floating up there, in a daze. Daydreaming. Level with the top of the grass. Tracks cranking along. Noisy as hell. And smelly. The gas fumes nauseating. Sitting up there, melting. Sun directly overhead. *Dear Lee, I don't think I can take a year of this heat. It's like being in an oven. No escape.* Off in the distance, mountains, and directly in front of us the bomb-cratered hill we often climbed and went down the other side of in order to get to yet another of the valleys our missions took us to. At the end of the elephant grass and the tunnel-like path we created (one that by nightfall would be heavily mined), we made our way over to the hill that for some reason had caught the full wrath of American airstrikes and artillery. I mean, what I remembered thinking, as we drove up the side of the barren, cratered hill that had obviously been cloaked in jungle once, is: What did this particular hill do to receive this? The V.C. and possibly even NVA regulars seeking higher ground had set up camp there we'd been told, but looking around I couldn't see any evidence of that. But I did think how at night when I was sleeping—or lying awake I should say—on my cot on Hill 58 and heard bombs and artillery exploding in the distance, that what I was seeing on this hill was the target. A shudder ran through me imagining what it must be like to be out where we were trying to survive being a victim of such destructive weapons.

* * *

That evening we bivouacked in a field surrounded by jungle, and I went out on my first night-ambush patrol—with the one and only Henry Ross, the Ross element. Remember him? Yup. He was back. In all his glory. Sharkey and he had had a rollicking good time on their "R&R" in Bangkok and were back in action. Brought him along a six pack, Hank did. On night ambush? That was allowed? No, of course not. But who was going to tell him he couldn't? He was already there behind Two-six waiting with his evening's refreshments when I arrived. Had an ample supply (much more than anyone else assigned to the patrol) of grenades, claymores, extra ammo clips also. So, Hank. He was there. And Finlay too! He wandered over from Two-nine-er. "Hi Allie," he said, smiling, when I showed up. It was almost as if he'd forgotten that bizarre exchange we'd had in the tent when I'd first arrived. A guy named St. James, whom I didn't know much about except that he was called "rabbit" because he liked to fuck so much.

"Wait a sec. Doesn't everybody? I mean. . . ."

"It's just that he's over there humping away every chance he gets. Like the rest of us, I suppose. I don't know. He fucks like a rabbit, what can I say?"

Let's see. Who else was on that patrol? I don't remember the other members who showed up behind Two-six in the dusk that evening except for Sergeant Perez, the T.C. of Two-nine-er, which was the track Finlay was on. Perez, who was to be our patrol leader, referred to a map he unfolded in front of us, nervously briefing us on our mission: "We'll be going straight outa here, and when we get to here," etcetera, etcetera.

"Good luck, Allie," Murph called out to me as we set out, "happy hunting."

In the darkening twilight where we looked like shadows moving around, Hank showed me how to set up and position claymore mines around the ambush site he'd told Sergeant Perez to choose. "Here we go, sarg. That grassy area right over yonder. Trees to our back and that nice little path over there."

It was actually a beautiful spot, though I didn't realize it until morning, when the sun came up coloring the sky in pinks and oranges and revealing one of the most beautiful vistas I've ever seen. Tiers of lush green rice fields, lake below, mountains in the back ground. Right out of a National Geographic picture.

In the fading light as we set up our ambush aiming the claymores away from the tree line toward the path—to, um, pulverize, destroy with the thousands of steel balls that would be released during the explosions, any hapless Asian man or woman or boy or girl who happened to be wandering by that teensy weeny portion of the earth's surface that Hank had suggested we occupy. But that's what we were there for, right? To kill. Kill and maim. See to it that the enemy died and became wounded for their country and not the other way around. But it was so peaceful. I hoped no one would wander by. I wasn't at all anxious to get some kills.

Snakes. Fuck. Oh, man, I don't like this. Sitting here all night on the ground. What's in that jungle behind us? And what's crawling around next to me here?

I remembered what the sergeant at the 90th Replacement Company had told us (along with highly recommending we use rubbers if we plan on mixing it up with the locals and grim warnings of what could happen if we didn't). "There are one hundred different types of snakes in Vietnam," he said, "ninety-nine are highly poisonous and the other one strangles you to death."

Great. I started imagining that there were snakes—bamboo vipers in particular—crawling all around me. I reached down and made sure the bottoms of my jungle fatigues were tucked into my boots (Bamboo vipers were called Johnny Two-Steps because of the number of steps you could take before you fell over dead if you were bitten).

When darkness finally fell, it fell hard and I couldn't see a thing, nothing, not even my hand if I held it two inches from my eyes. There would come a time when I would know, be able to feel it in my bones, when I was in danger or not; whether I had to be on high alert while sitting out wherever we were—or doing all the other guerilla-like activities we were engaged in daily; and accordingly, learning to trust the radar I'd developed—and hey—the fact that at times I was just too darn exhausted to give a shit anymore. (*Come on, come get me. I dare ya. Come slit my throat, end this, see if I give a shit. Sorry Mom, Dad, I didn't really mean that, it's just. . . .*) Accordingly, I pretty much knew when I could safely close my eyes and get some much needed, wonderful, glorious sleep; daydream, remove myself from the war for a while. Then snap back to reality when I had to.

Oh fuck, here we go again. Yer safety off, Allie? Yup. I'm

locked'n'loaded, ready t'go. Oh shit, this motherfucking place is just crawlin' with V.C., booby traps every motherfucking place we step. Careful, my man. You wander any further back, we *all* goin' home in a pine box. Take that back. A body bag. I got so I could sort shit out. Danger-wise. But that first, spooky, moonless night out where we were overlooking that view that I couldn't see, barely even knew was there—I was *wide awake*, bro. ALL. The. Night. Long. Yessum, wide awake, and every time I heard Hank snap open another can of beer across the way, I jumped, wondering what it was. Then I realized and thought, what the fuck's the matter with everyone, especially Sergeant Perez, our leader, that they allow that. Isn't he jeopardizing the safety of all of us?

Didn't matter. Hank did whatever the hell he pleased.

But. . . but. . . .

No buts, that's just the way it was.

At least Hank didn't scrunch up his empty cans and discard them so the gooks could use them as weapon material. And in the morning he gathered the cans, wrapped them in a towel and hauled them back to where the tracks were.

My wasn't that responsible of him?

*There it is! There it i*s! Guys were always saying that and I wondered what in the hell they were talking about: There it is! There it is! It sounded like a boring two-year-old.

And then, it *happened* and I *knew*. There it was! There it definitely, unequivocally, damn sure in fucking hell was!

Our platoon had come back the same way we'd gone out (making new tracks, avoiding the ones we'd made the day before) and suddenly, less than a mile from home, sweet home (Hill 58), an explosion made the ground shake in front of us.

"Oh my God, oh my God, was that. . . ?" Wiggs and I sitting on Two-three's back flap looked at each other.

"St. James," he said, "that was St. James."

"That's what I thought." It was St. James we had both seen soaring above the curtain of dust that had been thrown up in front of us by the blast as if he'd been shot out of a cannon; one of his legs flying one way, the rest of him another.

And as I watched that terrible spectacle in disbelief, prayerfully denying what I'd just seen, yet knowing that what I'd just seen was real, I remember thinking of St. James and me sitting next to each other on night ambush the night before—him showing me a picture of his girlfriend Donna. As he'd flown up out of that cloud of dust, I thought of him sitting on the back flap next to Danko as Double deuce broke through the jungle and into the clearing moments before; of him jumping down inside Double deuce's back and fetching beers for his fellow crew members. I remember thinking, what the fuck's he doing? Isn't that a major no-no? *Don't ever, ever, get down inside the back of one of these things when it's moving. Understand? Ever.* Then standing up and handing Sergeant Jackson a can of beer. Sergeant Jackson raising the can above his head in a kind of toast.

I couldn't see a thing. Only a wall of dust. My arms were shaking. I was breathing heavily. I knew that what had just happened to St. James was only the beginning; that what lay behind that curtain would change my view of the world unalterably.

Then, as the dust settled, I saw Double deuce had been flipped over and was lying on its back. Thirty tons.

There it is! There it is!

But where. . . ?

Sergeant Jackson. Is he underneath?

The upside down carrier was lying flush with the ground; its treads facing up.

"Oh fuck, the thing's gonna blow," shouted Wiggs. "That motherfucker's gonna blow and Harvey's in there."

"Stay put," said Simmons.

"Yeah, but. . . ."

And then, oh my goodness, the back door swung open and there he was, Harvey, the driver, climbing out the back. How in the hell. . . ?" And as all these years later I think of him standing behind Double deuce in a daze, looking around—Wiggs and I were standing inside the back of Two-three manning our machine guns in case of further attack. I try to imagine how it was for Harvey that day, May 23, 1967; I mean, driving along, making sure he stayed in the tracks Two-one ahead of him had made, daydreaming about whatever he'd been daydreaming about and then waking up and finding himself upside down in a dark hole; realizing after however long that that hole he was upside down in was the driver's compartment and that, oh shit, I hit a mine, the reason I'm upside down like this is because I hit a mine and I've got to get my ass out of here; and then working his way back thinking as he's crawling over ammo boxes and grenades and water and gasoline cans, remembering that any second, any second the gasoline, which was dripping all over the place and he could smell, was going to explode, which would mean receiving the same fate as his friend, Gibbons, who'd been trapped inside Two-five when it hit a mine and exploded in the Iron Triangle during Junction City three weeks before; then clamoring toward the back, his heart pounding as he tried to figure out how to pull up the handle and open the back door, and the incredible relief of having the door swing open and climbing back out into sunshine.

But the sarg. Where in the hell was he? Flashes of him only moments before, raising the can of beer St. James had handed him while sitting high and mightily—invincible looking—on a board he had set across the top of the turret; shirt off, coal black muscular body and face gleaming with sweat—if there is a God, I remember thinking, it's probably a big, black man like him.

St. James was lying in some grass off to my right. Thompson and Donnie were kneeling beside him. I saw him taking his last, gasping breaths before Donnie pulled the poncho liner up over his face.

"Oh shit, there he is!" Wiggs called over to me.

I glanced over to where Double deuce's turret, with Sergeant Tommy Jackson still sitting in it behind the fifty-caliber machine gun, had been thrown forty, fifty feet off to the right. Slumped over, his head resting on the fifty, the sergeant looked as if he was taking a nap, but he was dead. No one could possibly have gone for the ride he'd just gone on and lived to tell about it, though part of me was like, "hey Sarg, what in the hell you doin' over there, my man?" And I half expected to see him slowly raise his head like he'd just woken up and was going to look around, climb up out of the turret, and then shaking his head and smiling, walk toward those of us watching him and say, "damn! I surely am not recommending any 'a you try *that* anytime soon."

Man, just like that, that strapping, two hundred and fifty pound "bad ass"—*oh he bad, he bad*—sitting God-like up there in the turret (and ready to reach into your chest and pull out your heart if he had a mind to; put a whoopin' on ya). He wasn't a "bad-ass motherfucker" anymore; now was he? No. And—I hate to generalize—but some scrawny, emaciated one- hundred-pound weakling whose skinny neck Tommy could have reached over and wrung with one hand (*come 'ere you sorry little piece a shit*) had very likely observed what had just happened to the giant black man riding along cockily on his throne-like perch moments before and was high fiving one of his friends.

Danko, the left gunner—I'd been so preoccupied with what had happened to the sergeant and watching to see if maybe he was still alive; watching Donnie and Sanchez lifting the sergeant's heavy, lifeless body up out of the turret and laying it down on the ground next to the turret's side; covering the sergeant's face and body with a poncho liner. . . I'd been so preoccupied with what had happened to Sergeant Jackson and Harvey and St. James that I hadn't realized that Danko was lying on the ground only a few feet in front of me. Actually I couldn't see him. But as Donnie and Stacey ran by in front of me I leaned over the side of Two-three to see what was going on and saw Danko lying in powdery dust just to the left of Double deuce. Obviously the blast had blown him off the back flap where he'd been sitting, but instead of being thrown like two of his fellow crew members had been his body had apparently been shot straight up and then come straight back down. Well, almost. Just to the left. And though I didn't think of it at the time—I've thought of it many times later however—when his body came down, unless I'm missing some law of physics, it came down past the vehicle's treads, which, when the vehicle was flipped over onto its back, were facing upward. Following the blast he was lying on the ground next to the back flap that like the rest of the upside down carrier, was buried and looked like a small meteor had come crashing down and dug a hole in the earth's surface. Danko's back was broken. Like the backs of way to many other 11th Cav troopers. Broken backs, being paralyzed from the neck or waist down was the most prevalent wound when tracks set off mines. I think of them now, Simmons, Jiminez, Sheeley. . .Talbot, Cimino. . . Whatever happened to them? Are they still alive? What's life been like for them? I think I know. Or at least can imagine.

In order to create a landing zone for the medevac helicopters, Sergeants Cruthers and Plaski mine-swept each track off to opposite sides of where they were lined up in a column forming a circular, covered wagon-style defensive laager. Harvey, who had a bandage wrapped around his head and seemed to be still in a daze, helped Donnie load the litter with Danko on it into the side of the first chopper when it arrived, and then at the insistence of the L-tee who wanted him checked out at the hospital—"after what you just went through; the way you got that fucking bump on the side of your head"—reluctantly climbed aboard next to Danko and waving in a—don't worry I'll be right back fashion—off he went.

Then the next chopper came in and took away the KIA's.

Wiggs informed me when we got back to Hill 58 that Harvey had been the one up in the Iron triangle during operation Junction City to shovel into a body bag being held open for him the charred bones and ashes of his friend and fellow driver's burned body from the floor of the Two-niner's driver's compartment. Finlay had told me right off the bat how a second platoon driver had been burned to death when his track set off a mine and I'd imagined his body being overtaken by flames as horrified crew members stood by helplessly and watched; but my mind hadn't gone any further than that. It hadn't jumped to that final heartbreaking task, which I soon would find out included scraping the splattered, gooey remains off driver compartment walls after a rocket had exploded inside, so that loved ones at home could have something of their dead son or father or uncle or brother to bury.

Double deuce was too far gone to repair: so after removing personal belongings and weapons and ammo and cans of water it was set on fire. Hank, at Sergeant Morrison's request, did the honors. Climbing into two-six's turret he fired fifty rounds at the damaged track until it burst into flames and became just another one of the thousands of charred wreckages littering the countryside—a reminder of how a bunch of peasants could consistently wreak havoc on a vastly technologically superior Army.

* * *

The week after Double Deuce hit a mine, Two-three, the track I was on set off a mine in almost exactly the same place. Next thing I know I'm sitting on the ground in six inches of powdery dust wondering what in the hell just happened. Why am I. . . ? I looked at Two-three's back door and then up at where moments before I'd been sitting. Wiggs, who was still up on the back flap looked down at me, and then without losing eye contact swung his legs around, pushed off the side and jumped down. "You okay?" he shouted as he hurried over and knelt down beside me.

"Yeah," I said, "I guess. A mine?"

"Sure seems that way."

Let's see, arms, hands, legs, feet. Everything seemed intact. Donnie came over. He and Wiggs helped me up. I dusted myself off. Tana moved the vehicle forward so Simmons could check the treads for damage. Two of the tread cleats had been blown off directly underneath where I'd been sitting and were replaced right then and there. Wiggs and I climbed back up next to our machine guns (that's it? That's fucking *it*? I. . . I don't need to be dusted off?). And with Wagner and Ferrante minesweeping our tracks, we cranked back to Hill 58. Ah," a lost opportunity," I thought sitting on the back flap, not just *then* as we came back out of the "rabbit hole" and moved across the paddies, but for the whole rest of my tour. I mean, had I had the wherewithal after I was shot up into the air and suspended there for a few moments following the explosion (I do remember being in the air, I do, I do, hanging there, before being released and . . . plopping down into that soft bed of dust) . . . had I fully realized what was happening—oh my—do you think I wouldn't have straightened my arm and made sure I landed on, and broke, my wrist? Million-dollar wound, baby. *Nurse, a little more morphine, please. It really hurts.*

But alas, no broken wrist, not even a scratch, and I would be going *out there* many, many more times.

The next day—or was it two days after?—Sergeant Morrison got on the radio and asked Simmons to come over to the Two-six with his crew. He had something to show us.

And indeed he did. Though when we first arrived and saw the cylinder shaped chunk of concrete he was holding—that's what it looked like, a slab of concrete—we wondered what it was.

"What you got there, sarg?" Simmons asked as the four of us approached.

"You know what this is?" Sergeant Morrison asked, his eyes glistening.

"No, can't say I do."

Simon, a young, black gunner on Two-six looked over from where he was sitting inside the track cleaning his rifle and said, "Y'all a buncha lucky motherfuckers I cen tell ya that."

"That's a mine, isn't it?" said Simmons.

"Sho nuff is," said Simon.

Sergeant Morrison looked over at me. "It's the one—well—the other *half* a the one that. . . . "

"Sent me on my little journey?"

"Yeah. It was found. . . the third platoon found it right where. . . . "

Sergeant Morrison handed me the slab of whatever kind of explosive material it was. "This is it, Allie. If what you're holding had gone off. . . .

I have a photograph of me holding the sacred slab. Simmons took it with my instamatic. He took another of Sergeant Morrison presenting it to me. We're both smiling, standing by a bunker on Hill 58.

I showed it to my wife, Ruth, and my daughters, Emily and Julie and explained how if what they were looking at had exploded along with the half that did . . . .

"There wouldn't be any us, right Dad?"

"Correct."

"You wouldn't have been able to meet Mommy."

"That's true."

"How come it didn't. . . ?"

"How come I made it? How come I was able to come back in one piece?"

4.
China Beach

Early on while we were camped on Hill 58, Simmons asked me if I wanted to go for an in-country "R&R" at China Beach in Da Nang. None of the old-timers wanted to go.

"Wait a sec," I said, "how come . . . ?"

"You don't have to go."

"No, I didn't say that. I'm just wondering . . . is there something I'm missing?"

"Ya know, they offer these getaways, but like regular "R&R" you come back and it's like, oh fuck, *this* again. It's harder. Sometimes it's better to just stay put. Psychologically, that's what's going on. But you . . . ."

"I'm just getting started, right? Still a newbie. 'Hey, see if that Fucking New Guy wants to go up there.'"

"Chance to get laid. Lay back for a few days, sleep in. Order a cheeseburger. Eat some fries. Drink cokes and milkshakes."

"Okay, I'll take it. Sure."

"I'll send your name over."

Some guy from the third platoon—I don't remember his name, but can see his face. He was a fellow New Jersey-ite as it turned out. He and I hitched a ride in a two-and-a-half-ton truck to the Chu Lai Air Base five miles away. The driver, a young soldier with a "kicked look" in his eyes (that is, hell bent, shall we say, who was ready for *any* and *everything*) and a baseball cap on backwards, shouted, "Hold on tight, sports fans," to—I'll call him Jersey—and me standing in the back, then climbing into the cab next to his equally ready and rarin' t'go partner riding shot gun, slammed his foot down hard on the accelerator and held it there the whole way. We were haulin', bro. I mean, yeah, Jersey and I were pleased that we'd inadvertently signed up for the seemingly reckless, high speed joy ride. (Would we have preferred a helicopter ride to the Chu Lai base if that had been an option? Yes, but it was not.) Even though we were being bounced all over the place and each of us had come close to being flung out over the side and onto the ground several times as the truck was shooting up road dust over bumps and tore across fields and paddies, we were pleased that the purpose of such recklessness (beyond providing the driver and his pal their daily adrenalin fixes), was to avoid setting off mines and becoming an easy target for snipers and whoever might be in the jungle over there leading us with a rocket launcher. Did I—or do I still—have nightmares about being out there all alone, looking across the way as the truck bursts into flames and seeing thousands of NVA soldiers pouring out of the jungle and walking toward us? Do I still get a chill at that thought?

Yes. Yes I do.

At the Chu Lai Air Force Base after our adventurous ride (why were those clowns—who drove us back to Hill 58 in similar fashion, on our return trip three days later by the way—allowed to drive solo like that, without a convoy, I'll never know). We boarded an aircraft known as a Caribou. In order to lessen the risk of being brought down in a ball of flames by an exploding rocket fired by an enemy soldier positioned at the end of the runway, pilots of those big, clumsy, obscene looking birds, after leaving the runway, flew just above the tree line for several miles making it seem as though the plane was in trouble and those of us strapped in along the sides with no windows to look out of were in deep, deep shit. So *this* is how I'm going to die, I remember thinking, looking at my fellow passengers to see if they were harboring the same concern, crashing in a plane taking me to Da Nang for an in-country "R&R." No *wonder* none of the old timers wanted to go. They *did* know something. It felt safer staying back. Going out on missions. And then suddenly—what now?—the plane shot straight up, and went up and up and up, once again leaving me feeling doomed. And I didn't even think of all the other aircraft, not to mention thousands of artillery rounds constantly crossing the pilot's path (twelve o'clock, three o'clock, nine o'clock! Jeez); that unsettling awareness came later, on subsequent flights. Suffice to say I learned to block out all those concerns and closed my eyes and hoped for the best. What else could I do?

China Beach. The first thing I did when I got there—after I'd checked in and was assigned a bunk in one of the wooden barracks—was to ask around and find out where the best place to get laid was, right? Isn't this where—in soldierly fashion—I tell how I immediately left that China Beach scene—Fuck that, m'man!—caught a ride into Da Nang and—oh boy—the rest is history as they say?

No. Sorry to disappoint. All I wanted to do was take off my boots, put my rifle on the gun rack; lie down on the upper bunk I'd selected; stare up at the ceiling and day dream; close my eyes and drift off. Dream about—sure, females—girls I'd done it with. Well, the two. *Three.* Those evenings in Lexington, Kentucky. And those I, you know how it is to wish I'd done it with. Like Janey. Jesus, she didn't even know I was over there. Ah, yes, living inside my head, which soldiers do a lot. Growing up in Rochester, New York, my childhood there, and the going home process. Oh, the *going home process.* From the get-go, I started dreaming about what it would be like to have it all over and done with. To be . . . I had every detail worked out in my mind.

"I'm going into town," the guy from New Jersey—whatever his name was—entered the barrack and told me. He'd found a bunk in another barrack but in case I wanted to join him. . . .

"No thanks."

"Sure?"

He looked at me puzzled. That look I often got. "You jus' gonna…?"

"Lie here, like this, yes."

"Suit yourself."

I did.

One afternoon I took a break from just lying there on that top bunk and moseyed on over to the cafeteria.

"Mind if I join you?" I looked up at the young marine who holding a tray full of food was standing next to the table where I was sitting.

"No, course not. Have a seat."

He glanced over at the cheeseburger I'd only taken one bite from; the fries piled up next to it; the coke and milkshake to wash them down. "You was thinkin' along the same lines as me looks like."

He sat down and looked into my eyes. "Yer Army, ain't ya?"

"That okay?"

"Sure. It's just. . . like I say, it's mostly Marines here. What outfit you from?"

"11th Cav. Armor."

"Tanks?"

"Armored personnel carriers. Tracks we call them."

"And yer located. . . .

"Little bit south a here. Chu Lai. The squadron I'm in anyway. Our base camp's in the south. Thirty or so miles northeast of Saigon. Near Xuan Loc. How 'bout you?"

"I'm," we each nibbled our fries, ""I'm with the 9th Regiment, 3rd Marine Division. In Con Thien. North a here."

Con Thien, Con Thien, the name exploded inside my head. "Con Thien," I said to myself, "I'm sitting at a table talking to a young marine who's stationed in Con Thien." As I looked at him, gazed into his cheerful, friendly eyes—Jeez, are you even *old* enough to be doing this?—images of what I'd read in newspapers and magazines and seen on television flashed inside my head; a battered, rain-lashed hill up on the DMZ; flooded trenches; enemy shells exploding all over the place; medevac helicopters trying to get in and out without being struck by a rocket. Con Thien. I pictured this wide-eyed kid sitting in a foxhole, dashing for cover, diving into a trench to avoid being ripped to shreds by shrapnel. *This being everything the marine recruiter said it would be?* Part of me was thinking, cynically, oh you poor bastard, what's it like signing up to be cannon fodder? But another part was in complete awe. Con Thien. Con Thien.

We ate our cheeseburgers and talked. He liked being a marine and was proud. He'd seen a lot of his friends killed and even though it was nice having a little break here at China Beach, he missed his friends—those who hadn't been killed or dusted off with serious wounds—and he was anxious to get back. When we'd both finished eating we stood up and shook hands. I wished him good luck. He was heading back in the morning. Four, five years later, I was browsing through a book of black-and-white photographs titled, *War Without Heroes* by David Douglas Duncan, and came across a section about Con Thien. As I leafed through the photos Duncan had taken showing what it was like to be a marine at Con Thien in 1967, I came across a series of photos of Pfc. Richard Hughes eating an apple and recognized him immediately. He's wearing his poncho, has his helmet liner and steel pot pulled down over the poncho's hood, and has on those glasses I remember him wearing. Below the apple eating shots is a photo of two marines carrying a wounded soldier on a stretcher while slogging through mud. In the caption next to that picture—I bought the book so I can still refer to it—it says, "His rain-fogged glasses stared straight up into the heavy monsoon sky—apparently the happiest marine at Con Thien was dying, too." Standing in the bookstore, my heart sank, but then I turned the page and read the following: "'Dead! . . .Me? . . .Hell. I'm starved—they don't even feed you in this place!' Pfc. Richard Hughes sat on a litter, using his plastic spoon to clean mud from his boots. Mortar fragments had creased the back of his head—knocking him out—torn through his arm and ripped the seat from his dungarees leaving only minor wounds. When the medevac chopper arrived, he snarled with outrage at the litter bearers, 'Scram! I walked in—I'll walk out!' He limped away from Con Thien, where he had been content."

Question is, did he return to Con Thien after being released from the hospital. And if he did, which, given everything I know about him he would have insisted upon, did he survive after that? I could find out, couldn't I? Same as I did with my friend Doug Henning. Check to see if his name is on the wall. But I'm not going to. I like imagining him living in Kansas and showing his children—maybe even grandchildren—the photos Mr. Duncan took of him forty-six years ago at Con Thien.

At any rate, sure, it was nice to get away for a few days, a welcome interlude, but man-oh-man what (as I'd been warned) a complete and total bummer, a one hundred percent downer (a mind fuck) to suddenly find myself back in the field again. Instead of lying on the beach and then getting up and going into the ocean to cool off; or having a beer over at the EM Club; or enjoying yet another cheeseburger with all the fixins, and fries and a milkshake; or just plain "chillin," lying on that top bunk daydreaming, which I'd spent hours doing there, I was back in those jungles and rice paddies playing Russian roulette again; because you know what? That's *precisely* what the fuck we were doing, playing Russian roulette.

5.
Here We Go Again

Oh shit! Here we go again. The front of the track was climbing up the side of yet another tree. Higher and higher the track climbed as Tana (Santana) gave the vehicle more gas. The engine whined. The tread cleats underneath Wiggs and me dug into the growth below as, scraping away bark, the front end went up and up. Wiggs and I held onto our machine guns to keep from sliding off the back flap. Our track, the Two-three, was up front, leading, which meant our crew was riding point. I glanced back at Donahue, the driver of the Two-seven who was following close behind in the path Tana was creating. Taylor, the T.C. was reaching up from the turret and pushing away vines dangling from above as if he was spreading open a curtain. Millions of vines, intertwined with each other, dropped down from the tops of trees, and even though Santana was clearing a path, the ground the tracks were making their way over was thick with shrubs and bushes.

Simmons, pushing away vines and trying to keep his balance as the track became tilted at a forty-five degree angle, turned toward Wiggs and me holding on for dear life (we all knew that anyone who fell overboard would most likely become lost forever in the tangle below), and laughed. Finally, the tree the track had ascended made a loud cracking sound and toppled over. As the track crashed down on top of it, Wiggs and I were thrown forward. I couldn't see a thing. The V.C. could have been hiding two feet away and I wouldn't have seen them. *Sometimes the V.C.*

hang canisters of napalm or Willie Pete (white phosphorous), or grenades along wires so that when a track's antennae hits them it acts like a trigger and . . . .

Yeah, I know, I remember thinking many, many times when I was made aware of such frightening prospects. I get it: There are lots of ways to get killed or badly fucked up in this place, but surprising (knowing how I am) I didn't dwell on the endless anxiety-provoking information I was constantly being saddled with. Denial? Sure, to an extent. But as I think I mentioned previously, one can't live each and every second in such a high state of alert. It's too exhausting. The "crying wolf" culprit would become my own debilitating self. Mercifully, however, there often seemed to be some distracting occurrence or event when I was getting too carried away with what was or wasn't there in my surroundings—in this case the vine that had wrapped itself around my machine gun and was trying to tear it from its mount. "Hold on!" I shouted. "My machine gun. Stop! Tell Santana to stop. Back up a little."

Simmons, wondering why Two-three's engine was straining and whining so much, or why the vehicle wasn't moving forward, glanced back and saw what I was yelling to him about. I shouted over the intercom for Santana to stop. "Back up a little."

Santana backed up. Wiggs jumped down in back and came up with a hunting knife. As he was freeing my machine gun from the vine I felt something biting me. Ouch! Whatever it was had just taken a chunk out of my left calf. Two more bites. This time on my right shin. Fuck! I looked down and saw. . . ants. Large red ants were crawling around on my boots and . . . I pulled up my pants legs. Oh jeez, I reached down and brushed away several of the man-eating creatures that were crawling up my legs. Another bite. On the small of my back? Two more on my inner thighs. *I'm being eaten alive.* They were everywhere. I glanced down at where they were pouring out from underneath limbs and branches and debris that had fallen on top of the track. Frantically, I ran my hands up and down the inside of my legs; then, after brushing my arms—yes, they'd gotten up there too—and smacking myself in various places, I began jumping up and down. I kicked away the limbs the ants seemed to be swarming out of and then stomped them with my boots. Wiggs and Simmons watched me, laughing. Taylor, the T.C. behind us came over the radio asking Simmons what was going on and why was I doing a jig in the middle of the jungle? Like he didn't know, right? Like this was the first time he'd seen this? "My left gunner was attacked by ants," Simmons responded, "but it's under control now. Allie, wave. Show him you're okay."

"Fuck you," I said, looking around to make sure there wasn't a second wave coming at me. My whole body ached. I was covered with red, swollen sores. *Wounds.* My head was pounding. Yeah, "fuck you," I said. "All you assholes."

Then Sergeant Morrison, who was several tracks behind and couldn't see what was happening, asked Simmons what the hold-up was, how come we weren't moving?

"A vine latched itself onto my left gunner's sixty," Simmons replied, "wouldn't let go. Had to cut it free. Watch out for vines and red ants when you get up here. The ants dragged said gunner off into the jungle and are no doubt feasting on his ass."

"No doubt, Killer Two-three. I'll look for him. Thanks for the heads-up."

Breaking out of jungle. Moving along ridges. Coming down into rice paddies. Crossing rice paddies and moving past hedge groves. The sound of automatic gunfire suddenly; bullets clanging against my machine gun shield. Jumping down inside the back and firing my machine gun. Muzzle flashes. AK-47 tracers arching upward from the tree line. Coming right at me. The noise deafening. Slap on another belt of rounds, cock and fire. Twenty-round bursts. Eight sixties and eight fifties going. Pounding the jungle. Chew. Ing. It. *Up.* Gettin' some presumably. But how do you know? You often don't. Cries for Donnie, our medic. Gunships hovering over our heads. Then leaving and making way for the Phantoms. And oh shit, here they come, one after another flying in low over the tree line and setting napalm fires. Way, *way* too close to where we are. And finally the dust-offs—for several guys with gunshot wounds. One of them a guy who was always chomping on a cigar and playing cards; a ring leader type. The bandages covering his chest and wrapped around his neck are soaked in blood as the litter he's on is being carried past our track.

* * *

One morning we patrolled a bombed-out village. Grayson came over and asked me what I was doing. "You feel sorry for the motherfucker, don't you," he said, glancing down at the still breathing airstrike victim I was standing next to. He nudged the young Viet Cong with his foot; then, while the boy watched him with pleading eyes, he leaned over, glanced at the entrance to the tunnel both the boy and his dead pals had obviously been trying to make it into, and said, "Seems like you an' yer pals 'er a minute late'n'a dollar short, eh? A *second* late, looks like." Then, "Gal-lie! 'Ave t'say, you ain't lookin' so good there, Mr. Charles. Anyway ya slice it." He turned and looked at me. "Ain't that right there, Allie? Would you concur?"

Grayson was right; the boy wasn't looking too good. Blackened and swollen and covered with welts, from the balls of fire that had swept through the village and enveloped him and his friends as they'd tried to make it to the tunnel's entrance, it looked as if the flesh from his nose and forehead and mouth and around his jaw had melted, then hardened into the hideous mask he seemed to be wearing. And yet—could this *be*? Was this possible? From within the grotesque rearrangement of what I assumed had, less than an hour ago been a normal fourteen-fifteen-year-old Southeast Asian boy's face, the boy's big, dark eyes were gazing up at me. Well, at Grayson and me.

Grayson leaned over and spat on the boy, and then kicked him in the side with his boot. Hinman came over and did the same. Lacy and Jones upon seeing the boy ran over to the edge of the jungle and puked.

I have dreamed about kneeling down beside that boy and trying to comfort him; of giving him water; pouring the water ever so slowly into his damaged mouth so that he wouldn't feel as if I was trying to drown him. Watching the relief in his eyes as the water went down his throat and he began swallowing. But what good would that have done? It would only have prolonged his suffering.

I could have ended his suffering of course, the way I'm certain he wanted me to. And tell how closing my eyes and asking for God's forgiveness I tearfully . . . what? *Executed* him? That's what it would have felt like; firing a bullet into his head—then and there. On the spot—would have been the kind, merciful thing to do.

* * *

The day after we encountered the airstrike victims I was torn from my job as Two-three's left gunner, which I preferred to keep on doing thank you very much, and dragged from my comfort zone, which I'd been cultivating for the previous six weeks into what many have regarded as the most difficult and dangerous job in the Nam.

I was cleaning weapons behind Two-three when Sergeant Morrison came over the radio asking Simmons to send me over. He was standing behind Two-six waiting for me as I approached. "Allie," he said, reaching over and shaking my hand, "Isn't that what they call you?"

"Allie, yes."

"Come on in," he said, climbing into the back of Two-six. "Have a seat." I ducked my head and followed. He sat on one side; I sat on the other. He reached in into the cooler, pulled out an ice cold Pabst and handed it to me.

"Thanks," I said.

"You're welcome."

He watched me opening it. He had friendly, but somehow mischievous, dark eyes. They seemed to be twinkling from within his gleaming, coal black, mustachioed face.

"How would you feel about being my driver?"

"Your *who?*"

"My driver. Two-six's delta."

"Lousy," I said.

"Well, I'm sorry to hear that because starting bright and early tomorrow morning that's what you're going to be, my driver."

I looked at him, stunned. "That's it," I said. "I have no say in the matter?"

"That's correct."

"But…"

"No buts."

"Look, sarg, you're making a big mistake. A *big* mistake. I'm the most un-mechanically inclined . . . honest. I'm being straight with you."

"You'll do fine, Allie. Go fetch your stuff. You're assigned to Two-six now."

"Come on, sarg. What if I . . . . ?"

"Simon, Hank. Meet our new driver. You need any help bringing your shit over here jus' give us a holler."

Hank didn't care one way or the other if I or someone else was the new Two-six driver. So long as it wasn't him. Simon had an altogether different view of the matter, however. "Where'n the fuck you think yer goin' there, white boy?" he asked as I wandered over with my duffle.

"I'm…"

"I know, I know, you don't 'ave t'tell me. Yer are new driver."

Simon ran his eyes up and down me. "Tell me somethin'," he said, "you know what the fuck yer doin'? I mean," he pointed his head in the direction of the track, "you know how to drive that fucking thing?"

I looked into Simon's eyes, gave him a confident smile. "Yeah, I reckon," I said. "Reckon I can manage. Sure." I shrugged my shoulders. "Why not?"

Simon bugged his eyes out. "Why not? Why *not*? Because… because you're a sorry ass white boy, that's why." Simon shook his head. "Ain't this somethin'? I mean, can you believe this fucking shit? We lose our driver—a brother, as it so fucking happens—and who replaces him? *You*. Elmer Fudd. Who says—

wha'd you say there, Elmer? That you cen manage? Well," he pinned me down with his glistening, laser-type eyes, "you damn well, sure enough, had *better* manage, if yer gonna be drivin' *this* black man around. Which it sounds like you *is*."

So here's my driving saga. How for two months—from early June until the beginning of August, 1967—I drove the command track with Sergeant Willie Morrison sitting up in the turret and Simon and the Ross element perched next to each other by their machine guns on the back flap.

6.
No Say in the Matter

"Willie, m'man, don't let em *do* this t'me."

That utterance I heard behind me in the dark as I sat in the turret on guard duty. Sergeant Vega, the nasty, five-foot-four sergeant had been giving me a hard time ever since I joined the platoon and let's just say whose views on manhood and what was required to be an effective soldier in the Nam differed substantially from my own and whose views he sarcastically snarled at me each and every chance he got. This hateful, sorry-ass individual poked his miserable face inside the back of Two-six where, holding a lit flashlight in front of himself, Sergeant Morrison was reading a letter from his wife.

"Please, Willie, do something." Sergeant Vega who was at the time (I didn't know it), handcuffed and had someone guarding him, as he pleaded, "Don't let this happen."

But Sergeant Morrison, whose calm, assuring, steady voice I can still hear, told him there was nothing he could do. "You know how it works, Jose. You're a sergeant in the United States Army. That requires . . . you're supposed to be a leader, set an example."

"Okay, I agree," I heard Sergeant Vega say in a weak, pleading voice. "You're right. I messed up. But . . . ."

"You raped and then killed a thirteen-year-old girl. For the hell of it. For fun."

"Come on, Willie, you an' I know what the deal is. She was a V.C. She might very well've been the one who set the mine that killed. . . . "

"You don't know that she was a V.C. *All* Vietnamese aren't V.C. Besides. . . you better leave, Jose. Sergeant Hancock, take him away."

"But Willie, come on. Have a heart, man."

In the morning two MP's flew in by helicopter, arrested Vega for the rape and murder of a civilian (a thirteen-year-old girl he'd come across in a village during a patrol he was leading), and off he went. To Leavenworth by way of LBJ, I assumed. I wonder if he's still rotting in some cell there. I know that in the morning when I glanced over and saw him being shoved into the side of the chopper I was glad he was arrested and taken away and sorry for the life he had taken.

It was during that period that Hank got on the radio and informed the pilot, who was trying to lower the net of supplies dangling from a Chinook helicopter, that if he didn't hurry his ass up, quit pussy footing around with his beer, he was going to step outside and shoot the motherfucker down himself.

Oh wow! The pilot was not at all pleased by what he was hearing from Killer 26 whoever that was. I could see bullets arching upward into the air toward the chopper; rockets being launched at it also. Bringing down one of those giant Chinooks—woe! An extra bowl of rice for those comrades.

Despite the cover, I and thirty-one other M-60 gunners and sixteen T.C.s working their fifties were firing into the surrounding jungle—not to mention the eight Big Boys (tanks) interspersed among us and firing their big guns (whoa!), I couldn't imagine being on the wrong side of one of them, because whoever was out there catching the brunt of our considerable, wholehearted wrath were still managing to give the distressed pilot a hard way to go. And then—as he continued to watch tracer rounds arching up toward him and rockets being fired from the tree line—to have some clown (uh, that would be Hank), looking out the back and checking the pilot's progress as he spoke on the radio; to have someone down there on one of the command radios saying, "Spider 13," or some such thing, "this is

Killer 26, quit fuckin' with me and bring me my beer." (Yup, I'm *listening* to this shit as I'm standing next to him firing *his* machine gun.) The pilot had to be wondering whose side all those troops below him were on, for whom he was risking his and his crews' lives to bring supplies to.

Okay, what was I doing firing Hank's machine gun? And where was Sergeant Morrison? As the platoon leader, how could he let Hank do what he was doing?

I'd been washing up when the shooting started. We'd just set up a perimeter in a large grassy area at the northern end of the valley we'd been operating in. I'd cleaned my sixteen and performed track maintenance and was taking a field bath, meaning I'd filled up my steel pot with water from one of the cans we carried and had been warmed by the sun and nakedly soaping myself up behind Two-six when I heard the familiar sound of rotor-blades off in the distance. Next thing I knew a Chinook helicopter was hovering above the field we were in with a net full of supplies dangling beneath it. As soon as the pilot began to lower the net he came under fire and Sergeant Morrison who was up in the turret yelled at me to get my naked ass inside the track and begin firing Hank's sixty since Hank was off as per usual drinking with his buddies over at the mortar track, pounding down the last of our platoons' beers. I hurriedly threw away the filthy, soapy water, rinsed myself off by holding the can of water over my head, and then buck naked with balls jiggling, climbed into the back of Two-six and began firing Hank's machine gun. Sergeant Morrison turned, looked at me and laughed. Simon who was standing by his machine gun behind me did the same. "Jesus, white man, *that's* a sight."

"Yeah, well, fuck you. Where the fuck's Hank?"

We laid cover. Two Echo Troop platoons and a platoon from C Company. And then as I was nakedly firing his machine gun, Hank climbed into the back behind me, found the frequency he was looking for on the radio and let the pilot know loud and clear what he expected of him.

* * *

One afternoon Murph and I heard an explosion as we were drinking beer behind Two-seven on Hill 58 and looked over and saw orange flames shooting up from the wall of jungle across the way and then thick, black smoke billowing into the air above it. Shortly after, word came down that the third platoon medic had been trapped inside the track he was on when it burst into flames and had been incinerated.

"You know who that *was*?" Murph asked me referring to the unlucky soldier as we were sitting in the mess tent eating breakfast the next day; unlucky soldier who . . . Jesus! Was burned to death during his first mission.

"No," I said.

"*No*," he cried, disbelievingly. "Wha'd'ya mean no?"

"No." I looked into Murph's eyes. "I don't remember."

"Fuck, man. We just met him. Last week. Right *here*. Young black dude. Nice guy. Funny. He was from . . . I don't know, but we met him, we were sitting here talking, you, me . . . .?

Then it hit. Way it would do. Many more times. That recognition. I saw him, sitting . . . his face. His eyes looking into mine as he asked, "What's it like? I mean, how bad is it out there?"

It hit. "Oh no, oh man, not him? *Him? That* guy? No, not him. Oh man, jeez. *He's* the one? Fuck!"

I could be anywhere. I remember looking around in the dark and thinking, anywhere at all. Except I'm *not*. I'm *here*, sitting in this outhouse. In Vietnam. The Nam. And tomorrow I'll be out there again. Back in those hills.

That outhouse. At the top of the small rise above the sandbag bunker next to which I parked the track. Convenient. Especially for someone like myself who had a chronic need for a place I could get to in a hurry. Up that path in the dark. *Where's my fucking flash-light?* Sitting over one of those three holes for hours. Daydreaming. Wondering if a mortar round would come in and end it all for me the way one had for those two soldiers at base camp?

Mortars. Despite the high probability that one might find its way near to where I was sleeping, I still disregarded Sergeant Morrison's advice and slept on a cot behind the track; refused to sleep inside the bunker. Why? Because I couldn't stand listening to the sound of rats crawling around the wooden beams above me. I imagined them glowering at me with beady, pink eyes as, teeth bared they hung by their tails watching me. But one night we were attacked. The southwest side of the hill—the side of the perimeter occupied by the first platoon—was rocked with explosions and from then on I reluctantly slept inside the bunker with rats.

* * *

Approximately—well, let's see—fourteen months? Fourteen, fifteen months from then a young woman I was quite taken with said to me during a hike we were on, "That's all you wanna do is kill, isn't it?"

Oh wow! Oh man! Those big, dark eyes gazing at me (looking, oh yes, yes indeed, into my own) from within that pretty face of hers; her long, dark hair framing that face and falling down past her shoulders. All I want to do is *kill?*

We were hiking in the Flatirons, Gail and I, those steep, craggy rocks overlooking Boulder (was I really there? Or just dreaming again), and when I saw a mouse skitter among the leaves next to the path we were on I pointed my finger at it and said, "Pow!"

The two of us standing there. In the woods. Did I say to Gail—

as I have said to myself a million times since, "Look, Gail, I. . . that's not true. I. . . ."

Did I try to explain that. . . oh fuck! How do you explain? I mean, rats, fucking rats, crawling around. Staring at me. No. I said nothing. NOTHING. Just kept whatever was roiling inside me those days (who am I kidding, still roiling inside me TODAY at times) to myself.

She wasn't afraid of me I don't think. Even then. I mean, during the hike. Up there in those Flatirons. After all she'd gone on the hike with me. I hadn't abducted her. She'd had time to think about it and refuse. But didn't. I'm sure some of her sorority friends had asked her if she knew what she was doing. I mean, oh sure, I seemed nice enough, but . . . I mean (and what's scary is, it's true) what did she really know about me? Some mighty scary shit goin' down over there in those jungles and rice paddies. You never know—I mean you really fucking don't—who you're . . . .

So, despite whatever she'd been told, any warnings she'd been given, she'd gone on that hike with me. Ah yes, walking over to her sorority house and picking her up. Her coming down those stairs and looking over and seeing me. Sweet moment. Good, you're bringing some water and a snack. How thoughtful. Beautiful day for a hike. Haven't been up there . . . Been a long time since I was up in those Flatirons.

Why didn't I say anything? Set that pretty young lady straight. Defend myself. Why did I just shrug my shoulders, like, yeah, well, of course all I want to do is kill. I'm a Vietnam vet aren't I?

* * *

After I removed my goggles that were caked with dust and dirt and grime from my eyes so I could see, I wondered if maybe I'd mistakenly driven off the cliff as I was speeding blindfolded—that's certainly what it had seemed like—down the steep, dust-filled road at the side of a ridge and had taken Sergeant Morrison, Hank, Simon and myself through yet another rabbit hole.

"You pleased with yourself? What were you trying to *do*?" I tore off my CVC helmet so I didn't have to listen to Willie's scolding, patronizing voice. He'd been yelling frantically at me, ordering me to slow down the whole time I was spitting out dust and, admittedly, recklessly trying to keep up with the Two-one whose treads were throwing up thick clouds of dust I couldn't see through. I could hear threats from the peanut gallery behind where Willie was sitting in the turret also. But I didn't care; just held my foot down on the accelerator.

At any rate, there we were in some exotic place suddenly. White, sandy beaches leading down to a narrow inlet; jungle on the other side; the inlet opening gradually off to the left into the South China Sea. The ocean's sparkling water sprinkled with sampans and tiny white sails. Children playing in the tracks our vehicles had made; the barrels of our fifties and sixties jutting out over their heads and silhouetted against the blinding whiteness of the sand. Where'd you cuties come from anyway? Watching us, our every move, in your conical straw hats and PJs. More children pouring out from the jungle behind us. Old men and *mama sans* stepping out cautiously from the trees also. Kids selling cokes. Two little girls hawking rubbers—case anyone was interested in following them for a quickie somewhere. Not *them*, but . . . oh, those three young women standing over yonder, watching us. Waving. Any takers? Oh yeah! A whole fucking platoon, ready'n'rarin' t'go, but hold on, hold yer motherfuckin' horses. Sergeant Morrison, seeing what's going on is nippin' the whole thing in the bud, tells the T.C.s on the radio that this is not the time or place. No dice. Stay next to your track until it's time to take the ferry over.

A flat, wooden, barge-like ferry taking one track at a time over to the small clearing on the other side. While we waited, the gunners jumped down into the sand to stretch their legs. Aw, you fellas had it rough coming over here today, didn't you? Sitting on the back flap drinking beer. While I and the other Deltas . . . .

I felt a tap on my shoulder. It was Willie. "Here," he said, reaching over and handing me a cold beer.

"Thanks," I said. I looked up squinting into his smiling face.

"Man," he said, shaking his head, "you are one obstinate sonovabitch, you know that? I can't figure if you've got a death wish—an' by the way, if you *do*, please don't include Hank, Simon, and me in it, okay?" He looked into my eyes. "I know what you're trying to do, Allie. But it's not gonna work. Dig? Must admit I never thought training someone t'be my driver would be like breaking in a bucking bronco, but I guess it is. I admire your feistiness, in fact that's one of the reasons I selected you, I could see you had fire in yer eyes, but you might as well get used to it, soldier, so long as I'm ridin' up here in the turret, yer gonna be down below me there . . . ."

Yeah, yeah, yeah. I took a long swig of beer. The sun was blinding. Everything seemed silky, unreal. I took the towel draped around my neck and wiped away the sweat and dust and grime that had been ground into my face. There was always the sensation when I did that that there was a slight breeze even if there wasn't. Voices. Down below me. Shouts from kids playing in the sand. Out of the corner of my eye I saw a big, burly man shooing kids away; telling them to scram. "Didi mau," he shouted, waving his big, gorilla arms. It was Hank, of course. A large crowd had gathered around him. The kids seemed to have developed a game of running up and trying to touch him. It was as if they were trying to grab hold of a piece of him or his clothing as a souvenir to take back to their village. He tried to scare them away, but couldn't.

That spot. Where we caught the ferry. It was right near there, within miles that in—well—let's see, in less than a year the My Lai massacre occurred.

7.
The Batangan

It wasn't until many years after I came home that I read in fictional and nonfictional accounts of the Vietnam War that the "peninsula" as it was referred to—the place we were headed to on the other side of the inlet—was the Batangan Peninsula, a treacherous, mine- and booby-trap laden area in Quang Ngai Province, thirty-two kilometers south of Chu Lai where some of the war's fiercest fighting took place.

Anyway, there we were out on the Batangan Peninsula. Was that the time Captain Johnson lost a leg when the soldier he was standing next to set off a booby-trapped grenade while kicking in a door in a village? While pulling a "John Wayne" in other words. Rule of thumb: Stay clear of overzealous dudes who think they're actors in a movie set.

And was it during that mission that we lost the Two-five to one of the gazillions of mines in that place? How? In. God's. *Name.* Did we avoid not setting off more? Eyes glued to the tracks the vehicle in front of me were making. Staying vigilant even as my mind was wandering: *Dear Mom, Dad and Sue . . . Dear Lee . . . Dear L.T. . . Dear Janey* and so on and so forth. Shoulders hunched against the rim of the hatch for leverage, laterals forward, foot on the gas, moving us another inch forward, another foot, across yet another paddy, through more jungle. It was *going* to happen whatever it was; it was only a matter of time. If not today, then tomorrow. Or the day after tomorrow. Or two weeks from then. A month. It was going to happen whatever it was; let it only be a foot. Or a hand. A few fingers maybe. Couple a toes. Some metal in me; the ol' million-dollar wound—whatever one considered that to be. As time went on what was looked upon (dreamt about as a million-dollar wound) changed. One could imagine living without a foot in other words, if that would get me the hell out of there . . . But it was going to happen whatever it was—except that it didn't!

Dripping with sweat; soaked. Eyes blurry. *Fuck you, sarg. I'm doing the best I can.*

Hopkins, the firebug. I've forgotten about him. Torching huts in villages. Setting them aflame after being given the go ahead. Wow! The look in his eyes. Dude had found his niche. Right place at the right time. Out there on the Batangan. I can hear the roar of the flames, see the faces of the villagers who were evacuated, feel the intense heat as I sat in the driver's compartment watching. *They're helping the V.C., Allie. Wha'd'ya think?*"

And then there was the third-platoon gunner who was trapped from the waist down under a side of the track he'd been riding on top of when the mine exploded. The dude was lying face down, half of him crushed by thirty tons of steel that had been flipped over onto him, his other half sticking out like he was trying to crawl away but the weight was just too much. "Say, could someone give me a cigarette?" he asked calmly as Hank and I and several others approached him; and then to one of his fellow platoon members who placed a cigarette in his mouth and lit it for him, "how soon before y'all cen get this motherfucker off me?"

Since it wasn't advisable to hitch the track up to another and drag it off the victim, fucking him up even more than he already was, he had to wait for the squadron's wrecker to come and lift it off him. "You okay, m'man?" his buddies gathered around trying to comfort him. "Hang in there, help is on the way. Here. Have another cigarette."

And wasn't it out on the Batangan that time—we would go out there again after the old platoon left—that Riley died of shock after a rocket exploded next to him? It was a shame because he could have been saved. Though if I had looked down after an explosion and seen my guts spilling out, I doubt very much that I would have been any more comforted than Riley by the medic telling me to hang in there, they'd push all that stuff oozing out of me back inside, sew me up and I'd be as good as new. No, given my discomfort in even *hearing* about that sort of thing, then again having witnessed it over and over and over, I probably would have gone the way of Riley.

* * *

One day the commanding general of the Americal Division to which our squadron was attached flew in to where we were camped and Hank jumped down off the top of the track and said, "lock my heels and stand me at attention, motherfucker." The general, in exchanging salutes with Hank, said, "carry on soldier," then with the colonel for the second squadron, Captain Jacobs and the rest of his entourage, moved on to the next track.

* * *

One evening Simon and I sat and talked, him in the turret, me sitting on the side. Despite our rocky start, we'd managed over a relatively short period of time to develop a close friendship. Don't ask me when all this started, when our contempt for each other—or should I say lack of trust?—evolved into something more positive. He, no doubt, got a kick out of my stormy relationship with Sergeant Morrison and enjoyed watching me give the sergeant a hard time. Simon and Hank got pissed at me when I purposefully drove like a maniac—when the road rage Sergeant Morrison had instilled in me fully manifested itself (jolting them forward and back as I recklessly drove over paddy dikes—slam into the dike; slam the front end down; slam the back end down; repeat—or sped around outside the tracks the vehicles in front of me were making, in suicidal fashion). Simon was pissed and annoyed, but also sympathetic and understanding. So when I'd had enough badgering and being smacked by Sergeant Morrison's bamboo stick, I jumped up out of the driver's hatch and refused to drive, Simon could relate to that. When Captain Jacob's voice came over the radio as I was standing on top of the engine ranting and raving, Willie was sitting calmly in the turret watching me, smiling (oh, he had a big grin on his face). When Captain Jacob said to Willie, "what the fuck's going on up there? What's the hold up?" Finally, having said my piece, I climbed back down inside my hole and sped off. Simon related to that also.

At any rate, "You ain't too bad, considering yer a white man," Simon had finally confessed to me, and then he'd turned and said, "tell me somethin', Allie, you a college drop out?"

"How'd you guess?"

"How'd I guess? How'd I *guess*? Let's face it, man. Guys like *you*? Case you haven't noticed, it's mostly niggers fightin' this lousy, fucking war. Poor folks, like myself. From the ghettos. Where *race* riots are now taking place. Ain't that somethin'? Tanks an' personnel carriers rollin' down the street where I live. Bet there ain't no tanks and personnel carriers bein' deployed where *you* live. Guardsmen standin' behind their sixties and fifties as they ride by . . . Every day in the *Stars and Stripes* I'm readin' bout this shit. Seein' pictures. Photographs. Kinda makes me wonder what the fuck I'm doin' *here*. Got my *own* war. Anyway, like I was sayin', it's us ghetto folks fightin' this war. Good part of it anyway. And, of course, just to make things interesting, create a little tension—which, as you know, we got plenty of round here—the Army feels compelled to recruit a lot of ignorant white folk from below the Mason Dixon. Can't be fightin' no war without *them*. Can't fight no war without a whole bunch a nigger-hatin' Rebel white boys. Now can we? Anyway, *that's* who's fightin' this sorry ass war. *Not* . . . ."

The two of us were silent, watching each other. Simon peered deeply into my eyes. "So what's *yer* fucking story, my man? How does someone like *you* end up being in a sorry ass place like *this* with someone like *me*?"

"Well, ya see, Simon— . . . ."

For the most part I was a good driver—not the best damn driver in all Vietnam, which Sergeant Morrison fantasized I'd be. Like I've said before, what did that even *mean* being the best driver? Were we going to have a contest? For me there was only one criterion for that elusive title: Not setting off a mine or being blown to bits by a rocket. But all in all, despite those several temper tantrums when I abandoned all pretense of being a good driver and literally ran amok (drove amok), all in all, I sat sweating with my mouth shut in that narrow, steaming, torturous hole next to the noisy, hot engine and did what Sergeant Morrison asked me to do.

One day we came under heavy fire and I just sat and read until the shooting stopped and Sergeant Morrison asked me to start driving again. Sat and *read*? What're you talking about? I'd asked Dad to send me some books to read and he'd gotten a deal to have paperback books he'd selected shipped to me for free. My fellow platoon members were pissed that among the books I allowed them to browse through after they'd arrived in cardboard boxes—there were several shipments—there were no "fuck books." "*How Green Is My Valley? Northwest Passage? Lord Jim? Moby* fucking *Dick? The Good Earth?* What *is* this fucking shit?"

"Look, why don't y'all just go find yourself a nice, stanky ma-ma-san with no teeth t'put it into. I hope yer dicks fall off. I hope you get . . . ."

Like I said before, anythin', bro. Anything a-tall. The prevailing motto. For many. For *most*. Once during scout training at Fort Knox we had a pass and two friends of mine (one who'd gone to Duke, the other the University of North Carolina in Chapel Hill) informed me before we headed off to Louisville that, "uh, you know, I . . . we just wanna warn you that, um . . ." Jesus, man, spit it out. What're you trying to *say*? You're not inclined to discriminate when it comes to . . . Holy fuck, I remember thinking, listening to those two dudes a-hemmin'and a-hawin', what're you trying to tell me, that we're going to old McDonald's farm or something? Which wouldn't have surprised me in the least actually.

But reading? Novels? Not the easiest thing to do while sitting inside the driver's compartment of an armored personnel carrier during a firefight in case you might have thought otherwise. First the noise level. Imagine trying to concentrate with all that machine-gun racket, one of the guns (that would be the fifty caliber) being fired directly above your head. *Come on guys, have some consideration. Can't you see I'm trying to* read *down here?* Then, of course, there was the not so small matter of enemy bullets arching up at us from the tree line, blue tracers coming right at me, some of them clanging against the side of the track. Plus I had a tough time making out the printed words on the pages with the sweat that kept pouring down my face and getting in my eyes. My eyes kept getting blurry, making me see double. Nonetheless I managed. I'd wipe the sweat from my face and eyes with an end of the filthy towel draped around my neck and read a few more sentences. I was about half way through *Northwest Passage* by Kenneth Roberts, as the book's protagonist was describing London and suddenly it became quiet, the shooting had stopped and guess whose voice came over the intercom asking me if I was awake?

"What in God's name you doin' down there, Allie?"

Moving forward. Toward whatever. It was a good thing we didn't know what was in store for us, wasn't it? What lay ahead?

Yeah, mighty good thing. A blessing.

More paddy dikes. More knocking down trees. Up, up, and then Boom! down.

Easy, easy. Always trying to stay in the tracks the vehicle in front of me was making.

Times when I could hardly breathe, when I felt as if I was drowning, suffocating. Wondering, when will this ever end? *Will* this never end?

Daydreaming again. The going home process constantly going through my head. Where was I? Oh yeah, getting on a Freedom Bird. Arriving in Oakland. Sitting in that dining hall having my steak dinner.

But not so fast. A whole shit load of time and—God knows what—left before anything like those recurring "going home" dreams occurred. And weighing heavily those last days out there on the Batangan was the deeply distressing knowledge that the old platoon to which I'd become so attached, was leaving, going home, leaving guys like Murphy and me as the ones the new recruits already pouring in should go to; the ones with the knowledge and know-how.

Hi Ma! When Mom had this photo developed this is what she saw—her oldest son sitting on top of the track after I'd climbed out of the driver's compartment. This photo was taken in one of the valleys we went on missions to from Hill 58.

Howitzers whose thunderous, ear-splitting noise as they were constantly being fired on either side of me almost drove me insane. Boom! Boom! . . . Boom! Boom! Stop please.

The bridge at An Tan where I met Julie and her friends.

Chinook helicopter bringing supplies to troops in the field. This is not the helicopter whose pilot Hank Ross threatened to shoot down if he didn't hurry up and land with his beer.

The burned-out wreckage of a Marine am-track that had struck a mine and been dragged back to Hill 58. It was lying on the perimeter like this when we arrived. Welcome to Hill 58 Echo troop!

What remained of the mine that only half exploded when the Two-three, the track I was riding on top of, set it off.

Checking to make sure mines and booby traps weren't being smuggled to the Viet Cong. Photo taken while we were out on the Batangan.

2nd platoon tracks making their way through thick brush out on the Batangan.

Our platoon leader, Sergeant Willie Morrison and his driver (the driver of the command track)—me!

One of the guard stations at An Tan Bridge where the children from nearby villages would come and sit next to us on the sandbags.

One of the ROK (Republic of Korea) Marines we went out on missions with. They'd ride on our tracks with us (same as U.S. airborne troopers did sometimes) and deploy when we came under fire. The ROK's as we called them were tough and well trained.

Two-three, the track I was assigned to in its position on the perimeter of Hill 58.

Top Left: South Vietnamese paddling a sampan just beyond where the river emptied into the lake near An Tan bridge.

Bottom Left: Photo of me at Blackhorse base camp after we returned from six months up north. Just before I shot off my mouth in front of Captain Jacobs and lost my sergeant stripe. Oh well. Just get me the hell out of here!

The author and his beloved "Sherman" before he was shot and killed for yapping, making too much noise. There were some soldiers who got off on the myriad possibilities of expressing their sadistic tendencies. They came over to Vietnam that way; locked and loaded from the get-go.

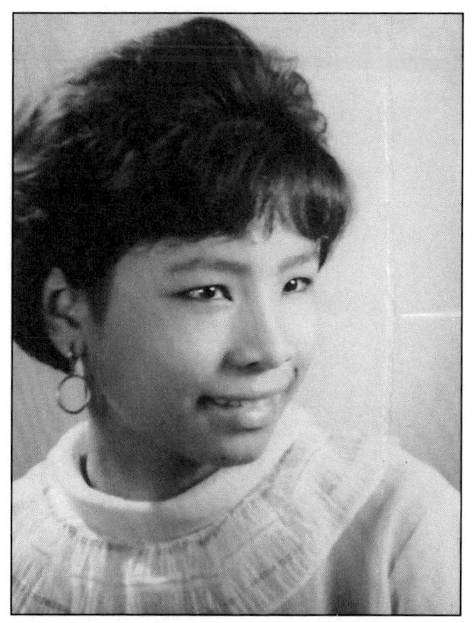

Photo given to me by Julie, one of the South Vietnamese children who came to the An Tan bridge from a nearby village.

Members of the 2nd platoon which I'd just been assigned to firing a fifty-caliber machine gun into the South China Sea as the LST we were on transported us along the coast from Saigon to Chu Lai.

Field mess tent. "Hold the SOS (shit on a shingle—creamed hamburger on toast) please."

Side view of the track, Two-three, in its position on the perimeter of Hill 58.

2nd platoon tracks moving out for a mission during the Tet Offensive. I had less than twenty days to go and wondered why I wasn't back at base camp; why was I still out there in the field?

My daughter Emily climbing out of one of the Chu Chi tunnels.

Back end of Two-three on the night perimeter while out in the field.

South Vietnamese children standing in the tracks our personnel carriers made just prior to their being ferried over to the Batangan peninsula. It was not too far from this sandy inlet that the My Lai massacre occurred.

One of our 2nd platoon tracks moving through a burning village during a search and destroy mission.

Crew member on guard duty in the turret of Two-three, the track I was assigned to my first six weeks in Vietnam. He's looking out over the rice paddies from our position on Hill 58.

8.
Tall Boots to Fill

The old platoon's DEROS (Date of Expected Rotation Overseas), otherwise known as their "wake-up"—that is to say, the day they'd open their eyes and realize their day had come, that their tour was over, and it was time for them to leave, go home, boogey the hell on out of there . . . The end was near, and then it came.

After we left the *Batangan*, we returned to Hill 58, stayed there for about a week and then drove to the beach at *Chu Lai* where we set up next to squadron headquarters. Leaving Hill 58 was very sad. In the same way I'd grown attached to the old platoon that was soon leaving, I'd grown accustomed to Hill 58, even thinking of it (everything was relative over there) as home sweet home when we returned from missions. *Ah, there it is. And here am I, still—well—still driving. Still . . . still, still,* still. As we were pulling out and the villagers from across the way gathered around us and waved; we waved back, I immediately missed the cone-shaped mountain looming off in the distance that always seemed to be watching over us and that I drew great comfort in spotting its green, jungle-covered sides and barren, beige-colored top. Whenever we returned from a mission, the top of the mountain was the first to catch the early morning rays of sun as the dreaded, already fiery orange ball rising behind me as I sat in the turret finishing up guard duty, spread across the paddies to the tree line where villagers from across the way were already setting out for their daily, backbreaking task. Indeed, I was eternally fascinated when at dusk, often as a night-ambush patrol was preparing to go out, I watched the same villagers who had set out twelve hours earlier trudging back, bent over with a log or some such thing. Even though the ROK marines (marines from the Republic of Korea) scared me with their over-the-top "kill anything that moves brutality" when we went on missions together, I wonder what would have happened if the ARVN's had fought with that same no-holds-barred mentality. I missed looking over and seeing the ROK marine camp on top of the hill that seemed to rise up out of the jungle across the way. And I missed our position on the perimeter and how the sun came up behind us and we didn't have to look over and face its glaring head each morning the way the first platoon over on the other side did: walking down and talking to the children, who in their conical straw hats and white pajamas came and stood on the other side of the wire, jabbering away, trying to sell us cokes and whatnot, gladly taking anything we reached over and handed them; tropical chocolate, and ham, and lima bean C-rats being the most popular give-away items. And then the children not leaving until just before dusk and then suddenly we'd see them walking back across the paddies as the sun sank behind the hills and their village, and turned the sky above them into a riot of colors. I missed the mess tent on the other side of the hill from where I was and the walk to it, watching and listening as Captain Jacobs told the mess sergeant one morning that if he didn't get his act together and start serving something a little more palatable he'd find someone else to feed the troops and assign him to a personnel carrier. I missed hearing Jackie Wilson singing the song, *Higher*, on Sergeant Morrison's battery-run record player and Sergeant Morrison and Simon and several other blacks from the platoon dancing and singing along with Mr. Wilson behind the track, "your love makes me feel higher than I've ever felt before," Hank wandering over to the mortar track where even though he was from L.A. ("come on Hank, you from L.A., bro"), the music being played on the radio by his southern drinking buddies during the Grand Old Opry Hour was more to his liking. "Go ahead, you fucking cracker," Simon would yell at him jokingly, as he went sauntering off, "go listen to that hillbilly shit." I missed the sound of artillery rounds whooshing over our heads after they were fired and then exploding off in the distance, or the hissing sound of flares after they'd been shot into the night air and the popping noise they made as they burst into flames lighting up the area. I missed sitting on top of the sandbag bunker near to us and reading letters, and writing letters myself. Oh Mom, I know how you suffered, how you thought of me constantly, each and every second, wondering if I was okay; wondering what I was doing that very moment.

"I just wanna know if I'm gonna make it," I remember Harvey saying to me six, seven weeks before he left, "and if I do, well what kinda shape will I be in. I mean, it's the not knowing that gets ya. Am I gonna wait till the end an' then have my dick shot off? Am I gonna spend the rest a my life goin' around blind, not being able t'see anything? Am I gonna end up paralyzed like Simmons? Or. . . ."

Sorry Harvey, I remember thinking, that's not how it works. Course, he knew that, we all did. But their day came. Quite a few actually had been given the nod. had won the lottery, beaten the odds, and with thirty days to go before their wake-up (the point at which commanders were required to remove combat soldiers from the field), they were sent back to basecamp to get ready for shipment home.

So, all of a sudden, new T.C.s, new drivers, new mortar crews, new gunners, new mess sergeant, new supply sergeant . . . new *every*-fucking-body.

And so long, sarg, so long *Simon*, so long *Hank*, so long *Harvey*. . . . Did I really know those guys? Sometimes I wonder. Those soldiers from that other life: Hank. *Sergeant Morrison*. Simon. *Finlay*. I only have a photo of Sergeant Morrison. How could that be? None of Simon or Hank? Or of Finlay? But, oh, I remember them and can see each of their faces clear as day. Can see Hank walking over and telling Cassidy to leave a villager alone. Cassidy glaring at Hank, like, who *is* this guy? And not exactly sure what to do. Hank shaking his head and saying, "now I ain't'a *hardly* bullshittin'," over all the bullshit constantly taking place. I can feel the tap from Sergeant Morrison's bamboo stick on my shoulder, and see his black, grinning face; and hear him saying "get back down in your hole, soldier."

And then, Simon, fucking Simon. I wonder whatever happened to him. Went back to living in downtown Newark I suppose. Listening to all that anti-war crap. But he was a cool customer. Smart. "You've got to find a way to go back to school, Simon," I told him. "*Why*? Because you are one smart motherfucker, that's why." Withstood all that racial shit that was constantly being thrown at him. Laughed it off. He was better than that. *Hey, a* black *president, Simon. How bout* that, *my man*?

God, I felt lonely. And I had some mighty tall boots to fill, didn't I? How was I *ever* going to get through the next—oh man—I still had two hundred and seventy days (a motherfucking *life time*) to go before my wake-up.

* * *

Boom! I was lying on the ground and someone was kicking me, yelling, "get up you sorry motherfucker. Get up."

Murph, it was Murph, I could tell from the voice. Jesus Christ! I thought, looking around in the dark, "what'd I *do?* One moment I was lying on my cot, dreaming and the next—

I got up tentatively, holding my hands out in front of myself for protection in case Murph, who'd rolled me off the cot, started kneeing me, pummeling me with his fists.

"Here's the deal, Allie," he said—I could see his eyes glowering in the dark—"while you were getting your beauty rest here, guess who's been out fixing one of those treads *that came flying off* asshole while we were being shot at. Hear all that racket out there? Surprised you could sleep through it. Well, not really surprised knowing you. What if we'd been overrun?" He looked me in the eye. I could hear shooting close by. Rockets, AKs, fifties, sixties . . . "Here's the deal," he said, "it's," he checked the glowing numbers on his watch, "it's not even midnight yet and," he glanced over at the mortar track whose right tread had been thrown off and Murph and the rest of the crew had spent the better part of two hours repairing while under intense fire, "an' guess who's gonna be drivin' that motherfucker up an' down that road for the rest of the evening?"

Well, let me think. *Me?*

Now, you may have noticed that the vehicle Murph swore he was going to have me driving throughout eternity was a *mortar track*. "What's that?" you ask and how did I end up being the driver of one of those? A mortar track was a standard armored personnel carrier except that it hauled around a mortar firing tube and all of its accompanying equipment, and whose assigned crew was responsible for carrying out nightly firing operations. Each platoon had one mortar track assigned to it, and the way it worked was this: While the "regular tracks" were lined up around the perimeter and their crews guarded an area, the mortar track was kept in the middle so that its crew could fire away at designated targets throughout the night. The way I ended up being the driver of a mortar track was: I accepted Murph's offer to be one.

Here's how it happened. Murph started by being groomed to be the T.C. of the second platoon mortar track a month or so before the old platoon left. Murph was one of those guys who even though he never finished high school you could tell he was smart as hell. He picked up the working mechanics of firing mortars just like that. No sweat. I used to go over and watch him and he'd explain to me what he was doing. Certainly not something I was readily able to master. Or master at all. Anyway, he asked me to be his driver for which I got a huge ribbing after I accepted. Let me rephrase that. Guys I'd been fighting with—the seasoned old timers like me then (there were about ten of us)—were somewhat resentful of me, even felt betrayed when immediately after the old platoon left, I too left the "fighting" members of the platoon to become a crew member on the mortar track, which in their eyes was traitorous, cowardly. Instead of going out on foot patrols and missions on our tracks each day I'd lay-up—that's how they saw it, as a lay-up—in the middle of some perimeter protected by them. I was, in their critical eyes, a self-preservation (got that right) opportunist in other words, the odds of being killed or seriously wounded in my new assignment having been significantly reduced. They indignantly called it "abandonment"; I saw it as leaving one not very safe job for another that was not, by any stretch, safe, but safer.

Fuck y'all, I'd thought, you do what you feel you gotta do and I'll . . . .

Look. Sure, I felt good about the prospects of not having to worry as much about setting off a mine or having a rocket explode in the hatch next to me, but as it turned out, due to the high number of disabled and destroyed tracks in each of the three platoons, the new company commander ordered that, until new vehicles came in, Echo troop's three mortar tracks were to function as regular tracks.

Great, huh? My best laid plans. FUCK!

Anyway, that's how I found myself driving along a dusty dirt road in the dark with Murphy sitting up in the turret firing the fifty as close above my head as he could without splattering it like a water melon. Ping, ping . . . ping, ping, ping, I could hear the AK-47 bullets striking both sides of the track and see the close-by muzzle flashes. We were back on the Batangan. We'd been charged with keeping "Thunder Road" (as the mission was called) open and free from mines for twenty-four hours so that, during the day, supplies could continue to be delivered to the Americal Division troops on the Batangan.

Needless to say, this wasn't what I'd expected. I'd actually accepted Murphy's offer to drive the mortar track prior to hearing that we'd be soon returning to the dreaded Batangan. Nonetheless, when I found out we were going back there, I'd envisioned staying put somewhere, watching Murph and his fellow crew members dropping mortar rounds into the steel cylinder tube we carried around with us and then listening to them explode off in the distance; not gallivanting around as per usual doing the same thing I did while driving for Willie Morrison.

* * *

Over the years I've had considerable hearing loss and am certain that it is to a large extent attributable to the loud noises I was subjected to in Vietnam. I would end up being exposed to the constant roar of artillery guns being fired at close proximity, which certainly contributed to my deafness; but, oh boy, the loud, deafening noise I experienced while driving that miserable evening out on the Batangan Peninsula was the biggest culprit of all. It was torture. Murph was torturing me that night. Sure, I'd messed up unnecessarily and had put him and the mortar track's crew in harm's way. I deserved to be punished. I knew better. Sergeant Morrison had drummed it into me that no matter what else I did, keeping up tension in the treads was the number one priority maintenance-wise. "Don't wanna end up in shit's creek without a paddle, now, do we, Allie?" Oh, the look on Willie's face when, in my mind, I told him what I'd done. Or *hadn't* done. First, I'd left my job of driving the Two-six he'd so passionately and methodically trained me to do—"you're going to do *what?* Drive the mortar track?—and then confessing to him about my failing to do the basic, routine maintenance he'd taught me to do.

"Willie, I'm sorry. I fucked up."

In the morning as the sun rose above the trees—six or so hours after Murph had rolled me off my cot—I saw the damage from what had taken place around me during the night. Up on the left side of the road a ways the third platoon's Three-nine was lying on its side and still smoldering. I'd seen it explode and go up in flames. While the drivers of several other tracks and I formed a circle around the disabled track, a medevac helicopter flew in and picked up the dead and wounded. All new recruits. I didn't even know the gunner who was killed. A bright light shone through the night as the helicopter came down so the medics and troopers helping load stretchers into the side of the chopper could see what they were doing. The increased intensity of machine-gun fire and grenades and claymores slamming into the jungle on both sides of the road allowed the pilot to raise the chopper and fly it away unscathed. Through the fog of cordite and mist I could see that the jungle in many places had been cut down into fields, and scattered around several of them were the arms and legs and hands of gooks that had poured out of the jungle and tried to climb onto our tracks. Their shattered, in some cases headless, corpses were already beginning to rot, and mixed with their fetid smell was the reek of burning oil and rotten growth and the lingering stench of napalm the Phantoms had swooped down and dropped, lighting up the night in fiery orange balls.

Back in the clearing where the second platoon was gathering—not too far from where I'd been torn from my sleep and dumped onto the ground—Murph and I climbed out of the holes we'd been confined to for the previous six hours—him from the turret, me from inside the driver's compartment—and looked at each other. "Sorry," Murph said, shaking his head and smiling, "but you *really* pissed me the fuck off last night."

"Really," I said, "I hadn't noticed."

9.
The Kids at An Tan Bridge

Our next assignment after the Batangan Peninsula was to guard a bridge that spanned a river just outside the small village of An Tan, located midway between Chu Lai and Tam Ky. The ARVN, who had a camp nearby, hadn't been successful in keeping the North Vietnamese and Viet Cong from blowing the bridge up several times, screwing up what was a vital supply route for the Americans, so Echo troop had been assigned to prevent this from happening again while also running patrols in the area. The way it worked was . . . like over there on Hill 58: One platoon would stay back and guard the base area while the other two went out on missions.

Besides having at least one crew member sitting in the turret of our tracks, which were positioned in various locations along the banks on both sides of the river, the bridge connecting the dirt road at a spot just before the river opened up into a huge lake, we took turns manning four guard stations: 1) a sandbag fortified bunker at the top of a forty-foot tower the Marines had built, where we climbed up the wooden structure by ladder, pushing our way up through a trap door that closed back down into part of the bunker floor and were able to see for miles; 2) the two sandbag bunkers at either end of the bridge where we watched to see if there was anything suspicious among the South Vietnamese constantly moving back and forth across the bridge, randomly checking what was in the carts being pulled across by water buffalo; 3) the baskets dangling from both ends of the yoke that the women balanced across their shoulders as they shuffled along, hunched over, the front and side baskets on mopeds and bicycles; and then finally 4) the wooden raft also built by the Marines that we'd sit in like a makeshift chair we'd constructed and watch for anything unusual among the sampans coming into the river from the wider waters after pushing off the bank and drifting to a spot underneath the bridge's steel girders where, if we didn't also keep a careful eye, we were likely to have a turd land on us.

A *turd*, yes. A human turd. As in being shat upon.

One of the kids from the village up the road, Julie, or Sandi, or Tommy, or Jamie, or Liz, or Janet (they'd all taken on American names in order to further endear themselves to us—their prayer was to have us feel sorry for them, which we did, at least most of us (how could we not?—and adopt them, take them home, remove them from the miserable life they'd been born into—that was their plan, their fantasy). One of those kids would suspend himself nakedly from the bridge's girders right above where one of us unsuspecting Americans was sitting on the raft scoping things out, trying to discern if that shriveled up old man waving to us as he stood paddling his sampan slowly under the bridge from the lake was just another papa-san bringing back some fish he'd caught or had a bomb or weapons he was smuggling in. While we were squinting into the blinding sunlight being reflected off the water and trying to make sense of the wavering figures floating by us on various types of dinghies, one of the kids would hang out over the edge and do his business.

Bingo! Nice shot there, Jamie. Bull's eye.

"Aw jeez. Fuck! Aw man. *Shit*!"

Exactly.

"Your friend's waving to you, Allie. Swanekamp (Swaney)

and I were up in the tower. I walked over to the side facing the road and looked down. Julie was standing by the bridge waving to me. I waved back. A line was forming behind the Two-eight, inside which the poor, pathetic, camp following girl/young woman who had been brought into the perimeter that afternoon had already begun taking on customers. Let's see, Dansbury, Chapman, Hall . . . Bugman, Crawford . . . *Staley*? You too?

"Look Swaney," said I, watching him hungrily eyeing what was going on, "Go ahead. I'll cover."

"You sure?"

"Yeah. Go ahead."

"Oh wow. Thanks. I owe ya."

I watched Swaney hurry across the perimeter, get in line behind Hitchcock and Watkins and then turn, look up, and give me the finger. I returned the gesture.

At the front of the line—twenty or so customers down—Dansbury was next. His time had come. He'd be *doin' it* momentarily. There was a young boy standing next to the track's open back door. Dansbury reached into his pants pocket, pulled out a bill of some sort and handed it to the boy, who slipped it into the purse he was holding along with the rest of his cash. Greer climbed out from the back of the track and Dansbury climbed in. Greer, who was always bragging about how he liked to live dangerously and "go in bare back" (not wearing a rubber) on account of—*it jus' don't feel right when I wears a rubber, know what I'm sayin'?* —staggered around for a moment, breathing heavily, still panting, and then thumping his sweaty bare chest as he hiked up his pants, cried out, "Whooie! That felt gh . . . ud. Reckon I'll jus' mosey my ass t'the back a the line an' get me some more a *that* action." Which, of course, he did.

Swaney finally made it to the front of the line, took his turn, climbed back up the tower, lit a cigarette, and then slumped down on one of the built-in benches. "Instead a bein' such a mamby pamby stuck-up sonavabitch, Allie," he looked over at me and said, "ya oughta come down offa that high horse yer on an' join us. Smooth's a fellar outright nice doncha know."

"Yeah, nothin' seems t'boost troop morale more'n a good ol' fashioned gang bang. Gang rape I should say."

"Fuck you, Allie. Jus' cause you . . . ."

"All you sweaty, grimy motherfuckers . . . How many, Swaney? How many'd she do it with before you? Thirty? Forty? Nice, man. Real nice. Makes me proud t'be an American."

Julie and Sandi, the two young girls who were often at the bridge, lived in a village just up the road—had wandered five, six miles away from the bridge and were sitting next to me under the flap I'd pulled down in front of the track, and Hampton had wandered over and told them to scram. "Shoo, Didi," he shouted, ducking his head so he could see us better and waving his arms. "I don't want no V.C. spies hangin' out next t'me." He gave me a glaring look. "What's the matter with you, Allie? What is it with you an' these dinks? You won't fuck em, yet . . . " That was the time we'd left the bridge, driven through An Tan, left the dirt road after about two miles, driven across a rice paddy filled with hedge groves, busted through jungle into a valley, skirted along the edge of the valley and up along the side of a ridge, driven across several small hills, and then busted through some more jungle into a clearing where, as I was pulling into our assigned position, I glanced over and saw Julie and Sandi standing off to the left next to the trees. Like, where y'all been?

Not too long after that unlikely encounter—how'd they get

there? How'd they know where we were going?—Julie brought a puppy from the litter her family's dog had given birth to—to the bridge. We adopted him. Called him Sherman. Julie let us keep Sherman overnight. We fed him, played with him, petted him under his big, floppy ears; let him lick us with his wet, generous tongue. Watched him stumble around clumsily on his oversized paws. Nice diversion. Until one afternoon Hampton, complaining that Sherman was yelping too much, and making too much noise, shot him in the head. "There," he said, as he sat next to Clayton on top of a bunker, "nuffa *that* shit," and Clayton, watching him, reached over and gave him a high five. "I concur, bro."

* * *

Sitting over one of the holes in the open-air latrine, as Tommy, Liz, and Jamie stood nearby watching—*top a the morning to ya, kids. Enjoying that sunrise over yonder?*—I read in the *Stars and Stripes* how a convoy from the First Squadron had been ambushed and then overrun just outside the 11th Cav base camp. *Overrun?* I remember thinking, imagining the fighting that must have taken place less than a mile from the front gate; Americans being mowed down as they jumped down from burning tracks to keep from being incinerated. *Overrun?* Eleven Blackhorse Troopers killed and more than twice that wounded. "Jesus fucking Christ," I'd shouted, "we're nothing but sitting ducks." And I'd thought of the Viet Cong and North Vietnamese hiding in the jungle just up the road listening to whatever hapless platoon was coming, waiting with their rocket launchers, mortars, claymores, grenades, and AKs for just the right moment to strike. *Now. Now. Now. Now. Now.*

After I commiserated with Swaney and Crawford and several other fellow second-platoon members as we sat on the wooden platform next to each other, I disgustedly threw the paper down in the dirt and said, "that's it. I don't want to do this shit anymore. I've had enough."

"Thrust'n'parry," said Swaney, standing up and pretending he was fixing a bayonet to the end of his rifle, "I'm ready;" then after shoving the bayonet forward and tugging it back like it was stuck and giving him a hard way to go, sat back down, finished wiping himself, then stood back up again.

"G.I. kill beaucoup V.C.," Tommy cried out, laughing as he watched Swaney pull up his pants and button his fly.

"Hand to hand," I said shaking my head. "Man," I stood up next to Swaney, looked over at the kids watching me hike up my pants, "I sure as hell hope we never get involved in anything like *that*."

Letter time. A whole stack. Let's see—ah! One from Jeff here. He get orders for his R&R to Australia yet? Letter from him coming from in-country, less than a hundred miles away. Cam Ranh Bay to—well—right there, where I was. Wherever the 2nd Platoon, Echo Troop, Second Squadron, 11th Armored Cavalry Regiment was. At that moment, the bridge at An Tan. The other letters I was holding—*how come you get so many letters, Allie?*—from back in the world; from Mom, dear sweet Mom, in Princeton; from Russ, from L.D., from . . . Willie?

Letter from Mom saying she'd seen the Eleventh Armored Cavalry Regiment mentioned in a *New York Times* article; how a convoy from the 1st Squadron had been ambushed right outside basecamp.

That's not where you are, right honey? You're still . . . .

"Up north, Mom," I mentally reassured her from the back of the track, "still at the bridge." Glancing over at the market across the river I thought of Mom anxiously waiting for my letters; her heart pounding each time she heard the mail truck; as she walked to the end of the driveway . . . none today. But even if there was a letter from me—Oh my goodness, those blue envelopes that had my fingerprints from that clayey red dust on them—what she was about to read had been written over a week before, the question was always as she began reading my words, what was I doing *right then*, at that very moment? Oh Mom, oh Mom, such suffering, the horrible anguish you live with each and every moment of every day. Unrelenting. Not knowing. Never, never knowing.

"What's so funny?" Swaney and I were up in the tower again and I was reading a letter from my childhood friend, Jeff Keller.

"This buddy of mine. Guy I grew up with in Rochester. He's in Nam too. In Cam Ranh Bay. We were trying to coordinate our R&Rs so we could go down under together. But it didn't work out. Anyway, for the most part, we don't say anything. Just make lists. Of names. Names and places. Someone or something that says it all. He writes down the name—which he did, right here, that's why I'm laughing . . . . Maudy Rathbun. Lord have mercy. Maudy's this old hag of a teacher we had in the eighth grade. Well, one of them. My parents had her as a teacher. And my grandparents too, probably. And here we go, oh my goodness, how does he come up with this shit? What's that show? This Is Your Life? Jim Peterson. Guy who came around and pinned our Sunday school attendance medals on us. Jeff was like a general he had so many dangling down from that sports jacket he wore."

"*Sunday* school?"

"Fuck you."

Russ wrote that he'd been discharged from the Army hospital at Fort Knox finally and was living in an apartment in New York City. But he was pissed. *I'm a gimp*, he wrote, *the Army doctors fucked me up. Royally. My left leg's shorter now.*

When I got home I visited Russ. We met—at his suggestion—in the lobby of the Pan Am Building. "See," he said, pointing to his leg after we'd greeted each other, "Look. Those fucks. I'm a gimp. I should sue those incompetent bastards. Good to have you back, Rick. Thanks for your letters. I've been using them. Drawing . . . from your material. In night class. I play the wounded vet. 'Yeah,' I say, 'we were out there on the Batangan Peninsula and,' I pause, looking down and shaking my head, 'suffice to say things got a little hairy out there.' Then I tell them how I woke up after a knock-down, drag-out fire fight one time and . . . see," he flashed his blue eyes at me. Handsome devil, Russ. I always took second billing to him when we went to Louisville or Lexington together. "Okay, go ahead," I imagined chicks saying reluctantly, "you can have the handsome one, I'll take that other guy." "See," Russ said, "I remember just about everything you wrote to me. You woke up from that fire fight and . . . I tell the class how I felt something touching me and looked up startled . . . ."

"It was pretty amazing. All these kids standing there, looking at me, some of them, kneeling next to me, pulling my ears. . . ."

"And you wondered how they got there, right? Where they'd come from. Well, that's what I tell the class. And they just look at me, like . . . they're trying to visualize this, same as me, same as I did."

August
Fort Knox, Kentucky

Allie,

Those kids at the bridge still shitting on you? I'm trying to picture it. Also, I'm picturing them showing up where you are in the field. You looking over and thinking, how'd they get here? Remember Schulte? He was killed yesterday. On Highway 31. Where else, right? Nothing's changed around here. Carol and I still live in that dumpy trailer. But I'm not complaining. No, no, not to you, anyway. Considerin' where you is and all. Take care, Allie. And keep writing.

-L.D.

P.S. Skaggs is going back over. Some guys are really into that shit I guess. From what you describe though it doesn't sound all that appealing to me. He, he.

August
An Tan

L.D.,

Yes, the kids are still taking target practice with their dumps. I have not been a victim however. Fortunately I'm not a prime target. Like some. These kids have a keen eye when it comes to who among us is most deserving. I'm going to Tokyo for a week. It was my second choice but I'm taking it anyway. Need a break. Word has come down that we're leaving the bridge soon and heading further north. Wish I could just pop over and have a beer with you and Carol. Watch this shit on your little TV rather than actually being in it. Down to . . . I'm not even going to say how many days I still have left until my wake-up. Too depressing. Take care. I'll keep my eyes out for Skaggs.

-Allie.

I wonder whatever happened to Julie and the kids who came to the An Tan Bridge. I, of course, thought of them when Saigon was falling. Did I ever! They would have been in their early twenties by then. I have a photo of Julie that she presented to me when we first arrived at the bridge. Yes, she'd spotted me right off, as a bleeding heart sucker, I suppose, and therefore a potential beneficiary. And it worked. I gave her food, even went into town with her and bought her a dress; a green "ao dai" that she picked out. Was I not only one of a long line of soldiers stationed at the bridge who she targeted, thinking, ah yes, definitely, he's the one? So be it. I knew what I was doing as I was doing it. The human interaction felt good. I needed it. A little warmth and tenderness in a world turned upside down. Protective, paternalistic feelings coming to the fore.

Though my wife was leery at first, we named our second daughter Julie. I convinced her that what Julie reminded me of was not the unimaginable horrors of that long ago, faraway place, but the still innocent, beating heart of a little girl I'd met there.

10.
Time Out

He was just sitting there in the sand, staring, a blank look on his face, eyes vacant, like, whatever it was inside his head that had made him who he was, had left, floated out into the hot, muggy air like an intrepid butterfly. Bound at his wrists and ankles, he sat slouched over with his legs stretched out in front of him. Two soldiers from headquarters were standing next to him, guarding him.

"Wow," said Hilton, trying to fully comprehend what he was seeing as we walked by. "*Gone*, man. Jesus."

"I know," I said, "frightening."

Hilton and I had just arrived at headquarters by convoy and were waiting to be driven over to the Chu Lai Airbase for the first leg of our trip to Tokyo and seven days of R&R. And there, sitting in the sand in front of one of the tents, broiling—no effort whatsoever to move him out of the blazing sun that was beating unmercifully down upon him—Jeremy Cooper.

Years later, seeing the same catatonic stare of a Vietnam veteran who was assigned to me in the mental hospital where I worked—I was his social worker—brought back the incident that had sent a fellow platoon member over the edge, and within a twenty-four-hour period, to go from being a playful, cocky, wisecracking nineteen-year-old soldier who enjoyed horsing around, bragging about how he was the driver of the fastest personnel carrier in the platoon, to being forevermore (as long as he remained on this earth, you could tell) merely existing in the catatonic state Hilton and I had seen in him on the beach.

"You killed him," I remember saying as I reached over and grabbed Jeremy's rifle from him. "You killed him. He's *dead.*"

"Naw," he'd looked down at Lyle, his grab-assing buddy since basic training, who I had just seen him shoot—in the back—moments before as Murph and I were walking back from chow, who was lying on the ground, bleeding, with an enormous hole where the bullet had blown apart his chest, and said, looking down and shaking his head: "Naw, he ain't dead. I 'as jus'. . . I 'as jus' teachin'm a lesson is all. Don't be pointin' no gun at me. Come on, get up Lyle. You ain't dead. Get yo ass up off the ground."

* * *

"Hi Lick. You valy handsome Lick. You buy Li Saigon tea? Li valy thirsty Lick."

Those sweetly uttered words coming to me softly, in a whisper almost, from the lips of a beautiful Vietnamese bar girl moments—*moments*—after Hilton and I sat down at a booth in a Saigon bar. Gazing longingly into my eyes—oh those big, dark eyes set in that pretty face—she stroked the back of my neck with one hand while dropping down—after rubbing my chest and stomach (for about ten seconds) with the other and . . . .

Wait a second you say. I thought . . . I thought you were going on R&R? To Tokyo.

Well, I *was*. And did. But first this most welcome interlude. My pre-R&R let's call it.

Before we even arrived at Tan San Knut Airbase in Saigon—

indeed, way back when Hilton and I first learned we were both going to Tokyo at the same time—he'd talked me out of following the usual protocol for soldiers going on R&R, which was to go to base camp, spend a few days there getting ready—having khakis cleaned and pressed so we'd look sharp representing our country, taking out money from the safe, etcetera, etcetera. "Look, man, we'll buy uniforms on To Do, have em pressed'n'ready t'go, so we'll be all set when it's time t'head over to Long Bien t'catch are plane. An' ya have yer cash, so fuck base camp'n'all that. Let's spend a few days in Saigon. See how the housecats live."

Hey, why not?

When I said that the evening I spent with Li was a welcome interlude—and it *was*, oh yes, indeed, it was (since I'd bought her about a hundred Saigon teas (shot glasses of Coca Cola) at whatever the exorbitant rate was, I was eligible to spend the evening with her, I also implied that it was only a warm-up for the *real* R&R coming up. But no. Trust me when I tell you that that wasn't so, that the seven days I spent in the coastal town of Atomi near Mt. Fuji were unremarkable—*got nothin' to report, Jack*—in that regard.

Okay. So what did I *do* during my R&R then, if I didn't spend every moment . . . ?

I bathed. Took long, hot baths in my hotel room. Tried to scrub myself clean. Which was impossible. I lay in that porcelain tub (my how civilized) with the back of my head resting against the wall; those green and pink tiles (yes, I remember), luxuriating in scalding hot, aromatically pleasing, sudsy water. Well, now that you mention it, the filth, that clayey, red filth, however much of it I was able to remove from my arms and legs and face and chest, clinging to the sides and then finally the bottom of the tub as the level of the water sank lower and lower after I'd leaned forward and pulled the drain plug, leaving me still sitting there exposed, like a ship wreck, then how I'd watched as the remaining, reddish, brown water swirled around between my shriveled up feet before being sucked down the drain. I'd sit like that for a long time, gazing at my hardened pecker (my one-eyed snake as we called them), sticking straight up, staring back at me and think of Li, how I wished she could be called in from the next room. *Come join me, sweet heart as I wash away—for the time being anyway—my troubles. I still have . . . oh my goodness, let's not think about* that *yet*; and then I'd stand up and take a shower, rinsing myself off first, then the sides and bottom of the tub, aiming the shower nozzle at them as I did my best to wipe away any remaining dirt with the bottoms of my feet; then putting the plug back in and reaching over and grabbing the bubble bath, compliments of the hotel, I'd draw more hot water and start the process over again.

But leave it to me—planning-wise (though it's not like I was able to seek help from a travel agent)—to go to Japan at the height of the typhoon season. On the second day of my R&R my buddies and I took the Kachi Kachi Ropeway to the observation deck at the top of Mount Tenjo. We were not able to see through the rain and fog over to nearby Mount Fuji, nor the—from what I've seen in pictures—spectacular views of Lake Kawaguchiko, one of the five lakes at the base of Fuji.

We went on a bus tour (my, how cornball and unsoldierly, eh?), visited the great Buddha, drove around Tokyo (where I thought, Wow! Twenty-two years ago we were at war with these people; this city was destroyed by our bombs), and then at a PX in Yokohama I bought gifts for Mom, Dad, Lee, and Sue, but due to a superstitious feeling that it would bring me bad luck (I was plagued by all sorts of superstitions in those days), I could not bring myself to purchase and have sent home—even at half price—stereo equipment, T.V.s, and cameras like most of the other G.I.s on the bus with me. All I could think of as I ran my eyes over all the great bargain items on shelves in front of me was Mom and Dad storing them in my room and then having to face them if I didn't come back; how having them there, waiting for me would have made it much worse for them, sadder.

"Mom?"

"Rick?"

"It's me, Mom. I'm . . . Hi Sue. Oh no, did I wake you up?"

"That's okay. Oh my God, I can't believe it's you; that I'm hearing your voice."

3:00 in the morning. Sue woke up startled in her room when she heard the phone ringing.

And on the other end of the line, in a hotel room in Atami, Japan, ten thousand miles away, I could hear Mom excitedly telling Sue, "It's Rick, it's Rick, it's Rick."

11.
Stepping Up

Sept 4, 1967

Dear Mom, Dad and Sue,

It was great talking to you on the phone from Japan last week. Sorry you were out of town, Dad. Again, Mom, Sue, I apologize for miscalculating and waking you and scaring the hell out of you—which no doubt I did—in the middle of the night. Anyway, so great hearing your voices. And now—well—I'm back here again. Like I never left. That's the problem with going on R&R too early. Not waiting until the very end so you can come back and be almost done. We're up near a place called Tam Ky—twenty-five miles north of the An Tan bridge—and the monsoons have started. Can't win around here. It's either dry, dusty and sweltering hot, or raining. Nonstop, relentless raining. Oh, by the way, I'm a track commander now. Yeah, me! Lt. Hansen approached me the day after I got back from R&R and asked me if I would be one of his T.C.s. "Are you kidding me?" I said to myself, looking into his eyes, "no. Absolutely not. No way." But what came out of my mouth was, "sure." I don't think I said, "of course."

So now, here I am in charge of the Two-seven. A sergeant. Well, I will be soon. I've been put in for promotion.

Well, have to run. Have a meeting with the CO. I'm leading the night ambush. One of them anyway. All my love,
-Rick

P.S. I've enclosed some film for development. Some R&R shots, then a few of this soggy place. The make-shift shelters we build (hutches we call them) to keep dry. But mostly my crew. Charlie, my driver, the kid with the big grin and my two gunners.

Sept 10, 1967

Hi Willie,

A few words from where the sun isn't shining anymore. Okay, you can wipe that smile off your face remembering how much I complained about the heat and sun. 'Bout not bein' able to breathe down there in the driver's compartment as you're beatin' the hell out of me with your stick. Ouch. That hurts, Willie. Nope. Jus ain't no pleasin' that driver of mine, you're shaking your head and saying. And thinking, my, my, he's still over there. That I am, Willie, that I am. Dealing with these monsoons. As a T.C. doncha know. With my own driver. Boy did I luck out. Grease monkey by trade. Kid from Des Moines, Iowa. Loves this shit, Willie. Needs no guidance in the maintenance department whatsoever. Just like me, eh? Oh go fuck yourself. Was tightening the treads with the grease gun when I met him. Looked up at me smiling, the expression on his greasy face saying—at least this is how I, his commander, interpreted it. Thanks for giving me the opportunity to serve my country in this way. Man, you got it, dude. And now, here, already, Willie, he's the best damn driver in all Vietnam. Came to me that way. Signed, sealed and delivered. "How often do I have to change the oil, Sarg?" he asked me. "Here man," I handed him the manual just like you handed Two-six's to me. Only I didn't tell him it was his Bible, Willie. Come on. Seriously? Charlie immediately began devouring it. Like it was a fuck book. Each to their own, right Sarg? Somehow I didn't find it all that interesting.

Wow, Willie. You named your son after me? Alexander Morrison? I'm deeply honored, but a little surprised considering the hard time I gave you. Not to mention trying to get out of driving after you left.

I miss you, man. Boy do I wish you were here to give me guidance. What do you think Hank's doing? No way anyone would ever hear from him, right. I mean if he contacted anyone it would be you. Yet somehow

I just don't see that happening. It's not his way. Every time I look out at this muck we're now having to operate in, you can hear the engines screaming can't you Willie as you're sitting at the breakfast table; or are you in the den with a Highlife, watching the Indians, who suck by the way. Yup, I still keep up with the box scores . . . every time I contemplate the mud we've got to go out and try not getting stuck in again, I imagine Hank standing next to me shaking his head and saying, "now I ain't a hardly *bullshittin'. . . .*

My best, Willie. All kidding aside, guys like you—soldiers like you—are the reason guys like me are able to get through this shit. Take care and keep writing.
-Rick

* * *

There it was. Tyler handed it to me in the pouring rain. I slogged back to the track through the muck, sheltering the envelope under my soaking wet fatigue shirt—the rain was coming down in sheets—then, after drying my face and hands and hair with a towel so I wouldn't drip on the sacred document I was holding, causing the ink to run, I plopped down on the seat next to the radio and now with the loud and familiar sound of rain pelting the tarp and stretched out ponchos above me and splashing into the puddles outside, I read the letter Dad had written to me. I could hear Dad's voice imagining him sitting at his desk, carefully choosing his words:

Sept 16, 1967

Dear Rick,

Your mother and Sue and I read your most recent letter and can certainly understand how discouraging it must be to enjoy a week or so on

R&R. I'm envious of the places you got to see—or not quite see due to the weather—and then have to not only return to the field, but do so during the rainy season. Which I must say sounds pretty miserable. Lee and I are sorry we missed your call from your hotel room in Atami, but your mother and sister were ecstatic to hear your voice and be able to talk to you.

Meanwhile, Rick, I want to congratulate you on your promotion to sergeant and newly found responsibility of being a track commander. Sergeants are the backbone of the Army (especially those in command positions) and your platoon leader would not have asked you to take on such a critical role if you hadn't demonstrated to him that you could do it. There's too much on the line to just appoint anyone. Anyway we're very proud of you, Rick, and you should be very proud of yourself as well. Good luck and I'm sure that your crew, who we've seen in the pictures Mom had developed, is glad to have you as their leader. Take care, Rick. Love, Dad.

* * *

Sept 17, 1967

Dear Lee,

I just got the most incredible letter from Dad, congratulating me on making sergeant. It scares me a little, Lee, because I'm pretty certain that the reason I told Lt. Hansen I'd be one of his track commanders when he asked was because I knew how much it would please dad. And it did. *Oh boy. Soon as I saw Dad's writing on one of the envelopes handed me during mail call—how come you get so many letters, anyway?—I knew what was inside.*

Where does this letter find you, Lee? In your dorm room? I can picture you sitting on the edge of your bed reading this. Thinking, yup,

Dad's proud of Rick alright. Noooooo question. Sergeant over there. T.C. Playing a leadership role now in that horrible mess. The war which you so adamantly oppose. That's okay. For me it's all about survival. Living from day to day, minute to minute. Yup, still here. Okay, let's see what the afternoon brings. Sorry bout so and so, but glad it wasn't me. Listen to me. Still have—wow!—let's not talk about how much time I still have left.

Rain's getting to me, Lee. Never stops.

By the way, I took out (led) my first ambush patrol. Ever mindful, little brother, of a trick the V.C. use. Which is: okay, I've described to you what a claymore mine is right? About the size of the top of a shoebox it's curved slightly outward and has 700 small steel balls packed inside C-4 explosive material. Quite a nasty thing to be on the receiving end of I would imagine. So we set them up outside our circle and supposedly—though I've never heard of it actually happening—the V.C. sneak up, turn them around and then purposefully make noise so we'll set them off. Ingenious, right? If they could pull it off. Just like that, eight Americans disintegrated. Which is what it would be. With you know who is at the helm.

Well, obviously nothing like that happened; however, as I was packing up the claymore I'd set ten hours before (ten long hours sitting out there in the rain, Lee, in the mud), I noticed that the wire was cut. Cut? Seriously? Yup. No question. Staley. Come check this out. Yes, cut. For sure. Out here—wherever this is. Cut. Some gook had crawled into our area as we were sitting there in the dark and cut the damn thing. What other explanation? And why? Just to show that he could?
Enough for now. We're moving out.
-Rick

* * *

Sept 29, 1967

Dear Rick,

It's always a great feeling for me to see that the letter you've written somewhere in the monsoons ten thousand miles away has found its way into my mail slot. No more dirt smudges with your finger prints in them for a while though I guess. Instead envelopes all wrinkly from being wet. Wow! Images constantly flying through my head. That night ambush you described. I sit in class and I'm mentally watching you. Sitting out there in the dark. My brother the sergeant; the track commander.

Dad is thrilled, Rick. Living vicariously. Sitting right up there in that turret with you. Mom, Sue, and I just want you to come home. Not that Dad doesn't. But he's diggin' it. A proud Pop. Stay cool, Rick. Remember those ABC's.

-Lee

* * *

Oct 10, 1967

Dear Lee,

We're leaving the north, finally. I guess someone finally figured out our tracks don't do too well in mud. Have a tendency to get stuck doncha know. Last three weeks a nightmare, Lee.

Picture our tracks out and about in this shit. Me telling Charlie over the intercom to not get stuck. But what's he supposed to do? You're GONNA get stuck if you're out here. One of us. So, it's pouring rain. Of course. It's the rainy season. And—what the fuck are we doing? We're on a mission. Which is to what? Make it from point A to Z without one of us getting stuck? Oh man, Lee. We're sitting ducks. Can barely move. Was surprised gooks weren't taking better advantage of the situation. But then they did. Oh boy, did they ever Lee. Three days ago, a tank from Hotel Company gets stuck in the muck and needs to be pulled out and we're sent to provide cover while a sixty-ton wrecker comes to do the job. Oh great. Now EVERYBODY'S going to get stuck. I'm riding up in the turret, soaked; drenched; rain pounding down (Fuck! I hate this shit) and I have a bad case of the you-know-what's and have fouled myself. Nothing new. You get so you just can't hold it in any longer. But please, do I have to get shot at besides? Guess so. We come under fire. So I'm up there firing the fifty, sweeping it back and forth, cursing. And we get stuck. Oh wait a sec. Maybe not. Charlie's got it, there ya go, keep moving. Good job. These things were not made to operate in shit like this.

And we hear a loud boom. Oh jeez, what the fuck was THAT? A mine? An awfully big one if it was. Sounded like a bomb went off.

Well it did. A bomb went off. Now Lee (by the way you don't need to tell Mom and Dad this), I've described to you what a thirty-pound mine can do (flip a thirty-ton personnel carrier over onto its back or side), but that sixty-ton wrecker that was coming out to help, the regular, every day, garden variety, thirty-pound Chicom (Chinese Communist) mine it set off happened to have been sitting on top of a fifty-gallon drum of gasoline. Lifted that wrecker into the air so when I saw it, it was lying on its side, smoking.

And sitting up top—well—riding up on the front of that wrecking monstrosity was the CO's assistant, First Lieutenant Harding. Never stood a chance. Nor did the lieutenant who was standing in front of the wrecker guiding it, motioning for the driver to come closer to the track that was stuck in the mud. The driver of the wrecker survived miraculously, but we just got word that he's paralyzed. Lt. Hardy and Captain Jacobs were good friends. In the same class at West Point. I have this image of them dreaming of their military careers as they're being put through the paces on the banks of the Hudson. Precedent for that kind of thing I reck-

on. And then, lo and behold, they end up not just being in the same outfit, but commanding a troop together. Both very likeable and sharp as can be, Lee. Sounds corny, especially coming from someone as jaded and cynical as I've become, but I consider it an honor and a privilege to be an NCO under them. They know their shit and do a good job of reigning in the assholes. Even though Captain Jacobs is obviously well aware of what can happen in war, you can tell he's really taking the loss of his friend hard.

Well, next time you hear from me Lee, it'll be from our base camp in the south. Where it's the dry season. So you'll be seeing my finger prints on my letters again.
-Rick

* * *

There we were at the Saigon docks again. Only this time driving *out* of the landing ship. It was the dry season again alright. Hotter than blazes. Sun beating down. We drove through Saigon; our whole troop; thirty-two armored personnel carriers and jeeps and trucks, up Highway 1, through Xuan Loc, and as we were lined up, slowly entering the gate at base camp, I could hear a band playing. Welcoming us, the weary warriors back from fighting in the north.

We drove around the perimeter, past the air field until we came to the Echo Troop motor pool where we lined up according to platoon.

The place looked different. There were wooden barracks now. The tent in which Finlay had given me such a bizarre welcome six months before was gone. All tents were gone. The sun's reflection off the metal roofs was blinding.

Seemed strange to be back. I remembered Captain McNulty briefing us for our trip north. Now that was over. I thought of what had happened up there; pictured the old platoon. I was a seasoned soldier now. And a sergeant.

I helped clean out the back of the track and then we cleaned our weapons. Charlie performed his maintenance. As he greased the treads I thought of how I had neglected to do that out there on the Batangan and the terrible consequences that might have occurred as a result. Then after a shower and shave, I put on fresh jungle fatigues, treated myself to a clean pair of socks and walked over to regimental headquarters.

"Excuse me, sir. Could you please tell me where I might find someone who plays in the Blackhorse band?"

"Sure. See that Quonset? And just behind that those two wooden barracks? That's where the band members sleep."

"Thanks."

* * *

"Rick?"

"Lonnie?"

"You're back."

"Indeed. Arrived this afternoon. Thanks for the welcome. I heard the band playing as we were driving in."

"Wow. Been a long time. I'm glad. . . .

"That I'm still up and about?"

"I heard stories. Thought about you."

"Yeah, well." I looked around. "Nice gig you got here."

"I'm not complainin."

"Good. I'd find it unsettling if you did."

We went over to the NCO Club where we bought each other beers; we talked as much as we could, given that there was nothing much for us to talk about really, and then I left, wandered back to my assigned barrack and never saw him again. Oh well.

* * *

It didn't take long after our return to base camp—less than a week—for me to open my big mouth and get busted. I don't even know what prompted it, some soldier from another platoon said something to me—don't ask me what—and I let forth with a long, hateful rant.

"What in the hell did you *say* last night, anyway, Allie?" Lt. Hansen asked me the next morning. "Were you aware that Captain Jacobs was standing close by listening? I guess you know what this means, right? Jesus. What the fuck's the matter with you?"

One of the hardest things I ever had to do was write Dad and tell him that I was no longer a T.C. That he could take all those dreams he was having of me being a sergeant and . . . .

Fuck! Here we go again. Okay, so I'd flunked out of school and—well—was put on academic suspension for a year. I'd pleased Dad no end by applying for and being accepted to Officer Candidate School, and then had dropped out of that program before it even started; and now this. Lee and I would talk about it as we walked on a beach near Colchester, England two and a half years later.

12.
Lost Innocence

"Dad was very proud of you."

Lee tilted his head away from the stinging ocean spray. "Still is."

I reached down in the sand, picked up a piece of driftwood and tossed it into the ocean. Together we watched it sail across the water and disappear in the waves. "It's awfully confusing to him. The burning of draft cards. Student riots. It frightens him. My going over there . . . I reassured him, I guess."

Thousands of seagulls were gathering on the beach. Lee and I watched the bravest among them flying across the water. They flew to a certain point, just beyond where the waves were breaking, then were stopped by the wind and had to turn around and come back.

Lee picked up a piece of shell, rolling it menacingly in the palm of his hand. "I guess we're surrounded."

I laughed. "This must be how Custer felt."

"I feel like Rod Taylor and . . . what's her name?"

"Tippi Hedron?"

"Tippi Hedron, yes. In the movie, *The Birds.*" Lee threw the piece of shell at the birds and they scattered. Moments later they were back.

"That squawking reminds me of you when you were learning to play the violin."

"That good, eh?"

"Yeah, that good."

Leaning into the wind, I thought about the photograph of Lee that Mom had sent to me while I was up north.

In the picture, which was like those on the covers of college brochures, Lee is walking down a flight of steps with a pile of books tucked under his arm.

I looked at him now. Long hair, and the same baggy pants he'd had on the morning I drove him to the Induction Center.

"He *was* proud. That letter I got from him, when we were up north; congratulating me on making sergeant. Enclosed was a snapshot of you. The one of you walking down those steps. Remember?"

"Sure. The one that was on the cover of the school newspaper." Lee smiled. "Times *have* changed haven't they?"

I nodded slowly, but did not say anything. Flashing inside my head were *Time* and *Newsweek* photographs I'd seen recently: massacred woman and children lying in an irrigation ditch at My Lai; a slain student lying bleeding on the pavement of a parking lot at Kent State; National Guardsmen standing steadfastly with their rifles opposite the hateful, glaring eyes of demonstrating students.

I reached down and pulled a blade of grass from the sand at the edge of one of the dunes. Carefully running the nail of my thumb along the center, I split it to make a whistle, and then absently threw it away. "When I became sergeant, I remember how proud I was." A faint smile formed across my lips. "Actually, I guess I just knew how pleased Dad would be."

Images of our father passed through my head. "In that letter I told you about, Dad described what an honor it was for someone like me, a draftee, to make sergeant; how the Army—you know how he gets—honor, responsibility, and all that . . . ."

We both chuckled. I remembered the carefully chosen words Dad had used in his letter. I could hear him in his confident, soothing voice, relating his views on the war, and then explaining in a loving tone how important it was to have young men like me . . . .

"He was right, you know, Lee. Dad was right. Without honor, responsibility . . ." I thought of myself leading a patrol through a village; sitting up in the turret—Track Commander! "It's important . . ." Once again, I recalled the words from Dad's letters to me. "'Important to have good officers, NCOs'"

We walked along silently. I thought of Lee in his dorm room, reading my letters and thinking about me, worrying about me, and then looking down at the sand, imagined Lee wearing a headband and chanting with angry students at peace rallies and antiwar demonstrations. Big Man On Campus. B.M.O.C. "That's what you'd be if you were still in college," I said to himself. "A hero. Hero to all those young women I've been dreaming about for the past two years; who I suddenly found myself sitting in class next to, and who, as I watched them strolling across campus, I thought, oh my, sweet Jesus, is this *real*?; am I really *here*? And finally, to all those young women—those I tried to get to know, anyway—whose facial expressions seemed to say—when despite my efforts to conceal the fact of where I'd been, they found out anyway—who *are* you? You . . . you one a them dudes, been up to *God knows what* while you were over there? You one of *them*? Did you . . . ? You a *killer*? How can I be sure you *aren't*? That you?—

"You *can't*," I shouted to myself. "You can't."

I glanced over at the pounding waves; they were getting bigger. As I watched them breaking close by, I remembered the searing looks I often got when someone found out I'd been in the war. Might as well have said that I'd just gotten out of prison; that I'd recently been released from a mental hospital.

I watched Lee walking. *Oh you'd be a hero, alright. Like Timmons and Hammond you'd be placed on a pedestal for standing up to our murderous government and refusing to go. For giving Uncle Sam the bird. For not giving in, allowing yourself. . . .*

I glanced at the two tiny moles on the side of Lee's face; *twins* we'd called them humorously when we were growing up, and imagined Cheryl and Diane fawning over Lee for—standing up! Refusing to go. At the same time, I heard Dad saying to me, "it saddens me, Rick, angers me no end to watch college students these days—your brother included, I'm afraid—protesting and carrying on, shouting their meaningless slogans, while brave young men like yourself . . . ."

Lee reached down and scooped up a handful of sand. He examined the sand as if it contained the answer to a puzzle. Letting the sand sift through his fingers, he turned to me. "Tell me something," he said, "your demotion—whatever it is you called it—when you spouted off. Held your own little anti-war rally. What did you *say*?"

"Nothing Captain Jacobs wanted to hear, *that's* for sure."

"So I gathered."

"Your brother the traitor."

"Certainly not how *I* viewed it.

"Anyway, that evening—listen to me babbling on—that evening up by the motor pool, I lost my cool—forgot my ABC's—and told Captain Jacobs, whom I liked and respected and trusted . . . that's just *it*, Lee, that's the crazy thing, it's because of officers like Captain Jacobs that I and others were able to get *through* that whole fucking mess and make it. Survive . . . and he kept the crazies under control too. No My Lai's with *him* at the helm. 'Aw, man, that mother fucker won't let us do *anything*? He won't let us have any fun a-*tall*.' At any rate, I told him and those who had gathered around and were listening, what a bunch'a fools we all were; how basically we were all suckers—*sucka*!—who had been duped and were . . . you can pretty much guess my spiel. Chief complaint: gasoline engines. Our carriers becoming funeral pyres. I pointed out—Captain Jacobs within earshot (I couldn't help myself) . . . I explained, in great detail, pantomiming—in case someone didn't get it, had missed it—why Diesel is used to burn shit. 'Because it doesn't *explode*!' I shouted. Then—long as I was on a roll (I knew I'd fuckin' blown it), long as I was going down—and from the glaring look on Captain Jacob's face, I knew I was—I explained to those gathering around me in the drizzling rain, how we were nothing but bait, going out each day in order to . . . What were we accomplishing? The V.C. could hear us coming for miles. Plenty of time to . . . Why are they making it so easy for us, they must've wondered. Rocket in a gas tank. Nice work there, Binh. Another in a driver's compartment. Oh Lee, the sickening feeling of sitting in the driver's compartment and hearing the familiar popping sound of a rocket being fired. Then the tense, horrifying moments as the rocket . . . This is how it worked. If you *heard* the explosion (which, thankfully, *I* always *did*)—following that . . . the swooshing sound the rocket made as it sped toward its destination—then you *made* it. Congrats! You got to go on—for what? Another minute? Two days? A month? Good God, Lee, how did I . . .? Anyway, if you *heard* the explosion, there you were! Still breathing. Wiping your sweaty face with a towel. Waiting for the next round. But if you *didn't* hear it—well—there wouldn't've been much to send home. Bits'n'pieces. What could be scraped . . . Anyway, I always felt . . . I'm pretty sure I told you in one of my letters how guilty I always felt right after I'd been spared. Not just that I was being allowed to go on, while someone else in the platoon wasn't, but that I felt giddy almost, struck with a sense of joy, that the sound of that exploding rocket meant someone *else's* misfortune and not my own. That *I* had survived and someone else *hadn't*. That someone *else's* family was going to be receiving one of those dreaded phone calls and not *mine*. For the time being anyway.

"Christ, Lee. Listen to me. Getting carried away. Like I did on my soap box. Gasoline engines. 'Aim for the gas tank. There you go! Beautiful. Perfect! See.' Guys jumping off the burning carrier. Trying to escape the flames. Easy targets. Several claymores aimed at them also. Command detonated. Timing everything. Gooks ten, Americans nothing. *Again.* And here come the choppers. 'Let's see if we can bring one of them down also?' You get the picture. I expressed some of these sentiments to you in my letters, if I recall. Fuel for the anti-war movement as it turned out. Right, Lee? Your brother being a primary source and all. But yeah, *bait*. I was all over that. And I think . . . I think the word expendable came into play also."

Lee waited until I finished, and then eyeing me, said, "Sounds to me, brother Rick, like you were a provocateur over there; a rabble rouser. And all that happened to you is—you lost a *stripe*? They didn't transfer your defiant ass down to the Delta?"

"Nope." I shook my head. "Just busted is all. Back to K.P. and burning shit. And taking orders. From an asshole as it turned out. That being the hardest part."

I raised my collar. The wind whistled in my ears. As we leaned against the wind, more seagulls lighted the wet sand next to us. I shooed them away, waving my arms and shouting, the way I used to do sometimes when the South Vietnamese swarmed around me in the villages.

"Di di," I shouted. "Di di mau."

"*Di di?*"

"Yes, di di. Di di mau. That means . . . ."

"Don't tell me. Get the fuck outa here?"

"How'd you guess?"

We both laughed. I watched the gulls returning, swooping back down on the sand. Some of them turned their heads as they strutted along and seemed to be staring at me. Thinking of how vulnerable the Vietnamese must have felt when tall, often angry American soldiers, swaggering and half crazed looking some of them, wandered into and searched their villages, and then of my own desperate need at times to have someone in charge I could trust and look up to (have *faith* in) in a world gone completely mad, turned upside down, I turned to Lee, and above the noise of the squawking gulls, cried out, pleadingly, "I was a good sergeant, Lee. The guys on my crew looked up to me. Depended on me. And I . . . " I shook my head back and forth dejectedly. "I let them down."

I took a deep breath. "Once again, our father—who lives across that great big body of water out there; who lives somewhere over there in New Jersey with Mom—was *right*. Dead on. If you, or Sue, or I don't stand up in this world and take the reins when we get the chance, the opportunity, someone *else*—not necessarily to our liking—*will*. And then . . . ."

Together Lee and I glanced out at the ocean as if we were

watching Mom and Dad moving about in their house three thousand miles away. "I felt for you, Rick," Lee said. "Would imagine one of the misfits you complained about messing with you, giving you a hard time."

I clenched my fists, holding them up to my chest, and then raising my elbows, pulled the pin from an imaginary grenade. Tightening my fingers, I swung my arm behind me; and then crouching low, eyes focused as if on a target, threw my hand forward in a lobbing motion.

Lee watched me, smiling. "Tempting, eh?"

"That it was little brother."

"But then—*ah ha*! You remembered your ABC's."

"In terms of doing something that menacing (which did run through my mind from time to time—every fucking *day,* actually), yes, I remembered my ABCs. Played it cool. With respect to keeping my highly controversial opinions to myself however—well—that's a different story."

I gave Lee a sad look. "Still bugs you, doesn't it?" Lee asked.

"Yes."

"Because . . . ?"

"Because of how it affected Dad. Might as well have . . . ."

"He was disappointed, yes. No question. Mostly he was worried about you though, Rick. Upset that *you* were so upset."

"That letter I wrote to him, Lee, trying to explain that all those things that he imagined me doing, that he was so proud of, I was no longer doing. Sorry Dad. Sorry Pop. I'm back to burning shit and being assigned K.P. And having . . . having a complete and total asshole in charge. And having my crew—my *former* crew . . . " I shook my head. "I didn't say any of that. Just complained about the war and my . . . Shit, Lee! Can't you just see him? Breaks my heart just thinking about it. Answer me this. When he got home from work whatever day that was—a thousand years ago at the end of that August—and Mom said, 'there's a letter from Rick, dear,' you think Mom, who'd already probably read it . . . what? Four hundred times?"

"Five hundred."

I nodded, smiling. "Five hundred. You're probably right. You think she broke the news to him so . . . ."

"So that he wouldn't go into shock?"

"Something like that. Oh Lee, how I agonized over what I wrote down on those . . . that thin blue paper while sitting inside that bunker. I practically used up a whole pad trying to figure out what to say . . . writing a few sentences and then crumpling the paper up and slamming it down . . . you think Mom tried to . . . you think she tried to ease the pain she knew it would cause him by . . . by telling him about it first, or. . . ? "

"She told him."

"Told him?"

"Told him, yes."

"You know?"

"I know, yes. She told me. She couldn't . . . ."

I thought of Mom harboring what she knew would be devastating news for Dad—or, at the very least, an enormous disappointment to him. I thought of Dad leaving his office and sitting on the train. Daydreaming. Imagining his son taking charge; fulfilling his role as a noncommissioned officer. *The Army doesn't just pick* **anyone** *to be a sergeant you know, Rick? Sergeants are the backbone of the Army.*

"Face it, Lee, I sucker punched him. Hit him right between the eyes. Might as well have. It's what he got for having confidence in me. For believing I . . . *Whammo*! Take *that* Dad! *Damn*! How *could* I? He had a vision, Lee. Of me stepping up. Being at the plate. So what do I do? Pull the rug out from underneath him. Instead of him being able to come home from work, kick off his shoes and read about me; learn about the most recent exploits of his son, Rick, the sergeant . . . . "

"You're too hard on yourself, Rick. Dad was disappointed, sure. But, as I said, he got over it. Immediately. Dad doesn't dwell on shit like that. He was more worried and upset because *you* were worried and upset. You were—and still *are*—his hero. *Believe* me."

Something wavering in the distance. A lighthouse?

Silhouetted against the dark sky, it seemed to be balanced on the long, thin line joining the land and ocean.

"Look how far we've come."

I looked back, and then reached down and scooped up a handful of sand. "Remember how we used to build castles? We'd build a wall around them, then wait and see how long it took for them to get washed away. When a wall would break we'd all try to fix it."

Another wave broke, sending water up next to where we were standing. I dipped my hand in the water, washing away the sand I was holding.

"Phew!" Dodging the water, I shook my wet hand at Lee. "It's cold."

Lee tossed the piece of broken glass into the ocean, throwing it at an angle, the way Dad had taught us to skip stones when we were growing up. The glass disappeared immediately, a bluish fleck in the choppy water.

Without saying anything, the two of us found ourselves walking back toward the weather-beaten shack we'd gone by earlier. The shack was barely visible from where we were, a small spot beyond which the coast jutted out, extending like a huge arm toward the sea.

"Wha'd'ya think? Mile, mile and a half"

"Something like that."

Lee reached down and picked up another piece of driftwood. He cocked back his arm, holding it behind him the way he and Sue and I used to do at the Jersey shore when our dog Andy was watching us (watching our *every* move), and then let it fly. We watched it sail across the water and then disappear in a wave.

"Where're you off to?" Lee asked. "Where art thou headed?"

I shrugged, turned, and in the midst of the long, confused and weary look I aimed at Lee, raised my hand, held the tip of my finger against the side of my head, and jerked my head sideways.

"*Not* funny," said Lee, watching me. "Not funny at all. Not one bit."

"Sorry," I said. "You're right. That was *totally* uncalled for. Shouldn't fool around like that. Not even . . . ."

Lee continued watching me, focusing on my eyes. Feeling uncomfortable (pinned down), I took a deep breath. "Look, you don't have to worry," I said. "I'm not going to do anything foolish. I promise. Not that selfish. Also, it wouldn't be fair to those . . .those who weren't so lucky. Awful lot of them. That would be letting them down." I paused, looking around. "I just want to become anonymous for a while, Lee. Get lost. Go . . . to Istanbul. Pull a *Lord Jim*. Steer a boat along one of the canals in Amsterdam, maybe. Drive a truck over in North Africa."

"Will you write?" Lee asked. "Keep in touch?"

"Best I can."

"Poor Mom. After what . . . "

"I know. I'm a shit, aren't I?"

"We both are. Oh how she suffered, Rick. We all did. Worrying. Not knowing."

"Moms are the ones who suffer the most. Who catch the brunt of it."

Lee moved his head up and down, and then peered into my eyes. "The phone," he said. "Every time . . . ."

"I can hear it ringing," I said. "Feel the suspense."

"It was considerable, believe me. Mom was afraid to lift that receiver off the hook."

"'Hello, this is . . .' I wonder how they *do* it; the officers assigned to . . . whoever's assigned that unfathomable task."

"Mom lived in constant fear of a call like that. 'Mrs. Alexander? This is Captain . . . ' Fortunately, whoever ends up making those kinds of calls never had to get in touch with Mom."

"Luck of the draw as they say."

"Wait a minute!" cried Lee, holding up his hands. "Hold on! You're not convinced that it was our prayers that kept you safe during those long, endless months, that . . . ?"

"To the contrary, little brother, I saw too much evidence of where praying and carrying the Bible around with you didn't seem to do much good. Don't get me wrong, *I* prayed incessantly and am truly, truly thankful for how things turned out. Nonetheless . . . . "

Lee looked around; sized me up. "Proof is in the pudding, Rick. I mean look at us. Strolling together on a beach. Whether through divine intervention, or . . . or luck of the draw—or a combination thereof, Mom—*you* and Mom (*all* of us), got through it."

I nodded skeptically. "And now," I spread my hands, indicating the long stretch of beach in front of us, "here we are—both of us—continuing to put our folks through hell. Some version of it, anyway. You over here . . . where are you, little brother, in exile?"

"Exile, yes. Sure. I'll buy that."

"And me? What am I, Lee—a fugitive? Richard Kimball?"

"Rick Alexander falsely accused . . . . "

"Of *what?*"

"Seeking justice . . . ."

"From *whom?*"

I looked over at Lee. Images of the two of us growing up together flashed inside my head; the two of us playing marbles—trying to win *steelies* and *cat's eyes*—in the back yard of our house on Grand Avenue; picnicking with our Mom and Dad and Sue and friends at local and state parks; getting off the bus together at the end of Merchants Road and walking home in deep (and getting deeper) snow—. . . .

I watched Lee and me entering the back door of our house, steaming from coming in out of the cold and stomping the snow off our boots, Mom down at the bottom of the stairs, helping us remove our gloves and woolen caps, our jackets and leggings.

I thought of Lee in high school and then in college; of Lee standing with friends at the bottom of a deep hole that was an archeological dig site he'd been working in since his arrival in Colchester. I mentally watched Lee reach down and carefully pick up and examine some artifact he'd been kneeling down and sifting through dirt for, and then remembered how in early November I'd driven him over to the Induction Center. Lee was referred to a sympathetic orthodontic student by an anti-war group, who fitted him with easy-to-put-on-and-take off braces. I had waited anxiously in the car while he went in for his physical.

"I'll be right out," Lee told me confidently, shutting the car door behind him.

Sitting sleepily behind the wheel of Mom and Dad's car, I watched Lee and several other figures converging on the steps of the building in the early morning dark. Forty-five minutes later, as the sky lightened, Lee emerged triumphantly. "Six months deferment!" he cried, climbing happily into the car. It was a story he relished telling. But that, of course, wasn't the end. At the conclusion of his deferment, realizing that Uncle Sam's long-range plan for him hadn't changed—and wasn't going to—that his government would soon be getting in touch with him again, Lee fled overseas.

I remembered Lee and me pulling up next to the curb in front of the Pan Am terminal at Kennedy Airport and helping Lee unload two large suitcases out of the back. After parking the car, I had walked back to the terminal and waited with Lee in a lobby crowded with young hippie-looking men and women until it was time for him to board a jet to London.

"This is it," Lee had said. As we'd shaken hands, Lee had had a determined look on his face. "I'm not coming back."

On the beach now, I relived getting off the train and wandering aimlessly along the narrow cobblestone streets of Colchester. In a small museum I spotted and entered moments before it closed, the woman behind the desk informed me that there were several archeological digs taking place locally and that the main one was being conducted right near there—in the center of town. I found the site easily.

Walking over to the edge of a deep, wide hole in the corner of a vacant lot, I looked down at Lee, Lee's friend Bill, and two other young men kneeling on the ground and digging the dirt around them with what looked like garden tools. Lee had been a picture of concentration, cautiously poking at the ground with the same look of curiosity and care on his face that I remembered him having as a child when he would stand for what seemed like hours peeling bark from trees.

He stopped digging for a moment. Using the ends of a towel wrapped around his neck, he wiped sweat from his brow.

Straightening his back and stretching his leg, he turned and said something to Bill, who continued digging behind him.

Lee looked up. Nothing.

He looked down, then back up. Still nothing.

He squinted, staring right at me.

Then it hit. "*Rick?* Is that *you?*" He was still staring. "My God, it *is*, isn't it? I don't believe this."

Walking along on the beach, Lee suddenly turned to me and said, "You feel that?"

I felt a slap against my forehead. Then another. "Rain," I said.

Lee was running. "Last one back to the car . . . " His challenge was lost in the wind, the roar of the waves.

As the rain swept in off the ocean, the two of us raced each other back across the sand toward the parking lot.

13.
Needles, Ice Baths, and Malaria

Boom! Down. Just like that. Whammo!

"Wow, man," Billy K. said to me later. "We're standin' in t'back a that newly built chapel, you, me an' the first sergeant; makes ya wonder, don't it? I mean that big, bad-ass dude slips in for some Christian guidance 'fore he gets back to the business a killin' gooks again. God'n'country, I guess. Bein' on the right side makes it alright. Anyhow, the chaplain's goin' on bout somethin'. Who knows, what can ya say in this motherfucking place? An' suddenly, I look over an' yer not there. So I step outside an'—what the fuck?—yer lyin' face down in the dirt. Looks like you took two steps then did yerself a nice little face plant."

That was the beginning of the cycle, when I would feel fine for twenty-four hours, leaving me and the medic to believe that the previous twenty-four hours of diarrhea, stomach cramps, and feverish chills were simply symptoms of a nasty bout with the flu that I'd recovered from. But then the said cycle kept shortening from twenty on, twenty off, eighteen on, eighteen off until it got down to four on, four off and finally I was sick all the time and it was pretty clear that I wasn't just having relapses.

Listen, take my word; don't ever underestimate the debilitating effect an injection from a mosquito can have on you. Oh, I saw many big, strapping, bad-ass dudes who were wishing to fucking hell they hadn't missed taking their malaria pills, and who, as they stumbled agonizingly, deliriously onto the malaria ward, were wondering what they'd done to deserve this.

Malaria . . . .

Look, I didn't *purposefully* not swallow my malaria pill one day if that's what you're thinking, in order to—well—miss all that good shit I've been telling you about; and take a break from the field. Nope. Had no idea I'd missed a day or two. Farley, our medic could be a nagging, persnickety asshole regarding those pills (as he was supposed to be—given that we all were "government issue" whose effectiveness the Army did not want compromised in any way), and we all gave him a hard time. "Go away. Di di. Leave me alone." But I was always compliant. As far as I knew. Put the fucken pill in my mouth as soon as Farley handed it to me, then swallowed. *There. Go bug someone else.* Nonetheless, I obviously missed a round—like I say, not purposefully. Hey, maybe I was off taking a dump when Farley came around. Who the fuck knows? And when after a shitload of blood work (drawn by an ancient-looking private who had the shakes—we called him the vampire) and beaucoup torturous ice baths to get my fever down, I was finally told that, yes, I did indeed, as expected, have malaria. My body was filled with it.

At any rate, one afternoon while the 2nd platoon was running escort duty, a guy we called Mousy—very witty, I know, but the nickname was right on—entered the tent that just had to have been a hundred and thirty degrees inside and found me curled up in the fetal position, shaking.

"You okay?" he asked, walking tentatively toward me.

"Look at me," I said—I knew it was Mousy by his voice, but I did not look up—"I can't stop shivering. I'm fucking freezing."

Mousy reached down and placed the palm of his hand on my forehead. "Jeez, man," he cried, "you're burning up. I'll be right back. I'm going to get the medic."

Fifteen minutes later the medic arrived—Mousy must have told him I was dying (which I of course was)—and drove me over to the aide station in a jeep; from there I was driven over to the 15th Medical Company, the base hospital, where I was admitted to the Intensive Care Unit.

As I already mentioned, the doctors were ninety-nine percent certain I had malaria, but until it showed up in my blood giving them absolute proof—*ah, yes. There it is. Finally*—they kept sending that shaky old private over to draw blood from me. I was a sick pup. I'd already lost thirty pounds, was down to 150, and didn't have the strength to take that hypodermic needle from the vampire and shove it up his sorry ass, which I wanted to do. *Oh no.* You *again*? But admittedly, despite this old private's obvious foibles (I mean, you had to figure, based on appearance—forty years in the Army and still a private? What does that tell you?); and with those bloodshot eyes staring at me from within a reddened face obviously ravaged by alcohol and a case of the shakes with his needle-wielding hand (plus the fact that since a child I'd been horrified by needles), can you see my concern? But this guy was good. I'm not saying I enjoyed having someone who shook because they desperately needed a drink, sticking a needle into my arm, but other than the fact that the blood he was drawing from me thrice daily—not to mention the finger pricks (*ouch! I hate that. Fuck*) didn't reveal the malaria that everyone just fucking knew was in me for almost a week, which was not his fault obviously; there were no real issues; the vampire was up to the task.

And those ice baths to keep the fever down. Until they knew for sure that malaria was the cause of my fever and could start the quinine, I remained a victim of torture. The orders passed on to the orderlies concerning me each evening were as follows (of this I'm certain): *Specialist Alexander. Bed number eleven. Over on the right there. Wake him up every two hours and take his temperature. Be careful. He may try and hit you. Let me amend that. He* will *try and hit you. He's gotten belligerent. Work in pairs. One thing you've got going he's easy to hold down. Weak as a baby. Zero strength. If his temperature rises to up over a hundred, give him an ice bath. Then put a fan on him. Don't relent until his temperature has subsided; is down under a hundred.*

Yup, those were the orders. How do I know? Because they carried them out. Oh so judiciously. Had I the strength I would have strangled them. Especially one. Who seemed to get off on the whole thing. Oh goodie an ice bath. I could hear the water being turned on over at the nearby sink; hear the water rushing out and filling the metal tray; hear chunks of ice being plopped into the water; hear the ice being chopped up; hear all of the above being wheeled toward me on a cart; hear the motherfucking fan being set up.

I know, I know, he was only doing his job. Saving my life actually. But as you've probably gathered that's not how I was viewing it at the time.

Of course I really had nothing to complain about did I? I mean an ice bath? Being stuck with a needle? Come on. What about . . . how about all those wounded soldiers lying on beds next to and across from me? Dying many of them. In rough shape. When you're in the field and you hear that someone who was dusted off two days before made it, you think, thank God, and leave it at that. Imagine them living happily ever after even though you know it's not true. They made it they made it; that's all that counts. But when you're on the ICU, you see firsthand what happened to them; wrapped in bandages now, you imagine them . . . smiling? Before whatever it was sheared off their legs; caused them to be paralyzed; removed their jaw and part of their face; tore open their stomachs and chests.

"Get. Me. The. Fuck. Outa here," I remember thinking as I listened to their last gasping breaths.

And they did. The moment I started the quinine I was transferred next door to the malaria ward.

The malaria ward. Two rows of hospital beds lining both sides of a Quonset hut. Female nurses making sure we swallowed our pills each morning. "There, now that wasn't so bad, was it?"

"No," I'd say gazing into blue, or green, or brown eyes. (The green eyes my favorite.) But I was lying. The stuff was foul. Made me feel sick. But no more ice baths.

"How you feeling this morning, Mr. Alexander?"

"Much better, thank you." *Sorry about my hard-on that's always sticking up, making a nuisance of itself. Reckon you're used to it however. I mean, damn, you don't even seem to notice. Or if you do . . . I know, I know, forty hardened peckers to contend with each morning, you gotta get past that. But the way you just snap your finger at it making it go down, kinda takes the wind out of a guy's sails.*

Oh shit, *you* again?

Doctor needed to check my blood count, so guess who showed up with his basket full of blood drawing paraphernalia? Arm shaking like all get out.

The nurses scolded us for just about everything we did; or didn't do I should say; not getting up and bathing (too much hassle, man, uh, you mean walk all the way over there?); not combing our hair (what hair?) and not answering letters. The *Princeton Packet* listed all the local servicemen stationed in Vietnam along with our APO addresses and I got tons of letters from all sorts of kind, good hearted people thanking me, wishing me well and letting me know that they were thinking about me during the holiday season. One particular well-wisher was a little girl—eight, I'd say—who asked me if I was scared and said she was praying for me. I thought of her and her parents and then of Sue and Lee and Mom and Dad and . . . it would have been nice if I'd come home and looked her up. Rang the doorbell of her parents' house and said, "hi, I'm Rick, the soldier in Vietnam who . . . ."

"Oh, my goodness, Rick. You're home. What a wonderful—let me get Tracy. Tracy?"

I'd thought of doing that, imagined Tracy coming down the stairs, watching me, this soldier who was at war in some far away land that she'd been writing to. But I didn't.

Major Thompkins kept giving me updates on the troops. The whole regiment was up at a place called Loc Ninh near the Cambodian border. The major showed me where it was on a map. Rough going up there apparently. I imagined 2nd platoon tracks busting through jungle; hauling ass across rice paddies; Charlie driving. *Take it slow, Charlie. Stay in the tracks the vehicle in front of you are making. Don't pull up next to a tree for shade. Avoid paths, trails, roads. Crisscross. Take the route less traveled. I know you're on top of the maintenance. No need to worry about that.*

Swaney, sitting on the back flap, smoking weed. Friar Tuck and Swaney passing the joint back and forth. *A tiny* mosquito, *Steve. Done me in. Yeah, I'm layin' up. Guess you could say that. While you . . .* I could hear him bragging about all the combat he was experiencing; how since he was involved and I wasn't, he was quickly gaining ascendency over me. *Well, you got it, my man. You are one bad, ass kickin' dude. And if you've indeed moved ahead of me in terms of what you've seen, I hope to fuck I* never *have the opportunity to catch up.*

But it did seem to be true, lots of bad shit going down out there; lots of casualties being reported; from all three squadrons. Mines mostly. Of course. Mines and booby traps. A helicopter shot down during a dust off. A rocket exploded in the fuselage as the chopper was rising and turning away. All three crew members killed; the pilot and two gunners; plus the three wounded troopers who'd just been lifted on board.

"So, where you from, Mr. Alexander?"

"New Jersey."

"New Jersey. Same as me. Where abouts in New Jersey?"

"Princeton. My parents . . . . "

Connie Francis handed me a pad. "If you'll write your parents' names and address and telephone number I'll give them a call."

"Really?"

"Absolutely." She reached over and shook my hand.

"Thanks."

"You're welcome."

As she walked over to the next bed (and the next hard-on), the tattooed fellow next to me had the tent thing going also. Doubt if there were any patients being visited who didn't. The song, *Where The Boys Are,* was playing inside my head. I was deeply in love and awfully disappointed that I wasn't going to be allowed to attend her concert that evening.

"Hello?"

"Hi. Is this Dorothy Alexander?"

"Yes, this is she, may I ask who's calling?"

"This is Connie Francis, Mrs. Alexander, the singer. I just got back from Vietnam where I visited with your son, Richard . . . ."

"Mom," I used to say, "When Connie Francis called did you really know who shc was?"

"Yes, of course."

"Come on, Mom. Really?"

"Yes, I knew who she was."

"And did you two have yourselves a nice little chat?"

"We did as a matter of fact. My dear friend Connie and me."

In my mind all these years later, I watch Major Thompkins telling me (as we're sitting on the edge of my bed), how the young man who I had become friends with—he was admitted to the ward several days before and assigned to the bed next to me—had left in an emergency and was being transferred to a hospital in the states. Tests had come back showing he had a rare disease known as black-water fever, an often deadly form of malaria that attacks the liver, and he needed special attention fast. "That's why he didn't say good bye, Rick." The major had startling blue eyes that seemed to look right through you. Oh he'd seen some stuff in this war; what was happening to a good many of those who were out there fighting in it. "He told me to say so long and wish you the best. He has a difficult road ahead of him, Rick. From what I've been told there's really no cure for what he's got. Can't just go the quinine route like," he motioned the rest of the ward, "like you guys. Unlucky fellow. Been over here—well—this is my third tour and he's the first case of black-water fever I've come across. What were the odds of *that* happening?"

Quite slim, apparently. I remember sitting silently and looking over at Jamie's empty, unmade bed. I imagined his plight. The urgency in the eyes of the doctors and nurses treating him; the frightened (terrified)—what the fuck is going on?—look on his handsome, young face. Dude was what? Nineteen? Twenty? Had just been assigned to a platoon. Hadn't been a T.C. for even a week. How long was this latest development going to keep him out of the field? A month? Wow, really? Aw, man, five weeks?

No, Jamie. Forever. You ain't goin' back. Your days of combat—how many? Three? Four?—are over. I just hope and pray to God . . . .

"The liver, Rick. What he has attacks the liver. So hopefully they get him back to the states in time . . . . "

"For what? To save it?"

"Yes."

"Otherwise?"

I hope you're out there somewhere, Jamie; that the doctors were able to do whatever they needed to do and . . . if you read this, let me know okay? I've thought about you a lot over the years.

In the same way that my friend Jamie had had horrible luck, Luke, who was assigned to the malaria ward to recuperate following his miraculous recovery from a snake bite—he'd spent six weeks in the Intensive Care Unit recovering from an emergency tracheotomy and throat surgery after a bamboo viper had bitten him on the foot. Wearing sandals, the *Stars and Stripes* tucked under his arm, he was strolling over to the latrine one morning. "See that fellow at the end of the ward there?" Major Thompkins pointed toward Luke who'd just arrived on the ward. "There is absolutely no explanation whatsoever why that young trooper is still alive. None. Other than—well—it's a miracle."

What a story.

If a fellow housecat (one of Luke's fellow headquarter troopers) hadn't seen Luke heading over to the shit house in his sandals for his mid-morning dump—no, you wouldn't have caught us line troopers traipsing around in sandals like we were strolling over to a beach house; if said fellow housecat hadn't stepped outside the tent and seen his friend suddenly draw back his foot, startled and then look around and topple to the ground, unconscious; if after seeing that, and then while rushing over to help spotting the highly venomous culprit slithering away and screaming for a medic; if a medic from the nearby aide station hadn't heard those desperate cries and rushed over to see what was going on . . . .

Bottom line. Because Luke was rushed to the ICU and operated on so quickly; because the treating physician knew immediately what he was dealing with, Luke lived to tell his tale.

Time moving slowly. But so what. I'm safe. Blocking out the fact that one day soon I will have to go back out there again. Face the music. And as if I needed to be reminded of that (what? Lest I fucking *forget?*)—Matt, Echo' troop's clerk showed up on the ward to see me one day.

"Specialist Alexander?"

I was sitting up in bed reading; hadn't noticed him walking toward me. "Yeah," I said.

"Hi, I'm Matt, Echo troop's clerk."

"Oh, hi." We shook hands.

"How're things coming along?"

"Okay, okay. Can't complain." He glanced around, as if assessing my situation; probably thinking, not bad, not bad, you've got yourself a nice little gig here. For the time being anyway.
Yeah, well, you think malaria's fun? Try it sometime, motherfucker.

"I have some bad news."

"From . . . out there?"

"From the field, yes."

"Echo troop?"

He nodded slowly.

"Second platoon?"

Again he nodded.

"Go ahead, shoot," I said, "let me have it."

"Two tracks," he said.

"Two?"

"Two-three and Two-nine."

"KIAs?"

"Four."

"*Four?*"

"'Fraid so. Your platoon got hammered."

"Mines?"

"Two-three a mine, Two-nine a rocket."

Oh, no. No. Please. I could feel it coming; see it in his eyes. "Charlie?"

That nod again.

No, not Charlie. Not him. Fuck. How . . . .?

Charlie had been cut in half when the Two-three flipped over and landed on him; a new guy who I'd only met once—Matt kept describing him until finally it dawned on me who it was. Then (as had happened to me before), it was like, Oh no, *him? That* guy? I remembered staying up late talking to him, telling him what it was like out there; telling him not to worry, he'd be alright. "Don't let these clowns scare you." He was catapulted into the air (the old being-shot-out-of-a-cannon trick I'd seen so many guys involuntarily perform) and had died from a broken neck after landing on his head. Harmon, Two-nine's right gunner, was sitting just above where the rocket exploded and—well—he and Sanchez, the left gunner . . . "You've been out there and seen all this, Rick."

Indeed I had. Opened up chests and bellies and stuff from

inside them hanging down, oozing out; blood gushing from a wound or forming like a big, red apple in their mouths; guys lying on the ground, twitching and squirming, not fully aware that they were missing an arm or that one of their legs, or both of them had been shorn off.

Oh yeah, I knew. And even though dead was dead—for those who'd been killed and were no longer thrashing around, suffering—"Am I going to die? I'm going to die, aren't I?—even though dead was dead, whether you went home in a pine box, or your remains—any that could be found—were shipped stateside in a plastic bag—*here, Mr. and Mrs. so and so. This is all that was left*—I cannot get out of my head the image of how Charlie was found after the explosion. I mean, there he is in my mind, driving along; his warm, friendly eyes gazing attentively at the ground in front of him from within his grease-smeared, dirt-encrusted face; and then . . . .

"Thanks for coming over and telling me," I said.

"Not what anyone wants to hear. Hate to be the one . . . ."

"Could you send me Mr. and Mrs. Haibach's home address?"

"Sure. I'll have someone bring it over."

"Thanks."

I walked with Matt to the end of the corridor and then stood and watched as he stepped into the blinding sunlight and then walked over to where he had parked his jeep. "Dear Mr. and Mrs. Haibach," I said to myself, and thought of a photograph Charlie had showed me once. It was from his girlfriend, Joan. Joan had decorated a garbage can with red, white and blue streamers and painted the letters, HAPPY BIRTHDAY, CHARLIE!!! I LOVE YOU, JOAN, on the side. She was standing next to the can, smiling and waving.

As Christmas approached, I received lots of Christmas cards, letters, and packages. Let's see, what have we here? Oh my goodness, a miniature Christmas tree. With tiny decorations on it. From . . . Oh wow! A homemade card with Sue and her high-school friends' signatures on them. And little notes. I pictured them all in our house's kitchen working on the project; Mom taking the package over to the Princeton post office. Or maybe Sue took it over and mailed it, along with her friends. They could all drive now; had their licenses. Whoa! What keeps you awake at night more, Mom and Dad? Me over here, or . . . ?

Thank you, girls.

Couple of fruit cakes. Nancy Rider sent me homemade bread. And—aw Mom—chocolate chip cookies?

Letter from Jack Wheeler. Best of friends him and me since—what Jack? Since we were two or three? Lived two houses down from us. At the end of Grand Avenue. Corner of Merchants and Grand. Next to that field there. Jack had been in Air Force ROTC while at Michigan State and was stationed at—I forget which Air Force Base. He enclosed a photograph of him in his flight uniform climbing to the cockpit of a fighter jet. Go Jack! Must be a rush flying one of those things. Also enclosed were photos from the canoe trip he and I took together in northern Ontario the summer before I was drafted. Let's see, in this one I'm standing in a campsite on . . . Lake Anima Nipissing? That's my guess. Oh man, to be able to just dip that tin cup over the edge of the canoe and . . . one day, if I ever get out of this place, we'll go back there, okay Jack? Maybe head over to Lady Evelyn Lake next time.

Greetings from Jerry Keller from aboard whatever Navy ship he was on. Headed to the Persian Gulf or some such place in response to—what else?—increased tensions in the Middle East. Some things never change, do they? And a letter from his twin brother, Kim, who was in the Army stationed at Fort Dix, where, hiding under his bunk bed on several occasions, he overheard drug deals going down in his barracks and feared for his life. *Mom, as you may have heard, Rick, wrote a letter to the Army requesting that I not be sent to Vietnam because Jeff is there and her request was granted. So, great! Here I am trying to survive in the middle of a bunch of gangland thugs. I think I'd rather be over there with you.*

Card from the Adams family; each of them writing a little note; Wendy, Debby, Bill, Hartson, Art, Nance, and Lynn, with Bill reminding me of our trip to New York City before I headed overseas; and how on stage-right next to us as we dined at the Copacabana, Johnny Mathis had sung a litany of old favorites. Imagining Johnny peering soulfully out over the audience as he fondled the mike, Bill and I sipping wine and finishing off our meal; me, Lobster Newburgh, Bill, Chateaubriand, I could hear Johnny's voice and mentally sang along with him, "*Chances are, 'cause I wear a silly grin the moment you come into view . . . .*"

Why didn't you tell me we were supposed to tip all four waiters, Rick? Come on, man, you're the one who's supposed to know stuff like that. Living near the big city and all.

Wow! That one waiter, the head honcho, I presume, followed us outside, didn't he? Chased our asses down whatever street that was. And what did we do? Like an asshole I reached in my pocket, took a twenty out of my wallet and handed it to the sorry bastard. Oh well.

Card from McGraw's; one from John and Hilda also; another one from my Mom's sister, Marion, and Uncle Dick; card from Uncle Bob.

As I sat on the edge of the bed reading the warm, encouraging notes inside the cards and then immersed myself in the picture of a winter scene in some cozy place like Vermont on the front of one of the cards, colorful Christmas tree lights framing the window of a room in an otherwise bleak, rundown building on the front of another, my mind became flooded with memories; Jack and I playing ping-pong in the tiny basement of the house Jack lived in on Brett Road, Tommy Edwards singing, "*One Hundred Pounds Of Clay,*" on the radio as I crawled behind Jack's father's workbench to retrieve a ping-pong ball that Jack had slammed past me (*one of the few, eh Jack? One of the very few*); Kathy McGraw and her father trekking across the street in a snow storm to watch an episode of the *Untouchables* on our black and white T.V. because theirs wasn't working; Dad fidgeting with the rabbit ears behind the T.V. to get a clearer picture, Bill telling Dad, "Don't worry. That's fine, Jim. Perfect," as the opening bootlegging scene being described by Walter Winchell (*October 1932 . . . during the depth of the Depression*) came to an end and Mr. Ness and his fellow agents (William Youngfellow? . . . Enrico "Rico" Rossi? Lee Hobson?) set out to bring down yet another notorious gangster. Then, Bill Adams and I trying to steal a Lowenbrau keg from the German pavilion at the 1964 World's Fair (didn't get too far did we Bill?) "Just set that down right over here by the gate if you don't mind," the security guard told us, and then thanked us. One had the feeling that that kind of thing was happening on a regular basis.

Jack and me riding the Cyclone and Parachute Drop at Coney Island; childhood trips with the Kellers and Adams' to Niagara Falls and Letchworth and Stony Brook State Parks; skiing with the Adams at Whiteface and Snow Ridge; vacationing with the

Kellers at Allegany State Park (the Kellers occupying a cabin on Barton Trail, the Alexanders staying in the one on Weller); Lee, Sue, and my cousins Ken, Phil, and Linda, and me playing capture the flag at our house on Grand Avenue, in Rochester, and then at their nicely wooded home in Westwood, Massachusetts (Lee, Ken, and Linda on one side; Phil, Sue, and me on the other); and then all our Christmases together.

I glanced across the ward; thought about what lay beyond the screen door at the end. "If anything bad happens to me during the next four months," I said to myself, "it won't be due to a lack of friends and family pulling for me."

Christmas Eve. As I lay on my bed under a clean sheet, I imagined Steve and Murph listening to the sounds of the jungle ten feet in front of them as they sat on guard in their turrets; and with thick, moist air pressing down on them in the pitch black dead of night, saying to each other over the radio, "uh, killer two-three, this is, uh, killer two-seven. Merry Christmas, over."

"Why, thank you, killer two-seven. And a very happy merry Christmas to you, also."

Christmas day. I'd read in the *Stars and Stripes* the month before—in between being stuck with needles by the vampire—how following the heavy fighting on whatever hill it was, soldiers from the 173rd Airborne used the stacked bodies of their fallen comrades as tables to set the trays with their Thanksgiving meals on them. I'd felt cheated that I was too sick to enjoy the turkey, mashed potatoes and gravy, cranberry sauce, shrimp cocktail, etc. that the Army prided itself on delivering to every soldier wherever they might be. (I had told an orderly to bring me a tray and had stuffed my face and then rushed out of the aide station and vomited, but now there I was feeling fine and ready to try again.)

"Yo! Slow down, partner. Damn. This ain't a contest ya know. Wha'd'ya think someone's gonna come take it away?"

"Yeah, you're right. Missed out at Thanksgiving. Bein' a little foolish here."

"Where ya from?" We were sitting at tables that had been set up outside; my recovering malaria pals and I.

"New Jersey."

"Sorry t'hear that. I'm from Reno. What I meant was, over here. What squadron?"

"Oh. The second."

"Gotta ask you. You ever. . . ?"

"Heard of Hank? The Ross element?"

"Holy fuck. How did you . . . ?"

"I could see it in your face; that that's what you were going to ask me."

"Jesus, man. That's what I call . . . what the fuck's it called? When . . . ?"

"Telepathy?"

"Yeah, man. You just laid a big dose a telepathy on my ass. Did you *know* him?"

"Oh yeah. We were crew members together. On the Two-six. Echo troop. I was the driver, he was the right gunner."

"Well I'll fuckin' be." This guy whatever his name was (Reno) kept looking at me as if I was a celebrity.

Obviously Hank's reputation had preceded him; his defiant capers were known far and wide.

I had fun recounting and reaffirming his exploits; had a whole malaria ward—patients, staff, Major Thompkins—gathered around me listening; taking it all in.

A week later—one of the early days of that wild and crazy

year, 1968—I was ready for discharge. My blood count was normal, my weight and strength were coming back, but . . . Listen, honestly, I don't remember when I first brought up thc fact that I had an ingrown toenail that was infected and had to be dealt with; but just before I was to be released, I showed Major Thompkins my right toe, which had become swollen to the size of a golf ball and was as painful and sore as it looked. As the major held my foot and ran his fingers gently over the reddened, pus oozing infected area, examining it I almost went through the roof screaming.

"How long have you had this?" the doctor asked, questioning why I hadn't said anything about it for the past five weeks.

Look, like I said, I don't remember when I first brought it up. I honestly don't. But it needed immediate attention, and that's what it got. During one of those early days, in 1968, I was wheeled into the ICU and operated on.

When I woke up—while I was coming to from the sodium pentothal—I heard someone screaming, "I want to die, I want to die!" It was the boy lying on the bed next to me. He'd also just woken up, only *he* in doing so had come to the realization that his legs were missing; that he'd lost both of them to a mine that had killed two of his buddies. Major Tompkins came over and dressed the kid down; really let him have it. The last thing in the world the other gravely wounded, dying soldiers on the ward needed to hear was hopeless, self-defeating proclamations like that.

Later, when I questioned the major's seemingly cruel, sadistic bedside manner, he replied, "We here at the hospital start acting from our hearts," the major told me, "start doing what feels right to us—rather than what we know is best for our patients—and the Mister Joneses—who come to us daily, I might add—all mutilated and wishing they were dead—it's over before they even get started. Might as well hand them a loaded forty-five. Ah, you're looking a bit skeptical there, my friend. But you're going to have to trust me on this. You start allowing . . . you give these badly wounded young men—*boys* for Christ sakes—a chance to feel sorry for themselves, and they *will* feel sorry for themselves. Rough business. Takes its toll. Can do a number on you. But . . . " The major glanced at the boy sleeping, then back at me. "Someday," he mused, "it would be nice to know that Private Jones here has, that he will have fought and clawed his way, done whatever it is he had to do, to achieve some kind of. . . normal life; that he will be happy, content. At peace with himself. And that he will look back and say, 'That guy, the major—whatever his name was—that guy who was in charge of the ICU . . . that he did what he had to do. That what Mr. Jones was witnessing; or rather, the *recipient* of, I should say, tough love."

Whoa! Heavy stuff, eh?

I was discharged a week later. On crutches. Orders for light duty. Matt picked me up in the jeep and drove me over to the Echo troop tents—well—no longer tents; barracks now; wooden barracks.

14.
Saigon's Been Hit!

I went back almost immediately and apologized. My woe is me ranting . . . it had had nothing to do with him; he just happened to be the one who'd walked over and handed me my duffle. *Sorry. Jeez.* He was doing me a favor for Christ's sake. And I blasted him. Really let him have it. "You were *asked* to bring this shit? Tell me . . . Pvt. Turner? Do you always do everything you're told?"

For that brief, depressing, unfathomable moment when Turner called my name and I looked over and saw him, realizing what he was carrying and what he was about to hand over to me; he might just as well have walked over and planted his fist squarely between my eyes.

"Look," I told him as we sat in the shade of the Two-eight after I went back and apologized, "it's kind of like this. Remember that sick joke goin' around in basic—well—don't know if you ever heard it; it's how the Army would break the news to you if your mother died. Drill sergeant says to the trainees standing in formation, "Okay you shit birds, all a you's got a mother take one step forward. Not so *fast* there Johnny.' Real fuckin' knee slapper, eh? And there at base camp less than twenty-four hours ago, Sergeant Pinkerton might just as well have said to me in front of the six or seven other rear echelon-troops, okay now, listen up. All a you's thinks yer stayin' here at base camp and not goin' back out to the field . . . Those who think they've *made* it an' are goin' home, take one step forward. Not so *fast* there Mr. Alexander.'

"That's how it seems," I said, glancing around (oh, I was back alright—fuck! Fuck! Fuck!), and then explained how it had all gone down. How after I'd gotten out of the hospital, Sergeant Pinkerton (Pinky) had asked me if I wanted to remain at base camp for the balance of my tour. How I'd said, "okay, let me get this straight, sarg, see if I'm hearing you right. You mean spend my last three months here at base camp and not go back to the field?"

"That's what I'm sayin', trooper. You've done yer time out there an' somebody's gotta stay back, so why not have it be *you* as opposed t'some newbie? Less ya miss it. Got a hankerin' te . . . ."

"No, no. *Fuck* no."

I told Turner how I drove a jeep, pounded in nails, and burned shit for several weeks, reveling in my good fortune (and doncha just know I wrote to Mom and Dad and Lee and Sue with this great news. "Halleluiah! I made it, I made it, I made it.") Then how Pinky called me over following formation one morning and asked me if I'd do him a favor.

"Sure. Of course."

Would I . . . ?

Oh man, hand-deliver a manila envelope to Captain Jacobs? *Uh, not exactly dyin' to. What if I get out there and . . . ?*

What could I say? Pinky explained to me what I had to do. Was I anxious? Yes. Did my heart keep trying to leap out of my chest whenever I thought about it? Yes again. Did I imagine myself . . . out there again? In harm's way? You bet. But the more I thought about it—hey, it was *going* to happen. I was going out there, the die had been cast, so do what ya gotta do. Which I *did*. What I'm trying to say, though, is, the more I thought about it (which was for twenty-four hours. I left the next morning), I warmed to the idea; was even glad. It was a chance to be with my friends who I hadn't seen in a long time and, yes, I was quite curious to see where they were.

So off I went. With a manila envelope tucked under my arm. The CO's currier. *Come hell or high water, Captain Jacobs, I will personally hand deliver this envelope to you.*

From the airstrip at base camp I flew via C-130 to Loc Ninh, a town near the Cambodian border sixty miles northwest of Saigon. At the airstrip there I climbed into the back of a two-and-a-half-ton truck with a dozen or so other Blackhorse troopers and was driven to regimental headquarters. From there I was driven by jeep to a jungle clearing where I boarded a Chinook helicopter and was flown to Second Squadron headquarters. While waiting at regimental headquarters I ran into Staff Sergeant Skaggs. Remember him? My pal from Fort Knox? He was glad to see me. And I him. He'd just arrived for his second tour. The chopper he had just gotten off I was hurrying over to board.

"Skaggs?" I'd said, identifying him as he and several other passengers emerged from settling dust.

"Allie?" He'd said, eyeing me suspiciously, "that *you* standing out here in the middle a nowhere?" He did a double take, adjusting his eyes. "Damn! It sure as hell *is* you, ain't it?" He hurried over, shook my hand and patted me on the shoulder. "Well I'll be." He looked around. "This just might end up bein' ol' home week. I ran into Timmons at base camp. Now you?"

"Yeah," I said, taking in the bleak surroundings, "quite a spot we picked for a reunion."

"Got that right. Listen, you goin' somewhere?"

I showed him the manila envelope I had tucked under my arm and explained my mission. "This 'ere envelope contains highly classified documents," I told him, "upon whose timely delivery by me could very well impact the outcome of the war."

"Well, they're in good hands," said Skaggs, "an' I'm glad t'see that the last eight months over here doesn't seem to have changed you."

We each gave a quick accounting of ourselves. It was "same old same old" at Fort Knox—he was glad to "*finally* get the fuck outa there and back here where I belong" (If you say so, Skaggs. If you say so), he told me to make sure that when I wrote to L.D. that I told him we'd run into each other ("at the ass end of the world, tell him. I mean, the *ass* end a the world"); he'd been assigned to H Company which meant he'd be a tank commander, in charge of a "big boy." And then we parted, went our separate ways. But before I turned and headed over to board the helicopter, I asked Skaggs about our buddy, Sergeant Carter.

"He didn't make it, Allie," Skaggs shouted to me over the noise of the helicopter engines. "He came over here a month ago. Was assigned to the twenty-fifth. Didn't last a week. Caught a bullet in the head on his first patrol."

A lot had transpired since Skaggs had told me how he'd lost his middle finger to a piece of shrapnel during a fire fight when he was over there with the First Infantry Division and I'd tried to imagine what it was like. Now I knew. Knew better than him. But he was a true warrior. Hope he made it. He's another one whose name I remember but that I refuse to look and see if it's in that huge wall location book at the Vietnam War Memorial.

It was amazing watching the war from above; seeing where it was taking place down below; a bird's eye view of the fields and jungle and rice paddies. I told Turner how strange it seemed to be flying above it all; knowing what those flashes were; those loud booms. How after we set down in a cleared area surrounded by jungle—oh that was bugaloo country alright; no man's land, the ass end of the world—I jumped down from the chopper into a field where I was greeted by a sergeant who told me to stay low and follow him. Holding my helmet with one hand, so the wind from the rotor blades wouldn't blow it off, clutching the envelope with the other, my rifle strapped over my shoulder, I ran crouched over to where ten or so tracks were lined up.

"Where you headed?" the sergeant turned and asked.

"Echo."

"Okay," he pointed to the third track over. "The Eight-five over there. Climb aboard."

"Which I did," I told Turner. "Can't say it felt good. To be doing that again. Deja vu kinda thing. Didn't I do something like that in some other life? Well, here we go again. Oh boy, talk about being plunged right back into it. The heat, the dust, a free taxi service through hell. And there—oh my—coming at me suddenly as if in a dream—there they were! Steve and Friar Tuck. Walking along in front of the second platoon tracks. On that God forsaken road. Minesweeping. The . . . Ah, so *this* is what you guys've been up to, where you've been, while I . . . . Out here on the Cambodian border. 'Steve!' I shout, waving my arms as they approach. 'Friar Tuck!' They can't hear me over the roar of the engines. I try again. This time they look up and see me waving. 'Allie? Is that you? Where the fuck you been?' And as they pass us, going the other way, first them, then the different crews . . . the platoon has changed. I don't recognize half them—well—it's hard to recognize anyone anyway, covered with dust as they are . . . everyone looks as if they're wearing masks.

"'Thank you, thank you very much, I very much appreciate it,

Specialist . . . Alexander is it?' Captain Jacobs thanked me profusely—much to my relief. I mean he didn't say—as I must admit I was afraid he might . . . of course I was afraid he'd tell me I had to stay out there; but no, not even close. 'Make yourself at home,' he said. 'Go visit your friends, have a few beers and you can fly back to base camp in the morning. Chopper'll come in an' leave—well—be ready to leave right after breakfast. Thanks again for bringing this out to me.'

"Oh man. It was good to see everyone again. I spent the night on the perimeter drinking beer and talking. It had been rough out there. But for the past few days it had been eerily quiet. Was something going on? Everybody had been bonding over all the bad shit that had been going down, so I kind of felt left out. Even my best pals, those I'd been closest to seemed distant.

"Oh well, fuck it! It's not like I'd gotten malaria on purpose. At any rate, morning came and I was up near the mess tent; near the LZ where my chopper would come and remove me from that awful place, in—well, let's see—according to Captain Jacobs, in a half hour or so. Fine breakfast, Ron. That's one thing, even in the remotest, most fucked up places the Army often manages to serve up some decent chow. Such was the case out there on the Cambodian border on the morning of January 31. Pancakes, eggs—over easy thank you—toast and jam, hash browns, bacon, sausage, OJ, coffee . . . I took my tray over and as I was chowing down, stuffing my face with all that good food (while waiting for my helicopter to come get me), a friend of mine was playing the latest Beatles album on his battery-run record player. 'You gotta hear this, Allie. I mean it's a whole new sound, bro. They 'as all on somethin' during this recording session I do believe. See what ya think.' You heard it, Ron? So you know what I'm talkin' about? Okay, so I'm listening, looking around—oh yes, we are definitely out in the middle a nowhere—and some guy runs out of the command tent yelling, 'Saigon's been hit, Saigon's been hit.' Say what? What the fuck's he talking about, Saigon's been hit? Is this a joke? Then he starts moving his hands up and down, yelling, 'Saddle up, everyone saddle up, we're moving out.'

"But wait a sec. Hold on. I have a chopper to catch. What the fuck am I supposed to do? Everyone's running around like chickens with their heads cut off. The cooks're taking down the mess tent. The command track crew's packing up. I'm just standing there watching. Wondering what to do. Wandering around like a lost child. Which I damn sure the fuck was. I saw a sergeant barking out orders and went over and asked him what I should do. 'Is the morning chopper still coming in?' I asked and he looked at me like I was crazy. "Ain't no choppers comin' in, son. Not here. Not sure if ya noticed, but everyone's pullin' out. Look'—a brief moment of compassion?—'I don't know what your problem is, who you're assigned to, what track'r'vehicle yer supposed t'be on, but I'd highly recommend, fer the time bein' anyway, that you find yerself someone t'hitch a ride with.'

"Which I did. Hitched a ride with Tex and his crew on the Two-eight. All night, Ron, the whole fucking regiment. From Loc Ninh up there on the Cambodian border to . . . to that POW camp the gooks tried to overrun just outside of Bien Hoa. Dead gooks, hundreds of them, their bodies . . . body parts scattered all over the place. Got pretty far though I must say. Up to the fence. Could hardly breathe. I mean nothing like rotting corpses to . . . In that fucking heat? Then we came here. To this lovely spot.

"Anyway, sorry I lashed out at you. It was uncalled for. And for what?—doing me a favor? But you know what? Truth be told, I'd a been sent back out here anyway. Probably would've flown out with you on the same chopper."

* * *

Holy shit! Here we go again; the tangtangtang of AK fire against my guard shield.

I jumped down inside the back of the Two-five and started firing my sixty—ah yes. There I was again, reaching down and grabbing belts of ammo, then loading, cocking and firing—as I banged out ten and twenty round bursts, I remember thinking, this is a city street I'm on, we're fighting in the middle of a city, and suddenly felt nostalgic for the good ol' days, when coming under attack meant being shot at from someone hiding behind trees or brush or a paddy dike; or having tracer rounds arching up at me, or rockets being launched so that I knew where to fire back. Receiving rocket and machine gun fire from somewhere inside one or several of the two-story buildings lining both sides of the street (behind me? In front of me?), added a frightening new dimension.

Street fighting. Probably in the northwestern part of Saigon. Up near the Phu Tho Race Track? Very possibly. I know this now. In retrospect. But I didn't then. All I knew was that I was back out there again, fighting . . . In and around Saigon, Long Bien, and Bien Hoa.

Obviously I didn't know at the time how much I'd been swept up in history. One moment I was through with the war, finishing my tour at base camp; and the next . . . there I was firing at windows and roof tops and doorways. Swept up in history?

I know now that what had just gone down on the morning of January 31, 1968, while I was eating breakfast and listening to the Beatles latest album out there on the Cambodian border (January 31 being the first day of the Lunar New Year called TET), main force NVA/VC units launched a major, coordinated, go-for-broke assault against the major U.S. military installations across South Vietnam. It was a rude awakening, not just for the usually rear echelon, got-it-made-in-the-shade U.S. troops who woke up that morning to the—what-the-fuck's-*that*?—sound of gunfire and 122 millimeter rockets exploding all around them, but to the people at home as well. And, of course, to the generals who, caught up in their wishful thinking—oh yes, we are kicking some serious butt over there in Southeast Asia, they'd been proclaiming, remember?—in the midst of all that fake optimism and reassurance (or maybe they really did believe all that crap; believed in their own fraud so to speak), hadn't seen it coming. But Mom and Dad, Lee and Sue, the Adams, Kellers, McGraws, my aunts, uncles and cousins . . . what were they thinking when they woke up February 1 and learned that, oh my God, all hell had broken loose over there. Just when we find out that Rick has pretty much made it, appears to be home free . . . wonder how these latest developments will affect him?

Mightily. Mightily. Couldn't Giap have waited another two months before trying to pull off such a foolhardy maneuver? Come on, man, did you have to launch your attack *right then*? While I . . . ?

Ah, those days. Fighting. In those streets. Eleventh Cav to the rescue.

Fascinating reading about it now; how we charged from Loc Ninh and Lai Khe to join the fighting around Saigon, Bien Hoa, and Long Bien. Let's see. What happened? The main body of attacking V.C. units was forced out of Bien Hoa and Long Bien and fled two miles north to a place called Ho Nai. As I'm checking this out on a map I'm visualizing where we were and hearing the sounds of battle; the cries for medic after an explosion; I'm watching the L-tee requested gunships firing rockets into a building from which the rocket that blew Double Deuce's insides out and flipped it over was launched; I'm looking through a fog of cordite at the destroyed building, which was nothing but rubble now, and then at the Two-seven as Double Deuce's two wounded gunners and dead T.C. are being loaded into the back.

Okay, what else? After withstanding a massive ground attack by the V.C., the Eleventh Cav, Ninth Infantry Division, and 199th Light Infantry Brigade forced the enemy out of Ho Nai and in the process killed nine hundred enemy soldiers, wiping out the Fifth V.C. Division that had apparently tried to overrun Long Bien.

All over Vietnam shit was happening as the NVA/VC came out of hiding to fight. Disconcerting and shocking to American generals as this was, it was also embarrassing because they hadn't seen it coming. For the duration of the war the American people would never believe another word they said. Oh, the war's going fine now? We've got them on the run? We're killing them left and right? Fuck you! You're nothing but a bunch of fucking liars, an incompetent bunch at that; nonetheless, ironically, strategically, what happened during Tet was what most American brass had been hoping for and dreaming about since that whole mess over there had started-- suddenly fighting the little bastards on America's terms, not theirs. By abandoning their successful hit-and-run tactics for a General Lee, go for broke, Pickett's charge type strategy, Giap had given the U.S. military a chance to kill more enemy soldiers than they'd ever dreamed of. Oh sure, Americans suffered heavy casualties during Tet and the following seven weeks: 4,114 Americans were killed, 19,285 were wounded, and 604 were lost. From a military perspective (in the short run anyway; regarding the battles that were fought during Tet), the U.S. not only won, but won overwhelmingly; decisively. Oh yeah, make no mistake, after those initial attacks where cooks and border guards and embassy and hospital workers were killed, the U.S. military came back and kicked some serious butt; the enemy was decimated; it had been like shooting fish in a barrel. Most frustrating for American soldiers prior to Tet had been their inability to find the enemy. Now they'd found them. And had acted accordingly. But at home; back in the good old U.S. of A, having been caught with its pants down (after all the bragging the generals had been doing about how well the war was going—oh yeah, the winning hearts and minds and S&D (Search and Destroy) strategies are working just fine, another year and . . . . But being caught so utterly and completely unawares did not sit too well with the American people. Now tell me? How in the world were the NVA/VC able to . . ? How'd this happen, they were asking. What could have been a welcome turning point in the war for the Americans ended up being a victory for the NVA/VC. We *did* have the gooks on the run; had destroyed a good portion of them and were in the process of flushing out any who were left. Inadvertently, of course, Giap's strategy had failed miserably. He thought the South Vietnamese would rally around his attacking troops causing an uprising against the Americans, but they didn't, and he lost most of his fighting forces. Yet, Tet had broken the will of the American people. Public opinion became: Get the Hell Out of There. *Now*. We can't win. It ain't worth it.

Wow! 4,114 Americans killed during Tet; 19,285 wounded?

Among those killed was—I don't even remember his name. But I can see his face. Oh yeah. I'll call him Gary because he was a tough street kid (or so he fancied himself) from Gary, Indiana. While wandering around inside the Green Beret compound we were camped at I came across several damaged tracks that had been pulled into our troop's motor pool and were lined up next to each other. Most of the tracks were burned out wreckages ready for the junk pile because noticeably unsalvageable, but two of them seemed perfectly fine; I couldn't figure out what was wrong with them, what they were doing there. Then I saw. And my heart sank. There were holes, perfectly round un-frayed holes the size of a silver dollar in the sides of each of the driver's compartments. Let's see, the Three-five and . . . and the One-eight. Third and First platoons. I didn't know who the drivers were and didn't want to know, just that they'd bought it big time. Remember? If you don't hear the explosion—which these two obviously hadn't (they'd probably heard a popping noise—as the rocket was launched from a doorway, or roof top, or window, and then that horrible "I'm coming to get one of you" whooshing sound; but not the explosion; their fellow Deltas had heard that and thought, whew! Not me. Once again I escaped and lived to fight another day.

Later, I ran into someone I'd known at Fort Knox and he informed me that one of the Deltas who'd been killed was the guy I'm calling Gary. Gary had told me once, before we came over (while we were sitting at a bar in Louisville), that he didn't want to get too physically messed up in the war; maybe lose an eye, come home wearing a patch. Yeah, man, wow, cool. Jeez, guess that's why the Army likes to get 'em young. Wounded, battle weary vet returning to the streets of Gary, Indiana with a black patch covering one of his eyes; telling war stories to his steel worker pals. But it didn't turn out that way, did it? Instead he ended up . . . .

That night—the night after I found out that Gary was the Delta of one of the stricken tracks I'd come across; that it was *his* body that had been splattered all over the inside of Three-five's driver's compartment, I got good and drunk at the Green Beret's NCO Club and must have not completely passed out because I remember being kicked in the stomach and chest as I was lying out in the rain near the club's entrance and hearing an angry voice say, "Someone needs t'remove this piece a garbage so we don't keep tripping over it." Steve informed me the next morning as I was recovering from undoubtedly the worst hangover I've ever had (and that mean, bad ass sun coming up from behind those hills too?—its powerful rays banging against my already pounding, aching head? Fuck!); Steve told me as I sat up on my cot slowly, moving my body as little as possible so I wouldn't have to move my head any more than I had to, that if Friar Tuck and he hadn't lifted me up and gotten me the hell out of there when they did—"just in the nick a time"—several Green Berets who were not at all pleased to have their watering hole temple desecrated by the likes of some non-elite, rank and file motherfucker like myself (what? They never got drunk and passed out?) were fixin' on (oh yeah, you could tell by the look in their eyes) opening their flies and peeing on my sorry, drunken ass, or possibly even doing me bodily harm. "Jesus, man," Steve said, watching me sympathetically (not like he'd never been there himself), "can I fix you an oyster sandwich? How bout, les see if I cen rustle up some ham'n'lima beans for ya. You prefer I heat em up, er you jus' wanna eat em cold outa the can?"

Less than four months from my drunken outing just outside of

Bien Hoa I was pissing off Green Berets once again after I'd had too much to drink—this time as I was being introduced to a former Green Beret named Dan Blass at a party in Boulder, Colorado. "Dan, this is my friend Rick," Dave, my former college roommate, said, and then as Dan and I were shaking hands (Dave had explained how we'd each just gotten back from Vietnam) and as soon as Dave mentioned that Dan had been a Green Beret over there, I looked Dan in the eyes and said, "Oh yeah? We used to piss and shit on guys like you."

Bad move. Next thing I knew I was waking up on the floor and Dave and Larry were kneeling next to me, saying, "you alright? You alright?" And as Dave's and Larry's faces were coming into focus, Dave said, "Jesus Christ. What the fuck's the matter with you, anyway? You have a death wish?" Realizing Dan was standing nearby, watching and listening, Dave held back on telling me what a bad motherfucker Dan was and how I was lucky to be alive. Later though, he said, "Wow man, you be fuckin' with the wrong dude. Sayin' shit like that to Dan Blass, I mean, come on, Rick, what were you thinking? That motherfucker eats nails for breakfast; he snacks on jugular veins. You're lucky he didn't reach in an' pull your heart out.

But all that was a myth. Not that Dan couldn't defend himself in extraordinary ways. (Green Berets were among the best, most highly trained soldiers in the world, their reputation for *getting it done* intact.) If he'd wanted to, Dan could've caused me grievous harm (rather than just cold cock me and knock me out), but he was a good guy. Later that evening—out on the back porch away from everyone else—he apologized to me and then confided that as anxious as he was to get back home after two years (he'd completed two thirteen-month tours in Nam) that whole world he'd left behind (this world he'd come back to) had changed; turned upside down and he often found himself wishing he was back fighting in the jungle again. (Fucked up as that was, he understood it, this world he'd come back to? He no longer had a clue.) That very statement, "don't fuck with me I'm a Green Beret bad ass"—along with being a former linebacker for the University of Colorado football team, made him a kind of celebrity among certain kinds of guys, the wow! That is one bad motherfucker. How come you didn't bring me back any ears types; but that returning warrior with a macho profile wasn't cutting it so well on college campuses in the spring of 1968; especially with babes. There weren't too many young women dying to get to know and cuddle up to what they perceived to be a stone killer. Guys like myself back from Vietnam—having gone over and done God knows what in many young women's eyes—were being shunned anyway; but to have been a Green Beret over there made you even more of a pariah than I was.

Dan was crying by the end of the evening. I'd only just started on this precarious "why don't you just go back on over there where you belong" path, but already I knew what he was talking about. I could feel it already; peoples' indignant, disapproving eyes on me.

Truth was a college town like Boulder—not a place to go back to after being over there.

At any rate, Dan and I became good friends; and as we talked and I got to know him I had a pretty good feel for what kind of a soldier he'd been, how he'd conducted himself over there, and it was the absolute opposite of that asshole psychopath who in an attempt to do some soldierly bonding with me ten years later turned to me as we were sitting at a bar after work and said, "I don't know if you were into the kill thing when you were over there, but . . . "No," I said. Remember? No, no, no! I *wasn't* and neither was my friend Dan.

The street fighting lasted only three weeks and then we were back operating in jungles and rice paddies again. Like I said before, the NVA/VC had fucked up big time, their frontal assaults all over South Vietnam had been a Pickett's charge type disaster. Yes, in the long run, the assaults had broken the will of the American people to continue fighting. Enough already. But Giap hadn't known that yet. He wouldn't until years later when it became clear that his go-for-broke strategy marked the beginning of the end for the U.S. in terms of the U.S. actually winning the war. For the time being, however—with yours truly back in action (Giap having totally fucked up the latter part of my tour with his reckless shenanigans. What? You couldn't wait two more months to pull that shit?)—the NVA/VC were on the run, in tails-between-their-legs fashion; during their withdrawal, however, they made it mighty clear that our continuing to chase them and try to weed them out, which we did, would be costly. And it was. Back to their old-hit-and run ways. Except a month or so after Tet they were no longer doing much hitting; they were mostly hiding. And in trying to track them down and flush them out we kept setting off the mines and booby traps they'd planted during their withdrawal.

If I'd kept a journal during those last few months I may very well have recorded the following:

February 21. A left gunner again. Riding on the back flap. Of Two-five now. Tex the T.C. He's okay; a little full of himself. So near and yet so far: 58 days until my wake-up. I just want to know. Am I going to make it or not? Be killed or—

well—not killed? Go home whole or . . . what? Riding on the back flap. Day dreaming. Sun beating down. I feel like a zombie.

February 23. Some new guy keeps bugging me to get high with him. Says he has some great stuff. "Come on, man," he says, "let me open your doors." "Go away," I tell him. "Dee dee! Dee dee mau!"

(Smoking. Let's forget for a moment taking long, soulful hits on whatever exotic Southeast Asian weed was being offered on a particular day; the highly recommended, "knock your socks off," elephant grass that that hippie dippy newbie was trying to get me to open my doors with; let's for the moment forget about "getting high" and talk about that most sacrosanct of rituals performed by soldiers, cigarette smoking. As far as I could tell I was one of the few soldiers in our platoon; (what am I saying?) in the regiment; the Army; the whole fucking Armed Services—who didn't smoke; who gave away his weekly ration of cigs. And that's why, as I've been describing myself going about my daily activities as a soldier: cleaning weapons; sitting inside the turret or a bunker on guard duty; burning shit; peeing or taking a dump, I haven't mentioned having a lit cigarette dangling from my lips, my head tilted slightly and squinting to keep the smoke from getting in my eyes. I haven't mentioned all those gestures associated with smoking; lighting up; taking long, soulful drags; flicking away the butts, because—well—I didn't smoke. Okay, so, was I the only soldier over there who *didn't* smoke, you ask? No, I wasn't. Simon, Hank, and Sergeant Morrison didn't smoke either. Can you believe that? A whole track crew of non-smokers? Purely coincidental, however. I wasn't asked if I preferred to be on a smoking or non-smoking track in case you're wondering.

With respect to getting high—other than by consuming too much beer—I'm glad I missed the last few years of the war when drugs like heroin became popular. As for myself; I didn't start smoking grass until I got home. But that was short lived. One morning completely sober, not high on anything, I ran out of a classroom when I imagined that the head of the guy sitting in front of me had exploded. It scared me. I figured if I could have hallucinations like that when I wasn't high, what kinds of things would I imagine happening around me when I was? So I stopped.)

February 26. Steve just found out that the baby girl that he thought was his isn't his at all. Poor guy. He was so excited too. Proud. I have a daughter. Me. A little girl. I'm not clear about who told him. He just put in for a hardship leave but the L-tee says even though he'll sign off on it he won't get it. Army's afraid if he went back home now he'd kill someone. Which is true.

Third platoon lost another track. Set off a mine. T.C. thrown out of the turret and killed. Driver died while being dusted off. Gunners made it, but I know how that goes. God knows what they're struggling with in some hospital. As for me, I'm never going to leave this place, am I? This is it, isn't it? I'm going to be here forever.

March 5. Minesweeping. This new guy and me. Showin' him the ropes. What's there to show? You listen for that beep. Then dig carefully. Hoping, hoping all the while that the mine you think you've detected isn't one that can be command detonated. If it is—oh well—see ya! I made it pretty far over here didn't I Mom and Dad? Further than most.

March 14. Night ambush. Along with—among six other platoon members—a guy named Lewis Von Raider, a new crew member who feels compelled to tell me how he enjoys fucking his brother's wife. He has an unusual dick when it's hard, he says, not very long but wide (with respect to the circumference I guess he means) and his sister-in-law digs that. Well, now, thank you for sharing that with me, Lew. Lew keeps falling asleep when it's his turn to be awake and each time I shake him, tell him what a worthless piece of shit he is, he opens his eyes and looks at me and says, "you're right, Allie, I am a worthless piece a shit, aren't I? Jeopardizing the safety of my fellow patrol members, I should be shot right here. You should fucking shoot me." And then he closes his eyes and goes back to sleep.

It's true you get so dog tired you can't help yourself and in that dog tired state it's like, fuck it. Come get me. If there's anyone out there wants to come slit my throat, go ahead feel free. We all get that way. And have to fight it. But to be that way right off the bat? I guess he figures that since I'm so short—hell, I'm down to what now? 33 and a wake-up?—I'm always going to be awake and take care of anything that happens.

March 19. Two-nine set off a mine this morning. Same old shit. You hear the blast and look over and all you see is dust. Then the dust settles and—oh boy, here we go again. The track's been flipped over. It was lying on its side this time. Medic! Medic! No KIAs but the three crew members who were blown off the track are in rough shape.

(Higgins, the left gunner on Two-three received a silver star for his "heroic actions" that day; for—you ready for this?—going inside the back of Two-nine and helping the driver crawl out the back before the track blew; before it burst into flames. But wait a sec. Hold on. It wasn't *going* to blow. Why? Because finally, *finally* our tracks had diesel engines in them; the fuel tanks were filled with diesel fuel. So going in to help the driver was nice and all, but a silver star? At home, telling about it, Higgins no doubt talked up his seemingly courageous actions to the hilt, leaving out the fact that that track he'd entered would not have blown in a million years.

Just before we returned to the south a friend of mine who'd incurred a barely discernable cut on his arm from a piece of shrapnel (I'll allow that it was a piece of shrapnel that had barely nicked the surface of his skin during a recent fire fight, though there was no way of being sure), stood proudly at attention during an awards ceremony and received (along with fellow Echo Troop members who weren't there; a dozen or so who'd been seriously wounded; among them, Simmons who'd been paralyzed and several KIAs being honored posthumously): a purple heart. "You've gotta be kiddin' me," I told him prior to the ceremony, "You're actually going to stand up there and have them pin a purple heart on you?" He was at home by the time the diesel tracks arrived and I could picture him embellishing how he'd won his award. As long as his enthralled audience didn't ask him to show them his scar, right? If he ever ran for office he could mention that he'd been wounded, his campaign manager could say he was a highly decorated Vietnam veteran who'd spilled his blood for his country, and it all made me feel kind of nauseous. But when Higgins was awarded the silver star for—however the citation reads: entering the back of an armored personnel carrier that had struck a mine blah, blah, blah, risking his own life in order to blah, blah, blah—I had a change of heart concerning Clay's receiving a purple heart. Sure, in my mind I watched Clay standing in that formation in the drizzling rain; saw the teensy weensy cut—no more than a blemish for God's sake—that he had received his purple heart for; but I also saw Hank and him crawling into the back of double deuce way back when, to help Harvey after double deuce set off a mine and flipped over onto its back. "Holy fucken Jesus,' I remember Wiggs saying as he watched them, "get the fuck outa there. That motherfucker's gonna blow." Simmons had told Wiggs and me to stay put and man our machine guns, which we'd done (otherwise we would have been right in there ourselves risking our lives). I think. I hope. Look, nobody ever knows what they're going to do in such situations, how they're going to react. It just happens, but I remember saying to myself as Harvey first, then Clay, then Hank were climbing out the back, "hurry, hurry"—we all expected that any second it would blow—and I thought of how other platoon members had crawled into the back to help when they could, never thinking for a moment of the consequences, of those trapped inside when a track burst into flames and no one was able to go in and pull them out before they were incinerated.

March 22. Worst assignment yet. By far. Please, please make them stop. Please. I can't take it anymore. Send me out on ambush. Minesweeping detail. How about a call out where we pull out in the middle of the night and go help someone who's come under heavy fire. Fuck. I can't take it. Why am I being tortured like this? The noise. That ear-splitting noise. Every ten seconds. The gun on the left or the one on the right. I'm going insane. Make them stop. Please.

March 30. Murphy left the field and went back to base camp yesterday. Why him and not me? Our wake-ups are almost exactly the same. Mousy, who's supposed to leave soon also, informed me this afternoon that he re-upped; signed on for another year of this shit. What? After all your talk? "Yeah," he told me, "when it came right down to it I got nothin' goin' at home. All that shit I been tellin' you, it's all a bunch a lies. Look at me, Allie. Yer one a the few guys I can talk to. Who listens to me. Face it, man, I'm a fuckin' loser. Least at home I am. Here? I don't know. I'm gonna miss you Allie." (Mousy, fucking Mousy. First time I saw him was way back there on Hill 58. Simmons and I looked over and saw this new guy standing behind the Two-one.

"Jesus, man, who the fuck's *that*?" I said. "That scrawny dude with the rodent-like features. And what's with the Australian bush hat and all, the tiger uniform?"

Just some strange looking dude who didn't have a whole lot going for him. Who I admittedly detested at first. But he grew on me; grew on all of us.

"Hey Mousy, m'man, heard you guys had a rough one out there on ambush last night?"

"Yup. Shore did. Got hit hard, man. Gooks everywhere. They 'as comin' at us left an' right. Ended up havin' t'fix bayonets."

"Well'd'ya kill a bunch?"

"Oh, a big roger on that. We 'as stackin' em up fer sure. Fifty, sixty I'd say. Found ourselves in an NVA stronghold."

"Well, I'm glad ya made it back safe."

I got a letter from Steve after I got home updating me on all the latest. After giving me a rundown—the Second Squadron had left the Saigon area and was back up on the Cambodian border; my friend Ron Taylor, the guy who I'd scolded for bringing my belongings out to the field at the beginning of Tet had been killed—a mine. What else? After telling me all that and several other things I don't remember, he wrote, "oh, and by the way, your buddy Mousy's gone. He just left one day, slipped out into the jungle and didn't come back. That makes him a deserter, I guess. Figured living in Saigon or some village with some gook broad and having all his needs taken care of that way—'Mousy stay with Li. No go back'—was a far sight better than what he could hope for in America. I wish him the best."

Seven years from then—during the communist takeover of South Vietnam in the spring of 1975—I thought of Mousy and wondered if he was still over there. As I watched the fall of Saigon on the news, I imagined him hiding in some room in an alley in Saigon; or living secretly in some village; or had he been captured or killed? Was he holed away in a prison cell somewhere?

April 3. This is getting ridiculous. Ten days to go and I'm still out in the field, still going out on missions; night ambushes. Have they forgotten about me?

* * *

Finally, when I got down to eight days, eight and a wake up (so fucking short I was practically invisible), I ambled my weary, worried ass over to the command track and informed the CO of my predicament. He was new so it was perfectly understandable that he might not have known that one of his troop members had gotten so "short" and was still in the field.

"Really? That's unacceptable," I thought he'd say, all the while checking the name on my fatigue shirt to see who this soldier was who was supposed to have been back at base camp twenty days ago, so he could go ahead and tell one of his aides to make damn well sure I was on the next chopper out of there. Had it been any of the COs preceding him, Captain McNulty, or Johnson, or Jacobs that would've been the case. But *this* mother fucker? Maybe it was because I was a foot taller than him, that he only came up to my chest (he was a motherfucking runt) that he dismissed me so summarily, sent me back to my track quicker than the time it took for him to look into my weary, pleading eyes and determine that he didn't want to be bothered by such a trivial matter. "Eight days," he said flippantly. "What's the rush? Sounds to me like you've got yourself a whole buncha time before your plane leaves."

It was a conspiracy. First Giap, and then this fucking clown. I'm going to be here forever, I thought. I'm never leaving.

"Don't do it, Allie," Steve cautioned me—he'd seen me walk over to the command track and knew what was going on inside me—"Don't! Put it down. It ain't worth it. He's only just beginning, so there's a good chance he's gonna get his anyway. Without you. An' that way you don't need t'spend the rest a yer days in a prison cell. Be holed up in Leavenworth or some such place. Fuck em. Few more days an' you'll be outa here. *Gone*, Jack. Ridin' home on that freedom bird. Headed for the world. That's all that matters. Let someone else frag his sorry ass."

Fortunately I took Steve's advice. Remembered—yet again—my ABC's. Two days later, one of the new T.C.s heard of my plight and, from what I was told later by a witness, read Captain Dickhead the riot act. "Six days? This guy's supposed to go home in six days and he's still out here? What does this say about us? This is what we have to look forward to? Maybe getting zapped with only . . . ?"

I was on a helicopter to base camp the next morning.

15.
How Would You Like Your Steak?

Before I boarded the helicopter I said my goodbyes. "Take it slow Steve," I said, thinking of all the shit we'd been through together; how one night when we were on night ambush I'd reached over and touched him to make sure he was still there; that I wasn't sitting out there in the dark all by my wee little lonesome. "What the fuck're you doin'?" he grabbed my arm and pushed it away.

"You there?" I said.

"Am I *here*? Course I'm here. Where the fuck else would I be? An' lay offa my dick."

"Your dick?"

"Yeah, my dick, my cock, you grabbed . . . ."

"I didn't grab . . . ."

"Yes you did, you . . . ."

"Hey, I like you, man. I have special feelings for you."

Flashing in my head also as I looked into Steve's eyes was the time we both had to look away from Staley's twitching, mutilated body after he'd set off a mine.

Friar Tuck was kneeling on the ground behind the Two-four cleaning his sixty. He stood up looking at me and I looked at him and we both just shook our heads. "Yer gettin' there," I said shaking his hand, and then we hugged. "Write and let me know what's happening back there in the world," he said.

"I will," I told him and then I walked over and said goodbye to Nelson and Eason, and then to Carlton and Tex, and then I was sitting inside the chopper waving to my friends, and they were waving back and, wow! Was this really it? Was it really happening?

At base camp while you're waiting for your actual orders—"don't worry, they'll be here," the troop clerk tells you. But you want to see them, actually lay your eyes on them to make sure. Meanwhile you walk around taking everything in, remembering what this huge, sprawling camp looked like when you first arrived there the year before. Over there—where that wooden barracks is now—that's where the tent you found Finlay in was; him lying there on that cot sweating, asking you if you'd mind showing him your dick. Had you going there, didn't he? You remember Harvey giving you the low down on this strange individual, who became one of your best friends, then recall Finlay saying, months later, "little more dust, please," as sitting in a field where the two of you had plopped yourselves down as the supply chopper was taking off, you each mixed the quarter inch of dust that had settled on your mashed potatoes and gravy and tough-as-leather roast beef and peas around with them, then shoveled the gritty concoction hungrily into your mouths.

And you, of course, walk by the mess hall, a wooden structure where the mess tent used to be, outside of which you'd taken one of those many deep breaths and sighs and said to yourself, "what have I done? What have I fucking done? I'm not ready for this." And you weren't. And then you think of Hank, the Ross element, the Defiant One and how right over there as you were going through the chow line—he was on K.P., serving—he looked you up and down like you were the sorriest looking individual he'd ever seen and said, "who'n the fuck're you?" and then tried to stare you down, but you wouldn't let him, you stared right back, and then he said, "stay away from me. Hear? I don't want no motherfuckin' newbie within ten feet a me. Understood?" And Harvey who was standing behind you said, "Come on, Hank, lighten up. This here's . . ." And he explained who you were—well—where you were from, that you'd trained at Fort Knox and knew recon—but Hank wasn't hearing any of it. You were a sorry-ass new guy until you'd proven otherwise.

"I made it, Hank," you say to yourself, imagining him sitting in a bar in L.A., downing shots, or carving meat in a butcher shop. "I made it," you tell him, "just like you. And with a little more luck I'll be stateside within a week."

Your orders come. Matt hands you a copy. You keep staring at it. You imagine—as you have been for the past year—the freedom bird that will be leaving the states soon to come get you, and as you watch it flying in and landing and then taxiing on the runway and stopping in front of the terminal where you and two hundred other soldiers will be waiting to come out and board it, you hear your name being called and look up and see Sergeant Hammond walking toward you. Okay, you think, what the fuck're *you* doing here? Other than to harass and make my last few days here miserable?

But ah, that's exactly why he *was* there. Okay, maybe the CO hadn't put him in charge of the rear; assigned him to Echo Troop's head house-cat position right around the same time you'd received your orders for going home just so he could do some last minute messing with you; possibly even get you killed or wounded. Maybe that wasn't the true purpose of having him removed from the field when he was (and being in the rear was the perfect place for him); nonetheless. . . .

"When're ya leavin'?" he asks as he's approaching you.

"Shortly."

"When. Exactly." He glances at the folded paper in your hand. "That your orders?"

You open the paper and hand it to him.

"Let's see," he studies it excitedly with his squinty, bloodshot eyes. He, like the CO, comes up to only your chest, which makes him uncomfortable you can tell. He hates you. Ever since you were a sergeant and he ordered your crew members to do something—you don't even remember what it was—and you waved your hands in front of them telling them to stop. "No way. No way in hell. I don't care what that mother fucker told you to do, I'm ordering you to not do it." Yeah. You and he didn't exactly hit it off. And now, here he is, he has a chance to get even. Have the last say. He looks at you, same way he did—where was that? Out on the Batangan? Or . . . Who the fuck cares. You wish you could just put a bullet in the motherfucker's head. Put him out of his misery. Put everyone who has to deal with him out of their misery.

"April 19 is your DEROS," he says. "And it's . . . Says 'ere yer s'posed t'be in Long Bien by the seventeenth. So you've got . . . you've got two days soldier until. . . . "

When he sees that you didn't report to your assignment—did he really think you would? I guess so—he reminds you of where you're supposed to be and you look him right in the eye—just like you did way back when, wherever it was, he was giving your crew a hard time—and tell him to go fuck himself. "Go ahead, report me," you say. "Write me up. Do what ya gotta do. Let me know how you make out."

"Wait a sec," you can hear voices lashing out at him. "Let me get this straight," even your asshole CO would've been on his case (if for no other reason, self-preservation; to keep from losing his command over promoting such foolishness), "you assigned a soldier who was down to less than seventy-two hours to convoy duty? To ride shot gun in one of Gulf Troop's deuce and a half's? Do you believe for a moment that the L-tee in charge of the convoy—or any of the soldiers on that convoy—would've allowed a trooper who'd gotten so short that he was counting down by the hour to go on such a dangerous assignment?"

Oh, the look on his face when after you'd had your little say you calmly strolled back to your barrack. But until you'd gotten out of there, had actually left base camp; even as you were hanging out at the 90th Replacement Company in Long Bien, waiting for your plane to arrive, you couldn't shake your gnawing—*now where in the hell d'ya think* yer *goin' there soljer?*—sense of foreboding that still plagues you to this day; that plagued you all through the sacred going home process, then even after you got home; while taking one of those nice, long, hot showers you'd been looking forward to, letting the water pour soothingly over you; over your head and neck and shoulders; while sitting at the counter in Jake's Diner enjoying breakfast; eggs (*three*, over easy, please), bacon, hash browns, toast (rye), coffee (black), fresh squeezed orange juice (oh my) before setting out for your 10:00 class. "You know, Murph," you say as the two of you are sitting at the bar drinking beer in the NCO Club the night before you leave base camp, "it's like ever since I was given—the *nod*—so to speak, told I could go, it's like, you remember those gangster shows, the *Untouchables* and what not? Well, there's always some low-on-the-totem-pole-type dude, some flunky sonavabitch who's been naughty, right? Broken a gangster code of some sort, some rule—betrayed the organization—and he's being brought into a room by a couple of thugs to meet with one of the crime bosses.

Frank Nitty, maybe. Remember him? And as the—betrayer I'll call him—dude who probably got caught with his hand in the till, cookin' the books, screwing the boss's wife or girlfriend . . . as he gets down on his hands and knees and apologizes, begs forgiveness for whatever he's done, tries to persuade Mr. Nitty or whoever is standing over him to spare his life, they're consoling him, telling him, 'it's okay, don't worry, we all make mistakes, just don't let it happen again.' Meanwhile, as Mr. Nitty is talking to the guy, he's also running his hand back and forth on top of the guy's head, patting him comfortingly on the shoulder . . . as he's assuring the guy that everything's going to be alright, he's also indicating to the two thugs standing over in the corner watching him—by pointing his head their way and raising his eyebrows—to, as soon as he's finished consoling this poor slob, right after he's through placating the sorry bastard, take him out and . . . ."

Murph looks at you. You look at him. This guy . . . from that other life. You gaze into each other's eyes. Smart dude, Murph. No question. Uneducated, but smart. Way he picked up on the whole mortar launching routine. "Go back to school," you tell him, "study math. You're a whiz."

Flashes. Of all the things that have happened.

You reminisce. "Remember the time Harvey got drunk and fell off the ferry?"

"Oh yeah. Out there on the Batangan, when . . . oh jeez, I remember looking out over the South China Sea after. . . following one of those fire fights and thinking, we've only just begun. That was when I said, 'fuck it,' with regards to marking off days on a calendar. Too depressing. Oh great, down to—what? Two hundred seventy-three I believe it was; two seventy-three and a wake up. It was already a miracle we'd lasted *that* long. And we still had a lifetime to go?"

You reminisce; take turns telling story after story after story—purposely avoiding some (no need to bring up the time he fired his fifty over your head all night because you'd fucked up on your tread-tension maintenance and one of the treads had flown off); you tell stories—about Hank (oh shit. Lots of stories to tell about that guy) and then talk about what you're going to do when you get home. "First thing I'm gonna do is look up sweet Anne," Murph says, and you picture him combing his long, straight, wet blonde hair the way you'd seen him do a while back when he was getting himself duded up to go on R&R. "What the fuck you doin'?" you asked, watching him in amazement, "trying to be Elvis? And what's with that curly thing you got goin' there, that's hangin' down over your face? Haven't seen the likes a this shit since high school when all the punk ass hoods would take out their combs in front of the mirror in the lavatory during smoke break and do themselves up the same fuckin' way."

"Fuck you, Allie. Yer jus' jealous on accounta that shitty lookin' mat *you* got stuck with up top."

So Murph was going to see sweet Anne. You wished him the best. You would just love to know what he ended up doing; how his life turned out.

Your plan was to go back to Boulder, Colorado, in time for summer school. Which you did. And almost immediately—well—within eight weeks proceeded to lash out hatefully at the world.

You lay on a cot behind the orderly room thinking, I hope nobody changes their mind (but ever mindful that they still might); you lie there the last night—well—the last night at base camp imagining what it's going to be like to . . . wake up and hear birds chirping outside your window; not constantly hearing guns being fired, their rounds exploding off in the distance; not worrying about that tell-tale whistling noise and the accompanying cries of, "Incoming! Incoming!" Especially on *this* night. Remember the mortar round that hit the shit house with two troopers in it a year back? Just a stone's throw—less than that—from where you're lying there counting the hours; down to just hours now. Five, four, three . . .Oh my God it's . . .it's four o'clock. TWO HOURS . . . one hundred and twenty MINUTES until wake up. That mortar round had come hurtling through the air that long-ago morning and struck the latrine and everyone just kept looking at each other when it was over and the dust off had come and taken away what was left of the two unlucky soldiers in body bags and shaking their heads and thinking, when it's your time it's your time. Ain't nothin' you can do about it.

You don't sleep. How can you? Okay, maybe you doze off because you open your eyes and it's . . . it's getting light out. How'd that happen? You wanted to catch everything. You look around; at the mosquito netting surrounding you (this is where the First Sergeant sleeps when he's at base camp, but since he's out in the field Matt tells you to go ahead and use it, why not?); the mosquito netting, the wooden rafters above; the wall to your right; you take it all in. And while Steve or Friar Tuck or Taylor—someone from the 2nd platoon certainly—is opening their eyes and looking around at the other members of the ambush they've been sitting on the ground next to all night (the sky lightening enough for them to see each other); while they're gathering their claymores and whatnot and coming in, you're studying a darkened, warped looking two-by-four, thinking, oh wow! This is it. It's here. Today's the day. And then an hour or so later you're driven by jeep over to the airstrip and flown by your least favorite air transporter, the caribou (because of the noisy, what-the-fuck's-going-on rattle it makes. And then the sinking feeling you have throughout the flight that something catastrophic is happening and you're about to go down) to Ton San Knut Air Base.

Simpson, Bronner, Carlson . . .Watson, Donohue. . . you're all running into each other and hugging and shaking hands like you'd just won the big game, the ultimate prize, which—well—you all obviously had. Carlson and Donohue had been in the same squadron as you, Carlson in Gulf Troop, Donohue Foxtrot. Bronner had been in the First Squadron that stayed back while the Second Squadron was up north. He'd just missed being on the Blackhorse to Long Bien convoy that had been overrun less than a mile from the gate (he'd been on another convoy the day before) and Watson had gotten his wish to be a door gunner. You remember as you're talking to him how you and he had put in for door gunner at the same time.

So, did you wish you'd gotten orders like him? That you'd had the opportunity to experience the war from up above?

No. That would have altered the cards of fate. He'd beaten the odds of however many times gooks had seen him just a sittin' up there firin' that sixty a his and tried to bring him down and had emerged with flying colors; look ma, I'm still here, no worse—physically anyway—for the wear. On the other hand, had he been doing what you had for the past year, odds are great that he wouldn't have been so lucky; that down in the muck and dirt (and all the other shit that was down below where you were) he wouldn't have been able to miraculously avoid one of those mines or booby traps or mortars or rockets or the AK fire like you had. And visa-versa, who's to say that one of those thousands of times you were hovering just above the trees had you been granted your—hmm, that looks kinda cool—wish, that a rocket or rounds from automatic weapon(s) aimed and fired at you from below wouldn't have had yours and your crew members' names on them.

At any rate, all five of you had made it, were standing in almost the same spot in which you'd last seen each other and said, good luck, God's speed and all that; you were all there waiting for that big freedom bird you'd all been dreaming about for a year to come take you out of there because lady luck had favored you for some reason. Any messing around with the deck by taking someone else's assignment; taking turns on K.P. so you didn't have to go out on night ambush; or visa-versa; getting sick or wounded at this time as opposed to that; setting off the one in a hundred million mines that if you hit it would only half go off; being inadvertently thrown back into the fray again when you thought you were done (because that asshole Giap wanted to give a frontal attack strategy a whirl) and things might very well have turned out differently; as they had for Bateman and Clark. And Cruthers. Bateman and Clark, KIAs. Cruthers, paralyzed.

You see their faces—remember them being on training exercises with you at Fort Knox; them standing in formation with you as you all found out what outfit you were going to.

Bateman's and Clark's names you would run your fingers across on the wall at the Vietnam War Memorial.

Cruthers . . . you thought of him then as you think of him now. Paralyzed. He and Hardy and Crawford and Simmons . . . and a whole host of others whose names you've forgotten. But you can see their faces; young, smiling . . . are any of them still alive? You kind of know—there is no way you could possibly *really* know—the sort of life they lived after they were dusted off. Cruthers lent you a rubber—well—*gave* you a rubber at a party in Lexington, Kentucky a month before you left Fort Knox. You and he were amazed that Freelander didn't show up at Oakland. His name was called while all of you were standing in formation and . . . "Wow!" Bronner said as the two of you headed for the warehouse-type building you were staying in, "he really didn't show." He'd said he wasn't going to, but none of you actually believed him. He'd said he was going to Mexico. Is that where he went? And is he still there?

You've forgotten to mention the recruit you met at base camp during those last few days there and how before he headed out to join the troops in the field he gave you a heads-up about returning to the world; gave you advice that coincided with a *Time* magazine article you had read. "Sorry to break it to you like this," the dude had told you, passing on the hard-earned advice that his brother who'd just gotten back from Vietnam had shared with him, "but you wanna get laid when y'all get home. Get yer dick wet? Ya don't say nothin' bout this place over here. Got it? *Nothin'*. Nothin' at all. Zip. Ya make like you was never over here. Like none a this ever happened. Don't wanna feed in to all that negative shit's been goin' on back home. All that negativity bout what most people thinks is goin' on over here. True'r'not, y'all a bunch a killers. Murderers an' rapists an' what not. In the minds a yer average chick. Wanna get in te someone soft's panties, someone with titties an' what not? Become a protestor. An anti-war activist. A fuckin' hippie. Chicks'll be all over yer ass. Won't be able t'keep em away."

In a month or so you will look over at the red-tile roofs of buildings silhouetted against a clear, blue sky. Also silhouetted against the sky, etched across the blue in a jagged line behind the campus and town, will be the Flatiron rocks, and high above the Flatirons, flashing familiarly as it slides across the sky leaving a long, thick, white cloud-like trail behind it, will be the silver streak of a jet. Watching the jet, watching it taking the northern route toward San Francisco as it begins heading over the mountains, you will think of the many times you've looked up squinting from down in some baking hot rice paddy, or while sweating in the steamy heat of a jungle clearing, and seen the similar winking flashes.

You will reach over and pick up a stick. Peeling the loose bark off, you will think, "too small fer stirrin'," and remember Sergeant Hannah explaining the art of burning shit. *Well, ya jus' pour this 'ere diesel in here, see, an' then put a lit match t'it. Simple's that. An' then grab this 'ere stick'n'stir. Ya gotta stir.* Glancing at your feet—your sneakers; *not* jungle boots—you will throw away the stick and recall how the V.C. would coat their pungii sticks with feces so that when a GI set one off, had a sharpened piece of wood suddenly thrust in through the side of his foot (*ouch!*)—the poison shot *straight* into the blood stream.

"That's right," you will mentally shout to a pony-tailed young man walking past you on the lawn, "*straight* into the blood stream. You will watch the dude padding purposefully across the grass; heading . . . heading for *where*? Where you *off* to, dude?—an anti-war rally? That where yer headed. You off to protest the burning of babies? The killing of innocents? All that murder'n'mayhem you hear's goin' on over there? The horrible atrocities, cruel, wrong minded, brain washed, out-of-control maniacs like myself are committin' over there? You goin' t'cheer on the

Viet Cong and North Vietnamese? Chant along with an enthusiastic, off with our heads, audience, *Ho, Ho, Ho Chi Minh, the Viet Cong are gonna win*? "You have *no* idea, m'man. *None.* None at all." The student will glance over at you, and then quickly turn away. "That's *right*," you will shout to yourself, watching the student, imagining what he might be thinking, "I'm just one a them crazy Nam vets y'all've heard about, sitting over here under this tree laughing and talking to myself—so *watch* out!"

Your last night in what was still South Vietnam, you and your Fort Knox buddies attend a concert, in which five or so South Vietnamese men playing in a band, do an extraordinary job of mimicking the Beatles, the Temptations, the Doors, the Rolling Stones, the Animals, and the Young Rascals. One of the songs the band plays as you and your survivor friends sit in the dirt on the side of a small hill watching—the group is performing on a small stage below you—is a rousing rendition of the Animals' *We Gotta Get Outa This Place.* It is, of course, an appropriate song for the moment, a real crowd-pleaser and all two hundred of you lucky, goin' home G.I.s are going hog-ass-wild cheering and singing along. Closing your eyes and listening, you swear, I mean, swear to God, bro, that it's actually Eric Burdon up there working you soldiers into a frenzy and not a scrawny little South Vietnamese man.

You and the two hundred or so soldiers standing in formation are told to go back to your assigned barracks and stay there. "Your plane, gentlemen, could arrive at any time, so be ready to get your asses out here at a moment's notice."

You walk over to your assigned bunk, which is just inside one of the nearby barracks. You've chosen the bunk up top. You take off your black shoes, the ones that go with your khakis. Been a long time since you've worn them. Since—well—R&R. They're covered with dust. At first you say, "Fuck it," but then you take an end of the towel hanging from your bunk and wipe them off. There. Now why in the fuck did you just do that? Not like they're not going to get dusty again. You leave your socks on. Arrange your shoes so you can step into them the moment you climb down from the bed. You imagine yourself doing that. Left foot. Right foot. Perfect. You pull out your shirt tails. Climb up on the top bunk. Look down at your shoes. Already to be stepped into. You glance at your socks that are on each of your two feet. Two of them. Quick body check. Let's see—arms, legs, hands, fingers . . . Nothing missing. Nothing. How'd *that* happen? You lay back. Prop your head on a pillow. Glance up at the ceiling. Think of where you are. What you're doing. Eleven months ago you lay on a top bunk the same way you're doing now. Except that it was in a barracks at China Beach, Da Nang, and you still had—oh my—three hundred and twenty days to go. You hadn't even gone to the Batangan yet. The Batangan. How in the fuck did you ever get through all that? Steve still out there. And Friar Tuck.

You must have dozed off. Because you're awakened by someone shouting. "We're leaving, we're leaving," a voice comes through the screen door. "Get up! Get up! The plane's here. It arrived early."

You leap off the bed. Slip into your shoes. Your bunk mates are hurrying past you, charging through the screen door. You follow. Become part of the stampede.

You run with your shoes untied over to where soldiers are gathering in formation. As you're stepping in line toward the back, you're tucking your shirt tails in. You bend over and start tying your shoes. Your hands are shaking. Your fingers don't work. Fuck! But you finish. And as you're standing up, you feel a tap on your shoulder. You turn your head. Look into the eyes of—oh, my God—it's Timmy. Timmy Cronin. The guy who a year ago you waited for your duffels to come down the chute with at San Francisco International Airport; who you flew over with after being at Oakland Army Base together; who you stood next to in formation as his name was called to go to the Ninth Infantry Division.

"We made it," he says, giving a thumbs-up. "Rick, right?"

"Yup. The Ninth, right? Timmy."

"You got it."

You have flashes of the two of you shaking hands and then him waving to you from the back of a truck as he and a half dozen other recruits are being hauled off to the Mekong Delta; him trudging through swamps, using lit cigarettes to burn leeches off himself.

"Gotta go," he says. "See you in Oakland."

You load onto buses. Get one more chance to see—no, you can't look out. The windows are covered by heavy, dark screens.

At Bien Hoa Air Force Base you step off the bus into (once again) blinding sunlight and are herded into what looks like an old hanger. You wait in line to be seated on one of the folding chairs that have been set up in rows. You don't recall any rhyme or reason as to who sat where; you don't remember being given a boarding number. Just that Carlson and you ended up sitting in the center of one of the middle rows next to each other.

You look around, trying to take everything in. Counterbalancing the endless list of "no mores" that keep flashing inside your head; the red dust that was always settling on you, getting in your mouth and eyes. The constant, panicky feeling that you were drowning in that hot, muggy air; feeling itchy all the time like there were bugs crawling on you; up and down your legs; in your crotch; along your arms and down the back of your sweaty neck. All those memories are there, bubbling over; feeling raunchy and filthy all the time, and tired, so dog-ass tired you barely gave a fuck if a V.C. crawled up and slit your throat—*go ahead, end this*; you're sitting there counterbalancing all those "no mores" with what you're looking forward to when you get home.

And then—oh boy—the door at the front of the hanger opens and here they come, the guys who just got off the plane.

As they walk tentatively past you, it's hard to look at them. You know all too well where most of them are headed; what's in store for many of them.

It's time to board. You remain seated while those in the front two rows stand up and get in line. One by one they step out onto the runway and as you're watching them, you're thinking, that will soon be me and imagine yourself walking up the stairway to the plane's entrance and being greeted by the pilots and stewardesses. "Okay," the sergeant in charge says, and points to the third and fourth rows. Twenty more soldiers stand up and get in line and as the last of them nears the door the fifth and sixth rows are told to go get in line and it goes on like that for twenty, twenty-five more rows—Jesus Christ, you're thinking, how long is this boarding operation going to take?—until finally the sergeant points to the row *you're* in and it's like, is he suddenly going to draw his fingers across his throat and say, "sorry. That's it. The plane can't hold any more." Is he going to say, "okay, you, you, you and *you,* go ahead" to the four soldiers sitting next to you. "But that's it. No more."

But you stay calm. Hell there's thirty, forty rows *behind* you still to go. "Remember your ABC's," you tell yourself taking slow, deep breaths.

And the next thing you know you're on the plane. *On* it, bro. Fucking *on* it.

You've walked up the stairway—well—across the runway first, that bad-ass sun beating down on you ONE LAST TIME, been greeted by the pilots and several lovely stewardesses (oh my. My, oh my, oh my) and are sitting by a window; poised one might say to catch—for real—the most crucial aspect of the going home process; the going home dream that's been in your head constantly for the past year. I mean, you can only savor so much what's going on. Look around and say to yourself, "it's happening, it's happening." Your heart is bursting with love for all mankind; for your family and friends who have been waiting and praying for this moment; for your fellow soldiers; for the three stewardesses whose eyes you just looked into as they greeted you; said, "welcome aboard." Especially the brunette. Come on, that wasn't just *any* look she gave you. "I've been blessed," you say to yourself gazing off in the distance. "Given life. And I will make the best of it, I promise. Help others."

Meanwhile . . . .

Not like the war's not still going on. There go two Phantoms. You know where they're going too. Oh do you ever! Your mind flashes on that napalm victim you came across in that burned out village. The boy's eyes gazing up at you from within his grotesquely-deformed, charred face.

"Go *get* some," you're supposed to say as you listen to the roar of the fighters' engines. But you don't.

The plane is moving. It taxies to the end of a runway and turns. You listen to the whine of the engines. The plane is shaking. The brakes that have been holding the plane back let go. The plane surges ahead. You feel yourself being pushed back against your seat. The world outside is rushing by. Suddenly you feel yourself being lifted; going up. Up some more. You're airborne. And down below—one more time; dust billowing up from a road; obviously a convoy of some sort, but you can't see the vehicles; and over yonder snuggled next to the jungle a sandbagged firebase, and beyond that, thatched roofs next to a river and then more jungle surrounded by rice paddies. Finally you're passing over sand dunes and heading out across the South China Sea.

"Something to drink, sir?"

Oh my, look who's standing there looking at you. The brunette.

"Coffee, please," you say, your heart trying to jump out of your chest suddenly.

"And how would you like it?"

"Uh, black. Black, please."

You watch her pour. She has small, dainty hands. Pink nail polish. She reaches over and hands you the cup. Your arm is shaking and you spill coffee all over your khakis.

"Oh, I'm sorry," she says—as if it's her fault—and immediately hands you several napkins. She pours water on the towel draped over the cart's handle and hands it to you.

"Thank you," you tell her, embarrassed; Carlson and her watching as you try and remove the stain. "Thank you."

"You're most welcome," she says. You hand her the towel looking into her eyes and watch her as she pushes the cart up to the next row of seats.

Does this mean she won't be accepting your hand in marriage?

Yokota Air Force Base in Japan (where you put away two cheeseburgers, a large order of fries, a coke and a chocolate milkshake in the terminal's cafeteria), the airport in Anchorage, Alaska (where it's snowing and you browse in a gift shop while the plane's being refueled), and then finally landing at Travis Air Force Base in Oakland.

Travis Air Force Base. Has that not been—since you departed from there a year ago—one of the key destinations in your dreams? Have you not been imagining the feeling of having the plane pull back and start descending suddenly while you're looking out the window and realizing that, this is it! You're almost there. You had in your dreams imagined looking out and suddenly seeing land at the edge of the vast ocean and being able to watch as you approach American soil. But you're not traveling across the ocean. You're coming down from Alaska, which means you're flying over land. Also—contrary to your dreams—you're approaching Travis in the dark. Is there a reason for this? At first—while landing, the halleluiah sound of the wheels touching the runway; as you're taxiing over to the terminal; while the engines are being shut off leaving you sitting there in silence—you don't think anything of it. But as you're climbing down the stairs that have been wheeled out to the plane and stepping onto the runway—well—not quite then maybe; more as you're being loaded quickly onto buses and being seemingly whisked the hell out of there and driven over to nearby Oakland Army Base, you wonder if sneaking returning soldiers into the country clandestinely has become the new norm. I mean it's not like you were expecting any fanfare, but Jesus Christ. Is this because of the soldier who was shot and killed as he was getting off the plane months back? You remember reading about that incident in the *Stars and Stripes* way back—well—you remember talking to Finlay about it so it was way back in June. Or July. How in front of cheering family members welcoming their son's return, an antiwar protestor picked off a soldier as he was getting off the plane.

So you've been whisked from the runway at Travis—that's

how it seemed—driven over to nearby Oakland Army Base and herded into a converted warehouse where those of you going to another assignment get in one line and those of you being separated (ah, you like that word) step into another.

But wait a sec. How long did you say it's going to take before I can walk the fuck out of here; collect my pay and . . . . *Seventy-two* hours?

But hold on, hold on. Chill. It's all part of the dream. Be patient—for even *this*. *Especially* for this. Remember, as you were sitting on the ground all night—doin' all that shit. Walking through steaming jungle—you imagined yourself being at Oakland Army Base for out-processing. Well, this is *it*. You're *here*. You know there are certain red-tape things that need to be done—*you're getting out of the Army, bro.* When you walk out that gate over yonder with your final pay and DD214 in hand you will be a free man; an honorably discharged war veteran. So you want them to get it right. No mistakes. Nothing that can come back to haunt you.

Oh man, it was right over there, in front of the main dining hall that you stood watching soldiers who were standing in line where you're standing right now. Soldiers who had just returned from over there and were waiting to go into the room you're about to go into for their steak dinner. Wow, you remember thinking as you watched them with awe and envy, they're done. They made it.

And now, a year later, that's *you* standing in line. You being told to go ahead, enter the building. You sitting at one of the tables. You gazing disbelievingly into the server's eyes and saying, "uh, medium well, please." You nodding and saying, "yes," to the question, "would you like sour cream with your baked potato?" You saying, "Italian, please," when asked what kind of dressing you'd like.

Yup—that's *you*. Gazing around the room; at the tall windows and high ceiling; the orange-colored walls. Cutting your steak; watching the bloody juice seep over into the baked potato. As you sit there poised to take your first bite, you look at the food on your plate—your *plate*, not tray (my how civilized)—and then you dig in, just like you did when your food was coated with dust from a helicopter that was landing or taking off and you mushed it around and ate it because you were hungry.

Now for the serious business of out-processing. Moving forward with your separation. Another physical? Go ahead Dr. Strangelove, grab my balls and ask me to cough one more time. The obligatory final briefing talk. Hey, give the young second looey a break. Dude's only doing his job. And, yes, as it turns out, he provided you with sound advice. Don't go into San Francisco. Go straight home. But if you *do* go into San Francisco, don't wear your uniform. Even though you have every right to be proud, having fought for your country, it's a fucked up world out there and . . . .

You were about to find out just *how* fucked up, weren't you?

Down to the wire. Collect pay at pay window, sign off on your DD214 and off you go.

Now you would have preferred to sit in the back of the cab and look out the window in silence, with your own thoughts. But no. While you were driven across the base then through the gate one last time, as you gazed down at the water, as you crossed the Oakland Bay Bridge, as you glanced over at the San Francisco skyline and then over at the surrounding brown hills, the cab driver and one of the other—civilians now—sitting next to you, tried to one-up each other with—who was the meanest, cruelest, most sadistic motherfucker in the valley—type tales. "Well, what we used t'do, see," the cab driver turns to the yahoo conversing with him at a light—fuck the rest of you obviously not wanting to go there pansies—and tells him how they used to take gooks up in helicopters and push them out. "An' the looks on their faces when they realized what we was doin', that we weren't just transporting their sorry asses somewhere; the look in their eyes as we gave em that final heave-ho motherfucker shove; I'm tellin' ya Jack, it was priceless; a sight te behold."

Yeah, yeah, yeah. Thanks for the ride, Mr. Badass. Maybe you can grab yourself another tour. Meanwhile, good riddance motherfucker.

In a rest room, at the airport, after you purchase your ticket, you take a long, hard look at yourself in the mirror above the sink. Thinking of the young couple whose eyes were glaring indignantly at you as you entered the airport lobby, you say to yourself, "not over, is it?" "No," you say, studying the lines and blotches of dirt still covering your older looking face. "Not over. Not by a *long* shot."

You dry your face and hands with several paper towels from a dispenser on the wall—*it's the* **little** *things,* **definitely**—then leaving the rest room, thinking of Simon and Steve—and Charlie . . . Friar Tuck, Sergeant Morrison, St. James, you walk to the end of a long, long corridor to wait for your flight home.

Watching out the plane's window (as you and only a handful of other passengers are moving stealthily through the night) you become mesmerized by the lights down below; the lights of American cities. You're flying over Denver; Chicago.

And then, there it is, first light; the sun suddenly shooting straight at you through the window. *Well, howdy there. Top a the mornin' to you and all that.* A different sun—from that other. Welcoming; calm and peaceful. Not like the—*oh fuck!*—the one Steve and Friar Tuck are still struggling with. No, no. Jeez, no. And there they are the wings that have been bearing you through the night; holding you up. The engines; and over yonder the horizon, golden now and stretching as far as you can see.

Down below, hills and fields and lakes and rivers—and then once again, that feeling, the feeling of the plane holding back suddenly and starting to fall, and before long you're looking at cars and highways and buildings and suddenly there it is! Oh my God, the New York City skyline. *Been waitin' for me, haven't ya? Waitin' for my safe return.*

You glance over at the stewardess who came over and sat next to you for much of the flight. She had a cousin who was killed in Vietnam. He was an officer in the 1st Infantry Division. You're tempted to get her telephone number. Give her a call. But you don't. You just say, "goodbye, nice talking to you," and walk into the TWA terminal.

Remember Dad? Right over there at the top of those stairs. We hugged and then you looked me in the eye and said "see you in a year." Well, the year's up and . . . you know those stairs you walked down and I stood and watched you before going to catch my plane; you crossed the lobby, then pushed through those revolving glass doors and went out onto the street—well—I'm heading down those very same stairs right now, Pop.

You ask the cab driver waiting outside the terminal if he'll take you to the Port Authority. He looks at your uniform, sees the expression on your face and says, "Sure. Climb in." Which you do.

At the Port Authority you buy your ticket to Princeton, New

Jersey. Gate number nine. Then as you're going down the escalator to get a bite to eat (you have some time to kill) you see a soldier with a Blackhorse patch on his uniform coming up the other way. He sees your Blackhorse patch also and you say, "what squadron?"

"Second," he says.

"Same as me," you say, "what troop?"

"Gulf," he says.

You tell him you were in Echo and ask if you can buy him a beer.

"Sure."

When he gets to the top he walks over to the down escalator and comes and joins you. He has an hour to kill also. He's headed for Perth Amboy. You both order food—cheeseburgers. Fries—then each end up buying the other a beer.

Standing outside the Port Authority building before you each head to your gate, you witness something that makes you both realize—in case you had any doubts—where you are; and what for you, is a harbinger of what's to come—a career working in mental institutions.

"Oh, so you like *him* better than me," a middle-aged man who has emerged from the crowd on 42nd Street is suddenly in your face, glaring indignantly at you, his lips pursed, his hand tucked limply under his chin. And then before your friend and you even get a chance to look at each other, try to figure out what just happened, the dude, never taking his eyes off the two of you—well *you*—proceeds to charge heedlessly across the street. "Holy shit," you say, as horns are honking and tires are screeching, "that motherfucker's gonna get himself killed."

You watch in amazement as the dude, never taking his eyes

off you—who does he think you are, his lost father?—careens along the curb on the other side of the street and then once more with squealing brakes and honking horns darts headlong into traffic, makes it to the other side, comes by and gets into your face again, and says, "oh, so you like black people better than me?" Whoa! This time when he charges back into traffic, you and your pal wait until he miraculously makes it to the other side so he has less chance of following you and then slip back inside the building through the glass doors and head for your respective gates. You do stop for a moment and shake hands and wish each other the best before losing yourselves in the Port Authority crowd.

"Riverside Drive," you lean over and tell the bus driver. He's the one who drove you out of the bus depot and through the Lincoln Tunnel down 95 past the oil refineries, through New Brunswick, down Route 27, through Kingston, past Carnegie Lake and now here you are at your stop in Princeton, New Jersey.

You're the last passenger on the bus. As you sit down on one of the seats up front the bus driver looks over at you and says, "Just get back?"

You nod your head.

"Kinda rough?"

Again you nod.

"Well, I'm glad you made it. I'm glad you're home safe."

"Thanks."

The bus pulls over and stops. The doors open.

"Thank you," you say as you're getting off.

"You're welcome."

The doors close. The bus leaves you standing there. At the corner of Nassau and Riverside.

You let a car go by and then cross the street. The smells of spring are everywhere. You breathe them in. Birds are chirping; you watch them darting from tree to tree. You watch squirrels chasing each other. The smell of freshly cut lawns; flowers in bloom; dogwoods; lilacs; white petals floating in the breeze; the sun feels warm and comfortable against the back of your neck.

You walk past familiar houses. People look over at you and wave. You listen to the sounds of children playing. A motorcycle roars by startling you. You can hear dogs barking. A new house is being built. The old one has obviously been knocked down. You try to remember what it looked like.

Riverside to Prospect, up Prospect to Woodside, down Woodside...

And there it is; the back of your parents' house. Just like you left it. Sort of.

Andy comes dashing across the back lawn to greet you and amazingly knows who you are. If he didn't he'd be chewing your leg off.

"What's up there, fella," you reach down and pet him under the ears. "Nice fella." Then you hear screaming. Sue looking out her upstairs bedroom window sees you petting Andy and is shouting, "Oh my God! It's Rick. It's Rick, Rick is home."

You walk over and hug your mother who was in the kitchen and has rushed out onto the back patio to greet you. You hug each other for a long time; this time—unlike a year ago—you don't have to peel yourself away to go off to war. When you let go finally you turn and as you're hugging Sue you hear your mom say, "your father, let's go call your father." Sue rushes up to the kitchen, dials the number and hands you the phone. Dad's secretary answers. "Grace?" you say, "that you? It's Rick. I'm home,

Grace. Is Dad . . . ?"

"Oh my God. Jim. It's Rick, he's home. Rick is home."

16.
The Pilgrimage: Postscript

Thick book. Enormous. Like a telephone directory.

Tears blurring my eyes so I can't see the small print.

"Move over, Daddy. Mommy will help you."

"Haibach, Haibach. First name?"

"Charlie. *Charles.* Charles Haibach."

"From...?"

"Omaha."

"Omaha?"

"Omaha, yes."

"And he died...?"

"December. He was killed in December. December..."

"14th?"

"14th, yes. December 14th. 1967."

"Okay, so—let's see—panel 44E, row . . . 33. Got that?

Julie turned and made sure I was watching. She even waited for me to nod my approval before reaching up and cautiously touching the letters in Haibach's name. "Go ahead, sweetheart," I whispered, "go ahead," and I knew that, in her hesitancy, she was just making sure I knew how seriously and reverently she was taking the ritual she had just watched me perform.

As I watched her, noting her reflection on the wall—noting, of course, the reflection of myself, standing behind her—I noted, also, off to my right, the reflections of the man in the wheelchair and the woman who was standing next to him.

Edging closer to the couple, I could now see that the man had a prosthetic arm protruding from his right shirt sleeve. Glancing downward, I saw that he had a prosthetic device jutting from each cuff of his trousers, also.

Suddenly, as if on cue, the woman leaned forward, letting the man reach up and wrap his arm around her. And then while the man began pushing against the armrest of the wheelchair with his "normal" hand, the woman helped him to wiggle up out of the wheelchair and stand up. It was a heart wrenching spectacle to observe—one that I sensed had occurred many times in that very same spot over the years.

As I watched the man steadying himself—still propped up by the woman and holding onto her, he was obviously having a go at trying to balance himself—I could see reflected in the wall the man's puzzled, but determined eyes, anxiously searching the smooth, black surface next to him. I knew, of course, what he was doing; he was zeroing in on the treasure he knew was contained in the wall and had discovered there many times before; he was trying to find the letters that made up a name, the name of some long ago, lost buddy of his—from that other life; and as I watched him, watched his eyes widen suddenly and become fastened to a spot on the wall, just above and to the left of where he was standing, I knew, having located two names and performed the same sacred ritual myself only moments before, the adrenalin-pumping rush he was experiencing.

The couple stood still, staring at the wall—mesmerized by a name obviously; and then, suddenly, the spell under which they both seemed to have fallen, momentarily, was broken, and the man and woman released each other. Once again, as if he'd been rehearsing, the man slowly, with the woman's help, withdrew his arm from around the woman's neck; and then, much the same way a child learning how to stand up and walk for the first time, is encouraged, but also protected by their mother, the woman backed away slowly, so that the man was standing on his own.

The man stood still for a while—gathering his confidence, I surmised, achieving the balance he needed for his next move—and then with the woman standing close by, watching, ready to help, if necessary, he slowly raised his hand up toward the name he'd been staring at, stretching and leaning slightly, until finally, with the tips of his fingers, he touched the first letter in whosever name it was. After pressing the tips of his fingers against that first letter—and moving them up and down along the letter's edges—he did the same thing with the second and third letters. As he moved the tips of his fingers over to the fourth letter, however, he lost his balance and fell back. The woman reached over and helped him. He paused for a moment, steadying himself, regaining his composure, and then, with obvious determination, raised his hand again. As he slid his fingers over from the third letter where he'd left off, onto the fourth, I could see that he was breathing heavily. I was too.

When he'd completed his ritual, he lowered his arm. As the woman moved closer, the man wrapped his arm around her, and she helped him back into the wheelchair. Julie, who was still standing close to the wall, turned suddenly to see where I was. When she spotted me, saw where I was standing, she ran over and stood next to me.

"Daddy," she said, "that . . . man in the wheelchair over there. You think . . . you think he got that way in the war?"

I reached over and pulled Julie close to me. "Yes," I said. Julie and I watched the woman reach down and help the man as he settled into the wheelchair. Wiggling back and forth, he seemed to be trying to attain a more comfortable position. When he seemed settled finally, the woman grabbed the handles behind the wheelchair and began pushing him forward. Julie and I watched as the two of them, along with their reflections, moved amongst the names on the wall. "What do you think happened to him?" Julie asked.

"Mine," I said. "Mine or booby trap."

Julie wrapped her arms around me again, and as she gave me another hug, I noticed that her eyes were riveted on the man. Lot to take in, I figured. Mine, booby trap (some exploding thing) that had torn the limbs off the body of what was once—like her father standing next to her—a young soldier in a long ago war. An awful lot for a ten-year-old girl to wrap her mind around.

But that's what she was doing, I was pretty sure. And as, Lord knows what disturbing images were crowding her young head at that moment, we both shifted our eyes to Emily and Ruth, who were still standing next to the wall looking at names. So many names.

Emily and Ruth turned toward Julie and me and waved, and Julie and I waved back; and then Ruth walked over and gave me a hug, and Emily, following her, walked over and hugged me also. And there we were, Ruth, Julie, Emily and me, embracing each other. And as I wrapped my arms around them—my wife and daughters—I glanced over at our reflections; the reflections of my family, along with those of other people standing next to the wall, and the reflections of the Washington Monument and the various types of brightly colored flowers that had been placed along the base of the wall. We stood there like that for a long time—mesmerized; in awe. And the next thing I knew, Ruth and I were back at work; Emily and Julie were back in school. And life went on!

Epilogue

By some twist of fate I survived and was allowed to go on and have a life. And though it took me a while to find myself after I came back, with a lot of help and support from friends and family, I ended up in a great place with a great career and retired after 33 years as the head of risk management in a psychiatric hospital. Along with me is my wonderful wife, Ruth, with whom I've been happily married for thirty-two years and with whom I have two wonderful, lovely daughters, Emily and Julie. My cup runneth over.

Emily and Julie. Until I had children of my own, I never fully appreciated the unrelieved anguish Mom must have felt worrying about me each and every moment of each and every day for the year I was in Vietnam. Constantly thinking about me, and wondering, what's he doing *right now*? At this moment. Is he...? Hoping and praying each time she heard the phone ringing that it wasn't . . . .

My sister, Sue, witnessed firsthand what Mom went through the year I was in Vietnam, during those endless, horrifyingly suspenseful days—at least from the vantage point of a mother anyway. From April 19, 1967 to that same date a year later: three hundred and sixty-five days of pure torture and hell. Sue was a senior in high school. Dad was often away on business. Lee was away at college so often it was just the two of them alone in the house together, looking at each other and dreading what each new day might bring. Tell me, how did all those mothers (and fathers, too, of course; and brothers and sisters and aunts and uncles and friends) do it, especially the mothers? It's the Moms who catch the brunt of the waiting. It's the mothers who hold on —for a year or years, and cope. According to Sue, it was Mom who would scour the newspaper each morning and then in the evening turn on the six o'clock news in the hope that she might discover some miniscule bit of information that would shed light on what I was doing and would provide her with a clue as to my safety and whereabouts. She'd turn on the T.V. and whammo! There it would be—the *war*. Remember? It would come on right before her very eyes: the close-up of a young soldier walking along on patrol, his eyes (was that *me? Is that* you, *Rick?*) looking out from underneath his helmet. And then suddenly there'd be shooting, the soldier would be lying on the ground, there'd be cries for medic and....

I believe Sue was more traumatized by the war than I was. She and her husband, Jim, have twin boys. As they watched their sons growing up (they are adults now), Sue was forever mindful (especially with the back drop of young Americans once again going off to war in faraway, previously unheard of, places and being killed and/or coming back seriously wounded and with deep psychological scars) of that excruciating year she and Mom spent worrying about me.

Oh Mom. Mom oh Mom oh Mom.

When Mom got sick and was dying of cancer, we all half expected Dad to be able to pull for Mom the same strings he'd pulled for me. (It always seemed to us that he had the power through his extraordinary faith and optimism to willfully guide me out of harm's way and back home safely.) Dad, *do* something! We all thought he could. *Do* something, Dad. But there was nothing he could do. Mom would look helplessly into his eyes—

her eyes glowing sadly, but lovingly from within her still beautiful, but gaunt now, suffering face—and he'd look back helplessly into hers.

While Lee was working at an excavation site in Colchester, England—after he'd left the U.S. to avoid being drafted—a Spaniard working at the site suggested that Lee go to his home town, San Sebastian, and get a job teaching English. Which is what Lee did. NOW, forty-four years later, he owns and runs an immensely successful English teaching school that he started. He has over a thousand students enrolled each year; has been married for thirty-eight years to Cristina, a Spanish woman he met while studying French at the University of Grenoble (ah! The capriciousness of life) and with whom he has a son, Pablo, and a daughter, Karen.

In 1976 (a year after I started working for the state of New Jersey), Sue, Jim, Mom, Dad, and I flew to Spain for Lee and Cristina's wedding; Ruth and I visited Lee and Cristina in Spain the year after we got married—1984; and Ruth, Emily, Julie and I have traveled to Spain to be with them three more times. Lee and Cristina have a cabin in the Adirondacks that they have been coming to each summer for the past twelve years. For the years prior to that (starting in 1970)—Lee (before he met Cristina), then Lee and Cristina (pre-children), and then the two of them with Pablo and Karen—would spend their summers with Mom and Dad at Mom and Dad's house in Princeton, New Jersey. Mom died in 1990 right after Julie was born. She got to spend two years with Emily and then hold Emily and Julie together on her lap. *Just before the end. The evening before she died, you, Emily, crawled up on your grandmother's bed amongst all the bags and connect-*

ing tubes. She jokingly referred to herself as the bag lady—and hugged her. And then we set you up on the bed next to your sister, Julie.... After Mom died, Lee, Cristina, Pablo, and Karen spent their summers with Dad at his house, and when Dad moved to Meadow Lakes (a senior living community) in 2000, they stayed with Sue and Jim or Ruth and me.

Glossary

AIT: Advanced Individual Training. Training soldiers received after Basic training.

AK-47: Automatic Kalashnikov, model 47 Soviet weapon used by North Vietnamese and Viet Cong soldiers. Considered to be a more effective, reliable and dependable infantry assault rifle than the M-16 issued to Americans.

APC (Armored Personnel Carrier): The M-113 APC referred to as a track. See track.

Article 15: Company level punishment from the Uniform Code of Military Justice that often involved extra duty. The ol' dig a whole and then fill it routine.

ARVN: Acronym for Army of the Republic of South Vietnam.

AWOL: Absent Without Leave.

Back-in-the-world: Slang for being back home in the U.S.

C-4: A malleable plastic explosive resembling silly putty. Often used for cooking as well as blowing things up.

C-Rations: Canned field rations, also called C-Rats.

Chicom: Abbreviation for Chinese Communist.

Chinook: A cargo helicopter with large rotor blades front and rear. Also called "Jolly Green Giants," they were often used to bring supplies to troops in the field.

Chu Chi: The Chu Chi district is located approximately twenty miles northwest of Saigon. It was south of the V.C. stronghold called the Iron Triangle, and was where the 25th Infantry had its base camp.

Chu Chi tunnels: A network of connecting underground tunnels in the Chu Chi district that were used by the Viet Cong as hiding spots during combat. The tunnels are now a tourist designation.

CIB: Combat infantryman's badge.

Claymore: An antipersonnel mine that's approximately a foot long, six inches wide, is curved slightly outward, and contains 700 small steel balls packed in C-4. They were usually set out in front of night perimeters and in front of each APC.

CO: Commanding officer.

CVC helmet: Headgear resembling a football helmet worn by track and tank commanders and drivers. The helmets contained radio earphones and microphones.

DEROS: Acronym for Date Estimated Return from Overseas: the date when a soldier ended his tour and rotated to the United States.

Deuce-and-a-half: A large truck that carried two and a half tons of cargo or troops.

DMZ: The De-Militarized Zone at the 17th parallel between North and South Vietnam.

Dust-off: Slang for a medical evacuation helicopter (Medevac).

El-tee, The: Nickname for the platoon leader, usually a lieutenant, or Lt. or L-tee.

EM Club: Enlisted men's club; the bar at base camp where the "rank and file" went to drink.

F-4, Phantom: Fighter jet that provided support for ground troops by swooping down and dropping bombs and napalm on the nearby enemy.

FNG: Acronym for Fucking New Guy; a replacement.

Fragging: The murder of an officer or NCO by a member of his own unit.

Get Some: Rallying cry to kill the enemy.

Gook: Derogatory term for the enemy; Viet Cong and North Vietnamese soldiers.

Grease gun: Tool that drivers of APC's used to inject grease into various points in the track's wheels and treads in order to keep up tread tension.

Housecat: Slang for "rear pogues"; soldiers assigned permanent base camp jobs, i.e. clerks, cooks who never left camp.

ICU: Intensive Care Unit in hospitals where the severely wounded and sick were cared for.

KIA: Killed in action.

KP: Kitchen policies

Laager: A temporary defensive perimeter of armored vehicles.

LBJ: Long Binh Jail, the U.S. Army stockade at Long Binh; also, of course, the initials of the 36th President of the United States, Lyndon Baines Johnson.

LST: Acronym for Landing Ship, Tank. Transport ship that carried vehicles (tanks, personnel carriers, trucks), cargo and troops to various destinations.

LZ: Landing Zone.

M-16: Standard assault rifle issued to American forces in Vietnam.

M-60: Medium machine gun that was mounted on either side of an armored personnel carrier. It was also carried on foot patrols.

M-79: Short-barreled, breech-loaded single shot grenade launcher.

Mortar Track: The armored personnel carrier designated to carry a mortar tube and accompanying equipment so its crew could carry out firing missions.

MOS: Military Occupation Status.

MP: Acronym for Military Police.

NCO: Acronym for Non-Commissioned Officers. By rank, Sergeant (E-5) to Sergeant major of the Army (E-9).

NVA: Acronym for North Vietnamese Army.

OCS: Officer Candidate School

ROK Marine: Republic of Korea marine

RPG: An armor piercing Rocket-Propelled-Grenade.

R&R: Rest and relaxation leave allowed once during the twelve month tour, usually for five days.

S&D: Search and destroy.

Steel pot: GI helmet.

Track: What we called armored personnel carriers.

TC: Track commander who sits in the track's main hatch usually a 50-caliber machine gun.

V.C.: Vietnamese Communist guerillas called Viet Cong; referred to by Americans as Victor Charlie, Charlie and Charles, i.e. Charles is everywhere tonight.

VTR: Large, treaded vehicle used to tow disabled trucks, tanks, and personnel carriers.

Willie Peter: A white phosphorous artillery or mortar round for marking targets; also used for its fire-starting effects and smoke screens.